RE-IMAGINING SHAKESPEARE IN CONTEMPORARY JAPAN

Related titles

Shakespeare in the Theatre: Yukio Ninagawa
Conor Hanratty
9781350087354

Early Modern German Shakespeare: Hamlet and Romeo and Juliet
Edited by Lukas Erne and Kareen Seidler
9781350084049

Shakespeare and the Politics of Nostalgia
Yuichi Tsukada
9781350175075

Shakespeare and Geek Culture
Edited by Andrew James Hartley and Peter Holland
9781350107748

Imagining Cleopatra
Yasmin Arshad
9781350058965

Shakespeare's Body Language
Miranda Fay Thomas
9781350035478

RE-IMAGINING SHAKESPEARE IN CONTEMPORARY JAPAN

A SELECTION OF JAPANESE THEATRICAL ADAPTATIONS OF SHAKESPEARE

The Three Daughters of Lear
(The Tokyo Shakespeare Company)

HAMLET X SHIBUYA ~ Light, Was Our Revenge Tarnished?
(Kakushinhan Theatre Company)

The New Romeo and Juliet
(The Shakespeare Company Japan)

Edited and Translated by
TETSUHITO MOTOYAMA, ROSALIND FIELDING and FUMIAKI KONNO

THE ARDEN SHAKESPEARE
LONDON • NEW YORK • OXFORD • NEW DELHI • SYDNEY

THE ARDEN SHAKESPEARE
Bloomsbury Publishing Plc
50 Bedford Square, London, WC1B 3DP, UK
1385 Broadway, New York, NY 10018, USA
29 Earlsfort Terrace, Dublin 2, Ireland

BLOOMSBURY, THE ARDEN SHAKESPEARE and the Arden Shakespeare logo are trademarks of Bloomsbury Publishing Plc

First published in Great Britain 2021
This paperback edition published in 2022

Copyright © Tetsuhito Motoyama, Rosalind Fielding and Fumiaki Konno, 2021

Tetsuhito Motoyama, Rosalind Fielding and Fumiaki Konno have asserted their right under the Copyright, Designs and Patents Act, 1988, to be identified as editors and translators of this work.

Cover design: Charlotte Daniels
Cover image: A scene from *Hamlet* (2018) by Kakushinhan, starring Kochi Yamato as Hamlet (by permission of Kakushinhan Theatre Company)

All rights reserved. No part of this publication may be reproduced or transmitted in any form or by any means, electronic or mechanical, including photocopying, recording, or any information storage or retrieval system, without prior permission in writing from the publishers.

Bloomsbury Publishing Plc does not have any control over, or responsibility for, any third-party websites referred to or in this book. All internet addresses given in this book were correct at the time of going to press. The author and publisher regret any inconvenience caused if addresses have changed or sites have ceased to exist, but can accept no responsibility for any such changes.

A catalogue record for this book is available from the British Library.

Library of Congress Control Number: 2020949608

ISBN: HB: 978-1-3501-1624-5
PB: 978-1-3502-1200-8
ePDF: 978-1-3501-1626-9
eBook: 978-1-3501-1625-2

Typeset by RefineCatch Limited, Bungay, Suffolk

To find out more about our authors and books visit www.bloomsbury.com and sign up for our newsletters.

The Editors

Tetsuhito Motoyama is Professor at Waseda University (Tokyo) in the Faculty of Law. Publications on Shakespeare and adaptation include, co-edited with Hiromi Fuyuki, *The Text Made Visible: Shakespeare on the Page, Stage, and Screen* (2011); and co-authored with Kaoru Edo, 'Strange Oeillades No More: *The Three Daughters of Lear* from the Tokyo Shakespeare Company's "Shakespeare through the Looking-Glass"', *Shakespeare* 9 no. 4 (2013).

Rosalind Fielding is a translator and researcher. Publications include 'Riots, Cherry Blossoms and Wheelchairs: The Performance Politics of Saitama Gold Theater' in *Performance Research* 24 no. 3 (2019), and she is an editor of *Shakespeare in East Asian Education: Schools, Universities and Theatre in Hong Kong, Japan and Taiwan* (Palgrave, 2021).

Fumiaki Konno is Associate Professor at Meiji University (Tokyo) in the Faculty of Commerce. Publications on Shakespeare and adaptation include, 'Charles Kean's Edition of *Henry VIII*: A Study of Its Base Text', *The Bulletin of Arts and Sciences, Meiji University* 524 (2017); and co-authored with Tetsuhito Motoyama, 'The Shakespeare Company Japan and Regional Self-fashioning' in *William Shakespeare and 21st-Century Culture, Politics, and Leadership: Bard Bites*, edited by Kristin Bezio and Anthony Russell (Edward Elgar, 2021).

CONTENTS

List of illustrations	ix
Preface	x
General introduction	1
Shakespeare and adaptation	2
Shakespeare's reception in Japan	4
Early Shakespearean translations and adaptations	7
Post-Meiji performance and translation	12
The Tokyo Shakespeare Company	22
Kakushinhan Theatre Company	26
The Shakespeare Company Japan	30
Introduction to *The Three Daughters of Lear*	37
Interview: Edo Kaoru	49
THE THREE DAUGHTERS OF LEAR	59
Introduction to *Hamlet X Shibuya ~ Light, Was Our Revenge Tarnished?*	147
Interview: Kimura Ryūnosuke	161
HAMLET X SHIBUYA ~ LIGHT, WAS OUR REVENGE TARNISHED?	167
Introduction to *The New Romeo and Juliet*	223
Interview: Shimodate Kazumi	233
THE NEW ROMEO AND JULIET	235

Appendix 1: A list of stage productions by the three theatre companies	271
Appendix 2: A list of Shakespeare productions in the Tokyo area in 2019	279
Bibliography	301
Index	311

LIST OF ILLUSTRATIONS

1. Naratani Yūki (Goneril), Sakō Yoshi (Fool), Edo Kaoru (Regan), and Makino Kumiko (Hell Wag) from the 1995 production of *The Three Daughters of Lear*. By permission of the Tokyo Shakespeare Company.   42
2. Tange Makoto (Fool) and Tsukasa Mari (Hell Wag) from the 2004 production of *The Three Daughters of Lear*. By permission of the Tokyo Shakespeare Company.   45
3. Maimi (Ophelia) from a scene recreating *HAMLET X SHIBUYA* in the 2018 production of *Hamlet*. By permission of the Kakushinhan Theatre Company.   153
4. Ishii Rina (Juri) and Takahashi Toshiki (Romio) from the 2012 production of *The New Romeo and Juliet*. By permission of the Shakespeare Company Japan.   223
5. Izumori Isamu (Rensu), Ishii Rina (Juri) and Takahashi Toshiki (Romio) from the 2012 production of *The New Romeo and Juliet*. By permission of the Shakespeare Company Japan.   229

PREFACE

This volume of Shakespeare-inspired Japanese plays from the late twentieth- and early twenty-first centuries is in many ways a product of the research collaboration between the Shakespeare Institute and Waseda University. We are indebted to the faculty members and staff involved in the collaboration at both institutions. It was initially through the suggestion and assistance of Michael Dobson, Director of the Shakespeare Institute, and Erin Sullivan that we approached Arden with this project. Morita Norimasa, Fuyuki Hiromi and Anthony Martin of Waseda University have also been greatly supportive of the project, and we were fortunate to receive funding from Waseda's Humanities and Social Sciences English-Language Scholarly Book Publishing Support Program in addition to a grant from Meiji University's Institute of Humanities.

Without the generosity of the three theatre companies whose works are included here, this book would not have taken shape as it has. Edo Kaoru and Okuizumi Hikaru (Tokyo Shakespeare Company), Kimura Ryūnosuke and Iwasaki Yūdai (Kakushinhan) and Shimodate Kazumi, Abe Michiko and Asami Norihiko (Shakespeare Company Japan) have been immensely helpful by answering endless questions from us and kindly allowing us access to information and materials that have not been made public or circulated widely until now. Gengi Shobō and Koko Shuppan, respectively the publishers of *The Three Daughters of Lear* and *The New Romeo and Juliet*, have made the texts widely available to the Japanese public and graciously granted us permission to use the published texts as the base texts for our translations, for which we are grateful.

We can neither thank Arden enough for taking on this book nor find enough words to express our excitement in knowing that these plays will be released by them. We owe special thanks to

Preface

Margaret Bartley and Meredith Benson, who have been most accommodating, showing us infinite patience through all the questions and delays.

Finally, we would like to thank the many colleagues and friends who have continued to offer encouragement, advice and help, and sometimes have been there just to lend an ear. Among them are John Oliphant, who helped revise the Scottish English of *The New Romeo and Juliet*, Hannah Osborne, who provided invaluable help in editing the draft, Matsuoka Kazuko, Koike Noriko, Fukuda Hayaru, Inoue Masaru, Ishiguro Taro, Nakajima Wataru, Uno Takeshi, Taki Tamako, John Jowett, Sarah Olive, Gaye Rowley, Suzuki Rieko, Sakamoto Azumi, Katō Kenta, Kanno Kimi and Geraldo Faria.

It is our hope that this selection of Japanese plays will spark interest in similar hidden gems of Shakespeare-inspired works in Japan today. They are one of the keys, as the gems in *The Three Daughters of Lear* are the keys to uncovering the truth in the play, to a better understanding of the reception of Shakespeare, not only in Japan, but also for our times.

In a quick note on style, we have followed the Japanese custom of having surnames precede given names for all Japanese names appearing in the text.

GENERAL INTRODUCTION

Looking at performance records of Shakespeare in Japan since 2010, there has been an average of over one hundred productions, parodies and adaptations per year. For example, according to data collated from event listing websites and the 'Tokyo Area Shakespeare Schedule' (iamnotthatiplay. sensyuuraku.com), there were at least 127 productions in the Tokyo region in 2016, not including international touring productions (such as those by OUDS or On Keng Sen), ballets, operas and workshops. These listings cover the wider Kanto region, comprising Tokyo itself and neighbouring prefectures Saitama, Kanagawa, Chiba, Gunma, Tochigi and Ibaraki, and as such is not an accurate representation of the total number of productions across Japan, but it does give a good representation of the scale of performance in Tokyo. A quick scan of the list from 2016 reveals titles such as *Romeo and Princess Kaguya*, *New Merchant of Venice*, *Macbeth/Cyborg*, *Merchant of OEDO*, *Romeo and me and Juliet*, *Macbeth in the Ring* and a revival of playwright Noda Hideki's 1990 play *Sandaime, Richādo* (*Richard III*), among others. Minami Ryuta has described Shakespeare as a 'database' that is accessible to Japanese artists, and this list – which is in itself only a brief snapshot of the bigger picture – is revealing of this trend of adapting, adopting and riffing off Shakespeare in contemporary Japan (Minami 2016a: 245).

The intention of this book is to introduce, contextualize and also reconsider the history and current practice of translating and adapting Shakespeare in Japan. This overview will be followed by three new translations of recent responses to Shakespeare's work from a diverse group of theatre companies and practitioners. The companies in question, namely the Tokyo

Shakespeare Company, Kakushinhan Theatre Company and Shakespeare Company Japan, represent different regions and generations of theatre makers in Japan, and although individually they offer quite different takes on staging Shakespeare in Japanese, they have in common their history of taking plays from Shakespeare's oeuvre and rewriting them, often with a particular audience in mind. We will look at the companies in more detail in the individual introductions, but before coming to that it is first necessary to frame the following discussion.

SHAKESPEARE AND ADAPTATION

There have been a number of studies on the practice of adapting Shakespeare, and also a corresponding amount of controversy around the practice, the terminology and the theory. Margherita Laera writes that theatre 'returns, it always does' but that is also 'repeats, and incessantly so. It repeats itself and the act of returning and rewriting' and in the process 'adapts itself to present contingencies and situations' (2014: 1). Rewriting takes place in many different ways, in performance, in repetition and even in deliberate silences, but the focus of this volume is on the process of adaptation. Adaptation has been described as a 'kind of interpretative intervention' (Laera 2014: 4), or an 'acknowledged transposition of a recognizable other work or works; a creative and an interpretative act of appropriation/ salvaging; an extended intertextual engagement with the adapted work' (Hutcheon 2006: 8) or as the 'borrowing and retelling of stories in new ways (repetition with a difference)' (MacArthur et al. 2009: xxi). Not only is the end result of adaptation under question, but also the different terms that can be used to describe it: Julie Sanders' list of terms includes version, interpretation, transformation, imitation, pastiche, parody, revision, rewriting, echo (2006: 18), while Daniel Fischlin and Mark Fortier note that adaptations have also been known as alterations, spinoffs, tradaptations and offshoots (2000: 3).

General Introduction

Perhaps one of the most commonly used alternative terms to adaptation is 'appropriation'. Fischlin and Fortier have argued that appropriation implies a 'hostile takeover, a seizure of authority over the original in a way that appeals to contemporary sensibilities' and that they are uncertain whether this label 'does justice to other, more respectful, aspects of the practice [they] are examining' (2000: 3), but as Laera notes, some 'artists and scholars prefer the term "appropriation" to define their work', particularly because adaptation 'suggests the idea of a derivative endeavour of lesser value than an "original" work' (2014: 5). She compellingly argues that it is perhaps 'more useful to think of adaptation as a synonym of appropriation, because it is too problematic to draw the line between a "faithful adaptation" and an "unfaithful adaptation"', adding that these responses are 'faithful or unfaithful to what, anyway?' (ibid.). In *A Theory of Adaptation*, Linda Hutcheon writes that as a '*process of creation*, the act of adaptation always involves both (re-)interpretation and then (re-)creation', which she says has 'been called both appropriation and salvaging, depending on your perspective', and crucially she writes that adaptation is a form of intertextuality and that 'we experience adaptations (*as adaptations*) as palimpsests through our memory of other works that resonate through repetition with variation' (2006: 8).

The plays translated in this volume are, in these terms, palimpsests of *King Lear*, *Hamlet* and *Romeo and Juliet*. In *Shakespeare's Creative Legacies: Artists, Writers, Performers, Readers*, Paul Edmondson and Peter Holbrook write that four hundred years on from 'the beginning of one of the strongest of all artistic legacies, we – artists, writers, performers and readers – continue to create and re-create Shakespeare' (2016: 1). In their *Adaptations of Shakespeare: A Critical Anthology of Plays from the Seventeenth Century to the Present* (2000), Fischlin and Fortier include the texts of twelve plays and then a longer list of other adaptations. The twelve main texts in the anthology include Welcome Msomi's *uMabatha* (1972), Heiner Müller's *Hamletmachine* (1977) and Paula Vogel's *Desdemona: A Play About a Handkerchief* (1994). In *Reinventing the Renaissance: Shakespeare and his Contemporaries in Adaptation and Performance*, Sarah Annes Brown, Robert I. Lublin and Lynsey McCulloch suggest that Shakespeare's plays and those of his contemporaries 'have found new articulation' by artists who use the plays to 'construct their own artistic projects, boldly and liberally reshaping the past to address the contemporary moment' (2013: 1).

The plays in this collection are likewise examples of this new articulation by artists as a response to Shakespeare and as such will appeal to those who are interested in both Japanese theatre and creative responses to Shakespeare. Each play engages with wider questions of Shakespeare in Japanese translation, the reasons for staging Shakespeare in contemporary Japan and the changing ways of responding to Shakespeare in performance. As already suggested at the opening of this introduction, adapting Shakespeare is a regular feature in Japanese theatre and has been since the earliest stages of Shakespeare's reception in Japan. These three plays, which deal with subjects such as community, disaster and social isolation, will now, we hope, also become part of the wider English-language creative response to Shakespeare and will, since in Fischlin and Fortier's terms adaptation is a 'process rather than a beginning or an end', form part of the way that 'Shakespeare's plays remain in process' (2000: 3).

SHAKESPEARE'S RECEPTION IN JAPAN

Daniel Gallimore and Minami Ryuta describe 'seven stages' in the reception of Shakespeare in Japan (2016: 484–96). This seven-stage theory builds on Anzai Tetsuo's 1999 idea of four stages: Anzai suggested that Shakespeare's reception can be divided into Meiji era adaptations, the *shingeki* period,

Fukuda Tsuneari's productions (1955–70) and then finally *shōgekijō* or the Little Theatre Movement (also known as *angura*, or Underground Theatre) (1999: 3–12). Anzai also later added a fifth stage that began with the opening of the Panasonic Tokyo Globe in 1988. An alternative method of dividing the reception history is to follow Murakami Takeshi's model, that begins with adaptations (1885–1905), adaptations and Tsubouchi Shōyō's translations (1906–20), Tsubouchi Shōyō's translations (1920s–1960), Fukuda Tsuneari's translations (1960s), 'rival translations I' (1970–74), Odashima Yūshi's translations (1975–85), and then a more diverse phase since 1985 with 'rival translations II' (1995: 240). For Gallimore and Minami, the seven stages are: Prehistory, *kabuki* adaptations, *shinpa* adaptations, early shingeki adaptations, mature shingeki replication of British productions, Little Theatre adaptations in contemporary style, and finally reinvention (2016: 485–86). Although they acknowledge there are overlaps between some of these stages, their model is extremely useful as a way of marking the developments in Shakespeare's history in Japan.

A more detailed description of Gallimore and Minami's schema can be found in their chapter in Jonah Salz's *A History of Japanese Theatre* (2016), but a brief overview of these seven stages is necessary for the following discussion. 'Prehistory', the first stage suggested by Gallimore and Minami, is based on the idea that there may have been undocumented interaction between Shakespeare's plays and Japanese theatre before the generally accepted timeline. Similarities between plots in one or two kabuki plays and Shakespeare have been cited as examples of this potential link, with the tragic lovers in *Romeo and Juliet* and in Chikamatsu Hanji's 1777 play *Imoseyama onna teikin* as the most common example. Some critics such as Kawatake Toshio have discussed these potential crossovers, citing early examples of trade and theatrical interaction in the seventeenth century, but equally critics such as James Brandon have argued that it is 'extremely improbable that playwrights before 1868 knew of Shakespeare's plays' (1998: 11).

Their second stage is *kabuki* adaptation, which covers the earliest stage of Shakespearean performance in Japan. The trend of adapting Shakespeare into kabuki briefly gave way to adaptations in the shinpa style. Shinpa (also written as *shimpa*) refers to the 'New School' of performance that spread during the 1880s as a response to the difficulties of staging newly imported Western plays in existing Japanese theatre forms. Shinpa, much less so than the following shingeki (New Theatre) movement, was a mix of traditional Japanese theatre and the then still unfamiliar Western theatre. It was a transitional theatre form whose key figures included Kawakami Sadayakko (1871–1946) and Otojirō (1864–1911), who (in)famously staged a scene from *The Merchant of Venice* in Japanese in Boston in 1900. As with the move from kabuki to shinpa, shinpa was largely replaced by shingeki from 1910 onwards. Although there were some overlaps between the two genres in the beginning, as the shingeki movement developed its focus became faithfulness to Western modes of performance, especially in terms of realism and authentic translation.

The angura period grew out of a reaction against what was seen as the limitations and repressions of shingeki, allowing for more freedom for directors and more attention to the bodies of the actors rather than on the prioritization of the translated text. The current stage has been described as that of 'reinvention'. Influenced by numerous factors including angura's rejection of 'authenticity', the growing Japanese economy, and several high-profile visits of overseas companies (such as the Royal Shakespeare Company with Peter Brook's *A Midsummer Night's Dream* in 1973), this stage has been characterized by its freedom and re-examination of previous performance trends. Particularly of note to the following translations is the rise in localized productions during this period, and the break with the need to be faithful to Shakespeare's text in either English or

Japanese. Contemporary artists also have a wider range of translations to choose from, including the older ('classical') translations from the Meiji period up to the 1950s, Odashima Yūshi's translations in a more colloquial style from the 1970s onwards, and Matsuoka Kazuko's poetic translations from the 1990s on.

EARLY SHAKESPEAREAN TRANSLATIONS AND ADAPTATIONS

The second half of the nineteenth century was a time of sea change for Japan, starting with the end of its isolationist policy in 1854. Then, with the *taisei hōkan* (return of political authority to the emperor) in 1867, the Tokugawa shogunate and feudalism came to an end. The Meiji period began in 1868 and continued until 1912, during which time the country started down the path to becoming a modern state. It was as the country stood on such a threshold that Shakespeare first caught the attention of the Japanese public. While the first written reference to Shakespeare in Japanese dates back to 1841, it was with the commercial success of *Saikoku risshihen* (*Stories of Successful Lives in the West*) in 1871 that his name became widely known. This is a translation of Samuel Smiles' *Self-help: With Illustrations of Character and Conduct* (1859), which introduced Shakespeare in terms of how his writings 'yield profit in the forming of our English character' (Takahashi 1997: 7). Once Shakespeare's plays started becoming available both in print and on the stage, people also turned to them for moral lessons that would unify and inspire them into building a new Japan (Kawato 2004: 62).

The plays were made accessible to the general public in three different ways. First, Charles and Mary Lamb's *Tales from Shakespeare* proved to be so popular that eighteen translations were published between 1883 and 1907 (Sasaki 1988: 511–16), ten annotated translations between 1886 and 1912, and seventeen different English readers between 1867 and 1877 (1988: 561–63). Kawato Michiaki argues that these textbooks were particularly important since they instilled in future translators a better understanding of the plays while promoting appreciation of Shakespeare among potential readers and theatregoers (2004: 76–78).

Second, Japanized adaptations of Shakespeare's works prevailed in the early part of the Meiji period. The first stage production of an entire Shakespeare play was Katsu Genzō's (1844–1902) 1885 *Sakuradoki zeni no yo no naka* (*Life Is as Fragile as Cherry Blossom in a World of Money*), a kabuki version of *The Merchant of Venice*. Based on a novelization by Udagawa Bunkai (1848–1930) of Charles and Mary Lamb's version of the story, the play makes use of the Japanese aesthetics of *kachō fūgetsu* (literally 'flower, bird, wind and moon', an idiom that expresses the appreciation of literary and artistic works describing nature) (Gallimore 2013: 174). Characters are given Japanese names and the setting is changed to Edo period (1603–1868) Japan. While this was a kabuki performance by kabuki actors, it was rehearsed in a non-traditional manner, according to Taira Tatsuhiko, with the actors delving into the moral and legal issues of the play (1994: 175).

Other popular adapted productions include Takayasu Gekkō's (1869–1944) 1902 *Yami to hikari* (*Darkness and Light*, based on *King Lear*), Kojima Koshū's (*c.*1870–*c.*1920) 1909 *Hibiki* (*Echo*, based on *Timon of Athens*) and Matsui Shōyō's (1870–1933) 1911 *Saiai no tsuma* (*Most Beloved Wife*, based on *The Taming of the Shrew*) (Anzai 1989: 4). The combination of traditional forms of theatre with modern ideas came much more to the forefront with the shinpa movement; shinpa started as an exploration of how kabuki could become a means to convey social and political messages to the audience (Powell 2016: 200). Kawakami Otojirō, one of the founders of shinpa, started *seigeki* (straight play) productions in which the excessive spectacle of kabuki was discarded so as to highlight the text. *Othello* (1903), written by Emi Suiin (1869–1934), was the first of these productions. By presenting Othello as a military general who is tasked with the mission to defeat Taiwan, 'the play "performs" Japan as an emerging imperial power' (Tierney 2011: 516). In November of the same year, Kawakami staged *Hamlet*, adapted by Yamagishi Kayō (1876–1945) with the help of Doi Shunsho (1869–1915). The tragedy was presented as a *sewamono* (a genre of *jōruri* and kabuki depicting the lives of ordinary citizens) with the political aspects largely expunged from the play and focus placed on the fall of a single family rather than a nation (Kawatake 1972: 221). Nonetheless, the production departed from the conventions of kabuki performances and was more in tune with the times. For one, it was not set in feudal Japan but in the Meiji period, and it also excised Hamlet's fourth soliloquy. While Takahashi Yasunari attributes this to the fact that 'a typically modern thinking man, was something unknown to kabuki' (1995: 104), it is also true that this choice was motivated by the desire to maintain a 'modicum of realism' (Powell 1998: 39).

The third group consists of straightforward translations of the plays. Tsubouchi Shōyō (1859–1935), the first translator of the complete works of Shakespeare (the first volume of his translations was released in 1909 and the final in 1928), is generally considered to be the first to have translated, as opposed to adapted, an entire Shakespeare play. He did this with his *Julius Caesar* titled *Shiizaru kidan: Jiyū no tachi nagori no kireaji* (*Caesar's Strange Tale: Residual Sharpness of the Sword of Freedom*) (1884). Although Tsubouchi does not opt to place the action in a Japanese setting, he takes liberties with the text by adopting the style of the traditional jōruri puppet theatre. As Gallimore explains, 'feelings are more effectively concealed in the traditional Japanese theatre but the narrative less ambiguous' (2006a: 2). The script for jōruri, known as *maruhon* or *impon*, provides the narration for the puppet performance, which is meant to be chanted to musical accompaniment. In order to make his translation more accessible to a readership not used to a story told without narration, Tsubouchi interpolated long narrative passages into Shakespeare's text.[1] This had a great impact on subsequent translators of Shakespeare and many followed suit, starting with Kawashima Keizō (1859–1935), the author of *Midsummer Night's Dream: Shunjō ukiyo no yume* (*Spring Fever, the Dreams of the Floating World*) (1886). Kawashima clearly acknowledges that his style 'is learnt from Mr Tsubouchi's *Shiizaru kidan*' (Kawato 2004: 271).

Tsubouchi eventually moved away from jōruri-style translations and focused his energy on rendering Shakespeare's text word-for-word into Japanese; this, ironically, did not result in the masses engaging more directly with Shakespeare's text but rather served to alienate them. In the 1890s, Tsubouchi made this shift to produce as faithful a translation as possible with the intention of 'enlightening the young men of the new age' (1978: 254). Tsubouchi writes of his *Hamlet*, which he completed in 1911, that in 'preparing for the upcoming performance of *Hamlet* with the Bungei Kyōkai (Literary Arts Association), I endeavoured to observe Shakespeare's intentions as much as possible' (1911: 339).[2] While the production, staged at the Teikoku Gekijō (Imperial Theatre) was a commercial success, Tsubouchi's translation became the target of criticism from literary scholar and novelist Natsume Sōseki (1867–1916). Sōseki dismisses Tsubouchi's work as failing to bridge a chasm that exists between the play and the Japanese:

> If Dr Tsubouchi demands that I explain what creates this chasm, I would reply it is England that is wedged between the play and us; that it is three hundred years that is wedged there; that it is also unfamiliar poetic language that is constantly wedged there. In other words, I would like to declare without hesitation that a

---

[1] For a detailed discussion of the actual translated text, see Kishi and Bradshaw (2005: 5–8).

[2] All translations of Japanese texts are by the editors unless otherwise stated.

man known as Shakespeare stands there and completely hinders our appreciation of the play.

(Natsume 2019: 394)

Sōseki goes on to express his indignation that Tsubouchi, 'so intent on his attempt to be faithful to Shakespeare, ended up being unfaithful to us, the audience' (Natsume 2019: 394–95).

Anzai attributes this difference between the two literary figures in their approach to Shakespeare to a difference in priorities. Tsubouchi was interested in the plays as a resource for modernizing Japanese theatre in order to create a Japanese equivalent of Shakespeare. For Sōseki, the theatre was of little interest and the plays were 'nothing more than a subject for academic study' (Natsume 2019: 27). They are nonetheless not completely at odds with each other, for Daniel Gallimore perceives nationalism and the desire for modernization as a driving force for both figures: 'In Shōyō's case, this nationalism expresses itself as an impulse to Japanize Shakespeare; in Sōseki's case, to value Japanese culture' (2006b: 175).

Ironically, while both Tsubouchi and Sōseki turned to Shakespeare as a catalyst for modernization, this move towards modernization drove Shakespeare from the stage. Tsubouchi was 'unfaithful to us, the audience' because he was convinced that making an accurate Japanese version of the plays available was crucial to the evolution of Japanese theatre. It was, however, not only translation that stood in the way of non-Japanized versions of Shakespeare being performed. Towards the end of the Meiji period, shingeki emerged, renouncing the conventions and commercialism of kabuki and shinpa and turning to social realism (Powell 2016: 212). Two theatre companies were responsible for starting this new movement. The Bungei Kyōkai was formed in 1906 by Tsubouchi and journalist Shimamura Hōgetsu (1871–1918); from 1909 to 1913 the company only staged three works by Shakespeare. In 1909, playwright, director and critic Osanai Kaoru (1881–1928), along with kabuki actor Ichikawa Sadanji II (1880–1940), founded the

Jiyū Gekijō (Free Theatre); not a single work by Shakespeare was included among the fifteen plays they staged until the time they disbanded in 1919 (Powell 2016: 211). Though Japan turned to Shakespeare in its efforts to modernize itself, once modernization was on its way, the plays were no longer suited for the social realism that the Japanese stage started to pursue. Instead, theatre companies preferred plays by contemporaries such as Ibsen, Shaw, Chekov and Gorky (Anzai 1989: 6). Although the works of Shakespeare did not disappear completely from the theatre, Tsubouchi's efforts to produce accurate translations relegated Shakespeare from the stage to the study, and it was only after the Second World War that productions of Shakespeare would thrive once again.

POST-MEIJI PERFORMANCE AND TRANSLATION

Following Tsubouchi Shōyō, the next influential Shakespearean translator was Fukuda Tsuneari (1912–94), a translator, critic and director whose translations became popular in the 1950s and 1960s and who translated nineteen plays. Gallimore and Minami suggest that Shakespeare was 'not considered as important as living Japanese and Western playwrights' until Fukuda's translations became popular (2016: 487). His first translation was *Hamlet* (1955), which he directed for the Bungakuza (Literature Company) theatre company. This *Hamlet* was famously influenced by the Michael Benthall production that Fukuda saw at the Old Vic in 1954. In this 'flawed attempt to find a way out of the shingeki impasse' (Minami, Carruthers and Gillies 2001: 3), Fukuda, who had taken detailed notes at the Old Vic performance, replicated much of the London staging in his own. This production, despite arguments by critics such as Kishi Tetsuo to the contrary (see Kishi and Bradshaw 2005: 74), is emblematic of the ethos of the shingeki movement, described by Watanabe Emiko as a '*reductio ad absurdum* of the categorical imperative of modernization-as-westernization' (2003: 82).

The Old Vic *Hamlet* had another impact on Fukuda's *Hamlet* since he used a 'somatic theory of theatre translation' that focused more on the sound of the 'spoken English' rather than the written English (Curran 2014: 5). He listened to the way Richard Burton delivered the lines, and also asked 'How did Olivier pronounce it in the film? How did Gielgud deliver the line on the recording?' (Fukuda 1994: 133). Consequently, he translated the play with an awareness of the text's future performance and how it would sound onstage in Japanese. Although Fukuda's translations are still occasionally used by contemporary artists, they are regarded by some as being 'a little too difficult and archaic for young audiences to follow' (Minami 2016b: 34), perhaps because as Sano Akiko suggests, while he thought it was 'necessary to modernize Shakespeare in Japan, he did not want a contemporary Shakespeare' (1999: 355).

There have been many other translations (marked in Murakami's model as 'rival translations I' and 'II'), but there are two figures that are really key to the following. The first of these is Odashima Yūshi (1930–), who was the second to translate Shakespeare's complete works. Odashima's translations were essential in the changing performance styles of Shakespeare in the 1970s, a change that was also influenced by the shōgekijō movement and tours to Japan by foreign companies. Rising to prominence during the 1960s and 1970s, shōgekijō rejected existing theatrical conventions, including theatrical space: performances often took place on the street, in tents and in other non-'theatre' spaces, allowing a new sense of freedom of expression. Odashima's translations were performed by director Deguchi Norio and his Shakespeare Theatre Company (STC) in Tokyo, beginning in 1975. By 1981 the STC had staged all of Shakespeare's plays, with Odashima translating at an incredible pace that saw him supply Deguchi with a translation 'almost every month' (Minami 2016b: 34).

Deguchi's productions are often referred to as 'Shakespeare in jeans' due to their laid-back simplicity: unlike the shingeki era's lavish productions and period costumes, the STC actors wore jeans and t-shirts and performed on an empty stage. The translations provided to the company by Odashima, full of colloquialisms and word-play (not used by Tsubouchi or Fukuda) and replicating 'the rapid tempo of daily conversation' (Minami et al. 2001: 3), went well with the speed and accessibility of the STC. Indeed, the increase in Shakespearean performance in the 1970s and 1980s (often referred to as the 'Shakespeare boom') owed much to Odashima's translations (Gallimore and Minami 2016). His translations are still regularly performed, and several internationally famous productions such as *Ninagawa Macbeth* (1980–2018) were presented using Odashima's work.

The second figure is Matsuoka Kazuko (1942–), the first female translator to take on Shakespeare's complete works. At the time of writing, she has translated thirty-one plays, with an upcoming new translation of *King John* marking her thirty-second. Starting in the early 1990s, Matsuoka began translating for theatre companies, including *The Comedy of Errors* directed by Peter Stormare at the Tokyo Globe in 1994. Her new translation of *King Lear* was performed in 1998 to celebrate the opening of the New National Theatre in Tokyo, under the direction of Uyama Hitoshi (1953–), and since 1998 Matsuoka's translations have been used in Saitama Arts Theater's project to stage the complete works. Her translation of *Twelfth Night*, the second in the series after *Romeo and Juliet*, was first staged in 1998. Matsuoka's translations are notable because female characters in her work tend to 'speak in [a] less feminine way, if not in masculine style', since she suggests that in previous translations women were often given speaking styles that were 'too modest and elegant' (Sano 1999: 364). Matsuoka's women are contemporary and equal to the male characters, at least in terms of their speech, and she has said that she was struck by the difference between previous translations and her own while she was working on *Romeo and Juliet*. Citing the humble style of speech Juliet uses towards Romeo in the existing Japanese translations, she writes that she realized 'that unique Japanese nuance wasn't actually in the original text' and that in the English text, 'Romeo and Juliet are on an even footing' (Matsuoka 2019). Her translations are also interesting because they attain their 'final form through discussion with directors' (Sano 1999: 362), with Matsuoka regularly attending rehearsals and sometimes revising her translation in response to the rehearsals. She also writes out by hand the entire original text before beginning her translation, suggesting that the 'action of writing something by hand connects your thoughts with your physical body. By writing the same words as Shakespeare, I felt a little closer to Shakespeare's own thoughts' (Matsuoka 2019).

Sano writes that Tsubouchi 'highlighted the similarities' between Japanese and Western culture, so that the Japanese audience 'could understand' and would want to 'learn more about it', whereas Fukuda saw it as 'his duty to introduce the true features of Western culture', correcting previous mistakes and misunderstandings (357). She adds that in Odashima's translations, 'the West is a close and familiar world. The two cultures are different but they can coexist' (ibid.). Similarly, for Matsuoka the act of translating Shakespeare into Japanese for performance results in the creation of what she has described as 'cultural hybrids' (Matsuoka 2016), an idea that is reminiscent of Beverley Curran's theory of translation as a 'process involving multiple languages speaking to each other' (2014: 1).

The availability of so many different translations, whatever their differences in style or motivation, has allowed the spread of 'reinventions' of Shakespeare: 'this unprecedented availability of translations has highlighted the instability of Shakespeare's texts in Japanese, encouraging some practitioners to stage their own versions' (Gallimore and Minami 2016: 494). To put it another way, the incredible number of responses, adaptations and 'tradaptations' owes much to the diversity of available translations that have encouraged a certain freedom with the texts and characters. It should also be noted that academic Kawai Shōichirō (1960–) has also begun his own translation of the complete works, which he began staging in 2014 with a production of *Much Ado About Nothing* as part of the 'Kawai Project', expanding the range of available texts still further.

In the current period of 'reinvention' there has been an outpouring of adaptations of Shakespeare. Besides the new productions created and commissioned by the traditional theatre genres (for example, Mansai Nomura and the *Kyogen of Errors* (2001), Ninagawa Yukio's kabuki *Twelfth Night* (2005) and the *bunraku* adaptation *Farusu no taifu* (*Sir Falstaff*), written by Kawai Shōichirō (2014)), numerous playwrights have created their own adaptations. Famous examples include writer and director Noda Hideki's (1955–) adaptations since the late 1980s (published in 1994 under the title *Shakespeare Wearing a Mawashi*, a *mawashi* being the band worn by sumo wrestlers), director Suzuki Tadashi's (1939–) adaptations (*Night and Clock* (*Macbeth*) in 1975, *The Tale of Lear* in 1988), writer Inoue Hisashi's *Tempo jūninen no Shakespeare* (*Shakespeare in the Twelfth Year of the Tempo Era*, 1974) and Nomura Mansai and Kawai Shōichirō's *Kuniusubito* (*The Country Stealer*, 2007), based on *Richard III*. There are countless other examples in various media forms, including *manga*, *anime*, television and film (most famously Kurosawa Akira's *Kumonosujō* (*Throne of Blood* (*Macbeth*), 1957) and *Ran* (*King Lear*, 1985)).

Noda Hideki, who is currently the artistic director of the Tokyo Metropolitan Theatre, based his adaptations on Odashima's translations. Suzuki Masae suggests that the basic concept behind Noda's 'localization' of Shakespeare is that a play 'will work better if it is drawn closer to the world of the audience' (2001: 137). Noda's plays include *Twelfth Night* (1986), *Much Ado About Nothing* (1990), *Sandaime, Richādo*

(*Richard III*, 1990) and *A Midsummer Night's Dream* (1992). *A Midsummer Night's Dream* was transposed to a forest at the base of Mt Fuji and intertwined with *Alice in Wonderland*. In *Sandaime, Richādo*, Noda moved the setting to a trial with 'Shakespeare' himself as the prosecutor in Richādo's (Richard's) trial. The trial is mixed with Shakespeare's own family history, in particular his relationship with his younger brother, and the world of flower arrangement. (For a more in-depth discussion of this play, see Suzuki's chapter in *Performing Shakespeare in Japan*, 2001). Noda has argued that in translated plays there can be difficulties in 'understanding the concepts behind the words' since words such as 'Count' 'do not sound familiar to us', and so he replaces the original setting with an equivalent Japanese one, introducing sumo wrestling in *Much Ado About Nothing* and flower arranging in *Richard III*, to draw 'Shakespeare's world nearer to mine' (Noda 2001: 220–21). Minami suggests that Noda's attitude of 'treating Shakespeare as source material rather than as authority' is representative of post-shōgekijō theatre (Minami et al. 2001: 10), and adds that Noda and other contemporary playwrights do not 'read Shakespeare for contemporary meanings, but they write contemporary meanings into Shakespeare' (Minami 2001: 157).

Inoue Hisashi's (1934–2010) *Tempo juninen no Shakespeare* is a play set in the world of the *yakuza* in 1841. A musical comedy, *Tempo* incorporates references to every Shakespeare play and in its first staging was five hours long (famously causing many in the audience to leave for the last train home) (Tanaka 2005). It was restaged by Inoue Hidenori in 2002 and Ninagawa in 2005, both using shorter versions. Ninagawa's production opened with a replica of the Globe Theatre being dismantled by Japanese workers dressed in Edo-period clothes, while the actors sang 'What if Shakespeare had never lived', a song mocking the prevalence of Shakespeare in Japan: 'Had it not been for Shakespeare, the shingeki world, which has produced few original plays, would be quite at a loss' (Minami

2010: 80). In a role combining elements of Hamlet and Romeo, actor Fujiwara Tatsuya delivered twelve different translations of 'to be or not to be' at breakneck speed, starting with Kawai Shōichirō's 2002 translation and ending with Charles Wirgman's 1874 translation, highlighting the instability of Shakespeare's most famous line in Japanese.

Inoue Hidenori (1960–), director of theatre company Gekidan Shinkansen, has directed a number of Shakespearean adaptations besides his 2002 staging of *Metal Macbeth* (2006), *Lord of the Lies* (2007), *Minatomachi junjō Othello* (*A Simple Othello in a Port Town*, 2011) and *Natagirimaru* (*Richard III*, 2013). In a piece on Inoue, Yoshihara Yukari asks 'Is this Shakespeare?', and argues that Inoue shows 'great mastery in un-Shakespeareing Shakespeare' (2010: 141). *Metal Macbeth* is a post-apocalyptic version of *Macbeth* set in the twenty-third century. Written by Kudō Kankurō, *Metal Macbeth* is a perfect example of Inoue's reframing of Shakespeare's plays as 'contemporary pop theatrical events', combining various forms of popular culture and contemporary references (Gallimore and Minami 2016: 491). *Lord of the Lies* mixes *Richard III* and *Macbeth* with kabuki and Japanese legends, and falls under the umbrella of what Inoue describes as '*Inoue kabuki*', or a 'neo-kabuki' style that utilizes traditional kabuki elements alongside popular culture. Described by Yoshihara as a 'patched-up hybrid' that 'depends more heavily on kabuki than on Shakespeare' (2010: 148), *Lord of the Lies* was written by Nakashima Kazuki and was first performed at the Shinbashi Enbujō Theatre, a theatre usually reserved for kabuki productions. Yoshihara argues that Inoue's productions raise the question that if plays are to be called 'Shakespearean adaptations, how different can they be from Shakespeare's original?', and suggests that these 'pop appropriations' of Shakespeare show that 'we are living in an age of globalization and commodification', where the 'line between 'proper' and 'improper' Shakespeare is hard to determine and defend' (2010: 152–53).

Another prolific site of Shakespearean adaptation has been the Takarazuka Revue. Takarazuka, an all-female musical revue founded in 1913, is known for its kitsch musical adaptations of plays, films, mythology and literature from every corner of the world. Takarazuka has performed numerous adaptations, including *Adventures in Love* (based on *Twelfth Night*, 1980), *Puck* (1992), *The Tempest* (set in 1940s Hong Kong, 1999), *Epiphany* (based on *Twelfth Night* and set in the Meiji period, 1999), *Rome at Dawn* (*Julius Caesar*, 2006), *The Lost Glory – Beautiful Illusion* (based on *Othello* and set in 1929 New York, 2014) and *FALSTAFF ~ Falstaff Plunged into the Story of Romeo and Juliet* (2016). In 'Juliet's Girlfriends: The Takarazuka Revue Company and the *Shōjo* Culture', Ohtani Tomoko discusses the importance of *shōjo* (young girls) culture to Takarazuka's productions, citing the replacement of Juliet's 'bawdy Nurse' with several young women (2001: 159). She suggests that Takarazuka 'does not aim to produce a canonical and authentic Shakespeare', which requires a 'faithful translation of the text' and expressing 'the English point-of-view on Shakespeare' (2001: 161).

We have considered the impact that changing theatrical styles and forms of adaptation have had on Japanese performers, but it is also essential to consider the dramatic changes undergone by Japanese society in the past few decades. The three plays in this volume all respond to these changes and also to a series of disasters and violent upheavals since the 1990s. As Barbara E. Thornbury writes, Japan's theatre 'of translation' can be framed within 'the history of ideological conflict that defines Japan's modernization' (2013: 169), but these translations and adaptations should also be framed within the 'social and seismic shifts' of the past three decades (Curran 2014: 50). The plays collected here respond to different events in different ways, but they share a wider social context: the stagnation of the Japanese economy is a key underlying thread for all of them. Following the devastation and widespread poverty of the early post-war period, the Japanese economy underwent a 'miracle' recovery and became the second largest economy in the world. The economy nose-dived after the 'bubble economy' (1986–91), a period of massive inflation and speculation, burst: the following decade is known as the 'lost decade', which has since expanded to the 'lost twenty years'. The 1990s also brought about further problems besides economic recession. In January 1995 the Hanshin area (the region around Kobe and Osaka) was struck by the Great Hanshin Earthquake, killing around 6,434 people and causing extensive damage, and then in March of the same year the religious cult Aum Shinrikyō released sarin gas onto the Tokyo subway, killing thirteen and injuring thousands.

While these events have maintained a degree of influence, and are particularly relevant to the Tokyo Shakespeare Company's *The Three Daughters of Lear* (first staged in 1995), they have been superseded by more recent issues and developments. These include the rise in global terrorism, the environmental crisis, a changing economy and the 'demographic time bomb' of a super-ageing population and declining birth-rate. Those who grew up in the 'lost decade' are sometimes known as the 'Lost Generation': a generation of people who have only known an economy 'in constant decline', who have seen the loss of the job security promised to the previous generations and who have a rapidly ageing older generation to support. Japanese society has also seen a rise in isolated or troubled youths (including the *hikikomori*, people who completely withdraw from society), violent crimes and further domestic terrorist incidents (Otake 2009).

Furthermore, the Great East Japan Earthquake, also known as 3.11, has had an enormous influence on Japanese performance after 2011. Kakushinhan's *HAMLET X SHIBUYA* (2012) and the Shakespeare Company Japan's *The New Romeo and Juliet* (2012) translated in this volume are excellent examples of this influence. On 11 March 2011, a 9.0 magnitude earthquake struck the north-eastern coast of Japan, causing a devastating tsunami and a nuclear disaster at the Fukushima Daiichi Nuclear Power Plant. Described as an event that was '*sōteigai*' (beyond all expectations), the disaster caused at least 15,898 deaths (with over 2,500 people still reported missing), the destruction of 500 km of coastline and billions of dollars in damage (Geilhorn and Iwata-Weickgenannt 2017: 1). The crisis at the Fukushima Nuclear Power Plant forced thousands of people to be evacuated from their homes in the neighbouring regions, and despite residents being encouraged to return to some towns in recent years there are many areas still designated as 'Difficult-to-Return Zones'. The invisibility of radiation, its 'pervasive presence' in the 'soil, the water table, the sea, the air', was both at the time of the disaster and at the time of writing, a source of great anxiety and distrust (Poulton 2017: 139).

The following three plays are examples of the different ways Japanese artists have responded to the changes in the theatre and in the world around them. Since adaptations of Shakespeare have been present in Japanese theatre since the earliest interactions between Shakespeare and Japan, these plays represent some of the uses to which contemporary artists have been putting Shakespeare: to question pervasive ideas in society (consumerism), to attempt to make sense of the world again after 3.11, and to provide encouragement and entertainment to stricken communities. Japanese adaptations have moved through a cycle, going from plays set in the then-contemporary Meiji period to plays set in contemporary Tokyo and beyond. As previously referenced, Curran has suggested that translation is a process 'involving multiple languages speaking to each other and pluralized identities' (2014: 1), and it is possible to see these different languages, texts and performance styles 'speak' to each other in the three plays translated here. Given the frequent bias towards Tokyo-based performance, it is also an opportunity to present the work of the Sendai-based Shakespeare Company Japan here in English for the first time.

General Introduction

THE TOKYO SHAKESPEARE COMPANY

An overview of the company

Edo Kaoru founded the Tokyo Shakespeare Company (TSC) in 1990.[3] Since then they have been presenting Shakespeare to the Japanese public through their stage productions of Shakespeare's plays, performances of original plays inspired by Shakespeare, and stage readings of selected scenes from Shakespeare combined with explanations about the play.

With regards to the first of these three, they have staged twenty-five productions of twenty-three different plays as of 2019. One of the distinctive features of their productions is that Edo has translated or adapted all but four of the plays herself. Of the twenty-five productions, thirteen have been adaptations in which the source text has been reworked. The second group consists of six plays that are part of their 'Shakespeare through the Looking-Glass' series. These are sequels or re-imagined versions of Shakespeare's works which Okuizumi Hikaru and Edo have scripted together. Edo has acknowledged *Rosencrantz and Guildenstern Are Dead* (1966) as an inspiration for the series (Edo 2013: 23). A reviewer of the 2008 Japanese production of *Rosencrantz and Guildenstern Are Dead*, in turn, connected Stoppard's play with the work of the TSC when quoting translator Matsuoka Kazuko: 'There are instances in which it is possible to better grasp the world Shakespeare creates from the view of characters other than the protagonists' (Takahashi 2008: 14). The TSC also holds frequent reading performances of Shakespeare. This started with the 'Tudor Cats on a Moonlit Night' series in 1996. The TSC has presented reading performances at the Yokohama Art Festival and the

---

[3] The Company was initially called *Shibaiya Edo Yashiki*. They staged two plays by Kageyama Raiju, the playwright for the theatre company Sōkihei, as well as five Shakespeare plays. It was with the 1995 production of *The Three Daughters of Lear* that they changed their name to the Tokyo Shakespeare Company.

Suginami Theater Festival. In 2012 and 2013, they held bilingual readings of *Twelfth Night*, *The Two Gentlemen of Verona* and *Romeo and Juliet*, in which Edo read her parts in English while one of the TSC's actresses, Tsukasa Mari, read Edo's translated text.

Edo Kaoru and Okuizumi Hikaru

Edo received her primary education in Makati City in the Philippines and her secondary education in Chennai, India; it was during these years that she grew to love Shakespeare and English poetry. After entering the International Christian University in Tokyo (ICU), she joined a student theatre society that specialized in staging English language plays and directed a production of *Twelfth Night*. Also, the experience of seeing Deguchi Norio's ground-breaking productions of Shakespeare as an undergraduate student has left an indelible mark on Edo's own work. While most non-Japanese plays at the time were performed with actors wearing wigs and prosthetic noses to appear non-Japanese (known as *akage-mono* or 'red-hair productions'), Deguchi's actors wore jeans and no make-up; he also eliminated sets and the use of blackouts to create quicker pacing. Having completed an undergraduate degree in literature at ICU and worked in foreign aid for a year and a half, Edo joined Deguchi's STC from 1985 to 1987. This was followed by a stint as the star actress of the theatre company Sōkihei before her decision to start the TSC. During this time, she also worked as an interpreter for British director Glen Walford when Walford directed *Measure for Measure* for Rhyming Theatre Company (1988) and she performed Cordelia to Brian Cox's Lear in a workshop at the Tokyo Globe. More recently she has been giving readings of plays at Meiji University as part of its Meiji Shakespeare Project.

Okuizumi is the author of twenty-five novels to date and professor of Japanese literature at Kinki University. In 1994 his fifth novel *Ishi no raireki* (*The Stones Cry Out*) won the

Akutagawa Prize. He has also received the Noma Literary New Face Prize for *Novalis no in'yō* (*Citing Novalis*) (1993), the Noma Literary Prize for *Shinki* (*Sacred Vessel*) (2009), the Tanizaki Jun'ichirō Prize for *Tokyo jijoden* (*Tokyo Autobiography*) (2014) and the Shibata Renzaburō Prize and Mainichi Bunka Shuppan Prize for *Yuki no kizahashi* (*Steps of Snow*) (2018). Many of his novels combine mystery-driven plots with esoteric knowledge and humour, all of which are also features of his 'Shakespeare through the Looking-Glass' series.

The staging of The Three Daughters of Lear

The Three Daughters of Lear was first staged in 1995, and this production toured to Sendai. In 1997 a new version toured Kushibiki and Mikawa, which are also in the Tohoku region in northern mainland Japan. It has since been revived three times, and was also staged by the Majin Project in October 2019. All the venues in Tokyo have been small theatres that seat less than 150 people.[4] Jean-Jean, the venue for the first production, is of particular interest as this was where Deguchi had started staging his productions of Shakespeare and where many avant-garde 'underground' performances also took place. The theatre was in the basement of the Tokyo Yamate Church. This explains the following lines in the Fool's first monologue: 'After all, what rises above us? Immediately above us. Indeed, a church. And it is common knowledge that below a church lies Hell!'

In all productions of *The Three Daughters* the only set was a well in the centre of the stage, and the stage properties would be limited to nails scattered across the stage, two pails, the Fool's portmanteau, a crown and a ring (changed to a shawl in the 2000 production). Satō Keiichi, TSC's company musician who has been composing for the TSC since 1991, played original music on a lute at the beginning and end of the play. The Fool

---

[4] When touring in the Tohoku region, the venues were public halls with a much larger seating capacity.

wore a black suit and a bowler hat; the Wag, a button-down shirt, shorts and tights; the daughters, evening gowns; Edmund, a Romeo-blouse and white tights; and Lear, a robe. While the costumes were decidedly Western, they did not pertain to a particular period and created the impression of belonging to a generic fairy-tale. This, combined with the almost abstract space of the stage, had the effect of not only making the audience part of the world of the play, but also encouraging them to engage directly with the spoken words.

There have been two significant changes made to the play since its premiere. First, the 1995 and 1996 productions excised much of the humour. Maekawa Shirō, the director, decided on these cuts since the initial script took nearly four hours to perform. Much of the humour was returned to the script in subsequent versions and to the 2013 published version of the text, but part of the Fool's opening monologue (in which he describes the journey from Shibuya station to Jean-Jean) has been lost.

The second is the ending of the play. In the 1995 and 1996 productions, the Hell Wag exited in Cordelia's clothes. The Fool called to him to leave the ring, and then found the ring still in his pocket. The lights blacked out as he looked perplexed. The 1997 version saw the Fool exit without learning the Wag's identity, while the Wag, still in Cordelia's clothes, was struck by the realization that he was actually Lear's youngest daughter. The 2000 and 2004 productions replaced the ring with a shawl. As the Fool noticed that he had not given the shawl to the Wag, Goneril and Regan appeared collecting nails; the Wag stared at them from the other end of the stage, before he bent down to start collecting nails too as the lights went down. A number of lines were also added to make clear the suggestion that the Wag may actually be Cordelia. The most recent production had a male actor play the Wag; this was part of the reason why this version did not end with the implication that the Wag was Cordelia.

The translation of the play in this volume uses the text published in *Mephistopheles no teiri* (*Mephistopheles's Theorem*). However, while the source text opts for the 2013 ending, this translation replaces the ending with the 1995 version with the line additions from 2000.

KAKUSHINHAN THEATRE COMPANY

Kimura Ryūnosuke and Kakushinhan Theatre Company

The word *kakushinhan* can be translated as a 'crime of conscience', a 'premeditated crime' or an 'act carried out while knowing that it should not be'; Kakushinhan Theatre Company themselves translate their name in English as 'Convinced Criminals'. The company, which as of August 2019 has staged over twenty Shakespearean productions, was established in 2011 by director and writer Kimura Ryūnosuke. Kimura's first play with Kakushinhan, *HAMLET X SHIBUYA ~ Light, Was Our Revenge Tarnished?* (2012), is translated into English for the first time here. The play's title refers to one of the main characters ('Light') and echoes the emphasis throughout the text on corruption and decay, inspired by Hamlet's 'unweeded garden' line. Despite its relatively recent start date, particularly when compared with some of the more long-running companies discussed in this volume, Kakushinhan has been receiving increasing critical attention in Japan and has even become well-enough established to run its own training programme, Kakushinhan Studio. The company falls within Senda Akihiko's 'zero generation' label for theatre-makers in Japan who emerged after 2000, when the economic bubble had already burst and who therefore share the 'social/economic background of the so-called "lost twenty years"' (Senda 2011).

The company began by staging Kimura's adaptations of Shakespeare in 2012, first with *HAMLET X SHIBUYA ~ Light, Was Our Revenge Tarnished?* and then with *Romeo and Juliet on the Seashore* later in the same year. Since 2014 Kakushinhan has largely used Matsuoka Kazuko's existing translations rather than Kimura's own adaptations, although the company still occasionally inserts extra dialogue and short scenes into these productions. Kakushinhan's 'straight' Shakespeare performances (used here only in the sense of a translation rather than an adaptation) began with *King Lear*, *A Midsummer Night's Dream*, *Titus Andronicus* and *Hamlet* in 2014, followed by *Othello – Black or White* (2015), *Julius Caesar* and *Richard III* (2016), *Macbeth* and *Titus Andronicus* (2017), *Hamlet* (2018) and *The Wars of the Roses* (*Richard III* and the three *Henry VI* plays running in repertory) in 2019.

The company also stages shortened productions under the umbrella of its 'Kakushinhan Pocket' series. Productions that are part of the Pocket series are around two hours long and have a smaller cast (roughly seven to eight actors) than shows in the regular series (for example, the 2019 *Wars of the Roses* had over twenty actors). The project began in 2015 with *The Taming of the Shrew* and has since also featured *Pocket Henry VI* (running in repertory with the 'non-' Pocket version of *Richard III* in 2016), *A Midsummer Night's Dream* (2017) and *The Winter's Tale* and *The Merchant of Venice* in 2018. Since 2016 the company have been taking the Kakushinhan Pocket productions to Kimura's home prefecture of Oita. Besides these regular activities, Kakushinhan has also occasionally held one-off events and reading performances, including a reading of *HAMLET X SHIBUYA* in 2019.

Kimura was born in 1983 in Oita, Kyushu, and grew up in Takarazuka in western Japan. He studied English and American literature at Tokyo University, where he directed Shakespeare for the first time (*Macbeth*). After graduating, he studied at the Bungakuza's Acting Institute, attended some rehearsals led by Ninagawa and acted with Deguchi's Shakespeare Company. For his first university production of *Macbeth*, he rented a video of Ninagawa's famous 1980 production, but stated that he was 'amazed because it was entirely different from William Shakespeare's *Macbeth*' (Tanaka 2017). Citing Ninagawa's use of a *butsudan* (family altar) as a prime example of what he found to be so different in Ninagawa's version, he explained that after reading a comment by literary critic Kobayashi Hideo about how he 'borrowed others' text' to 'present his own views' he was inspired to adapt Shakespeare's plays freely (ibid.).

The founding of Kakushinhan in 2012 was directly inspired by the 3.11 disaster. Kimura argues that although his generation is seen as 'quiet' and 'expressionless' no matter the situation, the 'zero generation' have in fact 'lived in a pretty intense world . . . a turbulent era, with events such as 3.11' (Yadorigi 2016). Describing 3.11 as a 'momentum' to start Kakushinhan, Kimura has suggested that the 'many serious' events that have taken place in recent years have parallels with the 'world of Shakespeare' (Kimura 2013). However, rather than addressing these events directly, Kimura approaches them through the medium of Shakespeare, whose writing he suggests allows directors, actors and the audience to 'grasp "something"' through the theatre (Yadorigi 2016). Kimura wrote two plays during the early stage of the company which were both adaptations of Shakespeare; these were *HAMLET X SHIBUYA* and *Romeo and Juliet on the Seashore* (2012). Since 2014, however, he has used Matsuoka Kazuko's existing translations, occasionally inserting extra dialogue or short scenes, because he wanted to take 'a more direct approach to Shakespeare's language' and he believed that her translations 'vividly reflect the contemporary Japanese ethos and its language from a female perspective' (Eglinton 2016).

The staging of HAMLET X SHIBUYA

HAMLET X SHIBUYA was first performed at GALLERY LE DECO in Shibuya, a small white box space used for exhibitions and performances. Kimura largely left the space as it was, adding only some scaffolding around the existing columns. Although very little set was used, the stage space gradually became cluttered during the performance with ordinary objects from everyday life, including umbrellas, chairs and toilet rolls: a technique that Kimura has continued to employ throughout his productions. The large Chorus arranged the props, bringing them on and off stage as required by particular scenes. The production used its large cast to fill the stage, and also relied on contemporary music, instruments (including drums) and frequent use of blackouts and lighting changes.

Every character that appeared in the production was dressed in contemporary-style clothing, particularly noticeable in the Chorus who gradually filled the stage during the opening scene carrying shopping bags and umbrellas and dressed in familiar styles and brands, from Hello Kitty sweatshirts to high-school uniforms. The Chorus often spoke as one or split lines between them, and often spoke loudly and disjointedly on top of one another during scenes where they were not the focus of attention, providing a noisy and chaotic sense of daily city life. Throughout the production Kimura used blackouts and dim lighting, with some scenes lit only by electric torches carried by the characters, echoing the script's obsession with 'darkness'. The production also frequently used several long strips of white, red or black material as an effective stage prop. When the crossing attack was first recounted, Chorus members lay on the ground and were covered by the large white sheet, only to slowly stand up and, still shrouded under the sheet, become the ghosts of Ophelia who torment Shibuya.

The company restaged *HAMLET X SHIBUYA* as a script-in-hand production in spring 2019, again at GALLERY LE DECO. This later production had only six actors, with the lines of the Chorus split between them. Compared with the densely populated stage and actors speaking over one another that had characterized the earlier production, the reading production was a quieter, more intimate affair that cleverly used small props such as toy police cars and cut-out paper figures to represent the multiple characters and overlapping events. Maimi, who played Shibuya in the 2012 production, was here cast as the sex worker, with Shimada Jumpei as Shibuya and Suzuki Akinori as Akihabara. The performance contained some changed lines and ad-libs, including Kōchi Yamato (as the Ghost/Police officer) who in his list of Shibuya 'motifs' referred to the location of the performance, close to the newly rebuilt Shibuya Stream complex, as the 'now cleaned up' neighbourhood.

THE SHAKESPEARE COMPANY JAPAN

Shimodate Kazumi and the Shakespeare Company Japan

Shimodate Kazumi, a professor at Tohoku Gakuin University in Sendai, established the Shakespeare Company Japan (SCJ) in 1992 with the financial support of twenty-nine donors. From the beginning the aims of the SCJ have been focused on representing the culture of Tohoku on stage and building a wooden theatre like the Globe in Tohoku, where they can get local people interested in the theatre and provide opportunities for them to enjoy productions of masterpieces from around the world. Surprisingly though, initially the company had no actors and it took them more than three years to stage their first production. In the meantime, Shimodate went to Britain on sabbatical and conducted research on Shakespeare at the University of Cambridge (1992–93). During this sabbatical he also learned how to produce and direct Shakespeare, and he had a chance to meet the Royal Shakespeare Company's Head of Voice, Cicely Berry, and to participate in her workshops some years later. After returning to Sendai in 1993, Shimodate translated *Romeo and Juliet* into the local dialect and eventually the company prepared for their first production of Shakespeare in 1995.[5] At

---

[5] In 2002, Shimodate was appointed Directing Fellow of the Globe Theatre in London and directed a special production of *Savage Sensuality*.

this stage they set about recruiting and auditioning actors who could speak both standardized Japanese and the Tohoku dialect.[6]

In 1995, they performed a version of *Romeo and Juliet* set in Tohoku, at British Hills, a resort and English language training centre in Fukushima. Although the performance met with a favourable reception, one comment from the audience alerted Shimodate to the importance of adapting rather than translating Shakespeare's works for the local Tohoku people: 'I enjoyed it very much, but why is Tohoku dialect spoken, when the setting itself is Verona in Italy?' (Shimodate 2017: 43–44). Since then, all of their adaptations have been set in some region of Tohoku or Hokkaido, and consequently there have been frequent references to local culture in the works. For example, the company's second production of Shakespeare was an adaptation of *A Midsummer Night's Dream*, which localized the comedy into a story about Matsushima Bay in Miyagi Prefecture, with its small islands, and the fairies in the woods of Athens were thus changed into the nymphs of the sea and Puck into a goblin known as *kappa*, which is a familiar figure for the local people.[7]

The SCJ has staged thirteen different translations and adaptations of eleven works of Shakespeare. Some have been revival productions of revised works, such as *The New As You Like It in a Hot Spring Inn* of 2008, which is based on an earlier 2001 version. They have performed their plays not only in Tohoku and Tokyo, but also in Britain: *Macbeth in Osore-zan* (*Macbeth of Mt. Osore*) was staged at the Edinburgh Festival Fringe in August 2000. In August 2019, the SCJ was invited to

---

[6] According to Shimodate, the actors are all 'amateurs', not professional actors, in the sense that they have a day job or are students. Members of the SCJ, including the technical staff, work as professors, high school teachers, nurses, accountants and so on, balancing their work and the troupe's activities.

[7] For a detailed analysis of the play, particularly in terms of the sound of the local dialect, see Gallimore, *Sounding like Shakespeare* (2012) and 'Speaking Shakespeare in Japanese' (2010).

perform *Ainu Othello* at the Tara Arts Theatre by its Artistic Director, Jatinder Verma.[8]

The language

The SCJ's scripts of Shakespeare are all written in the Tohoku dialect, which is quite different from standardized Japanese, particularly in terms of vowel sounds, suffixes, intonation and vocabulary. While Shimodate himself speaks the dialect of Shiogama, a coastal town in Miyagi Prefecture, other members speak the dialects of other areas in Tohoku. Shimodate writes scripts in his local dialect first, which each actor then 'adjusts into their own dialect' (*Ainu Othello* 2019: 15). For the SCJ, according to its website, the local vernacular is an indispensable medium which they believe enables them 'to express a deeper and broader interpretation of Shakespeare's world' and 'to create a new slant on Shakespeare's plays both in Japan and abroad'.

Shimodate also aims to explore the artistic potential of Japanese dialects. In the beginning of the Meiji period, it was imperative that the newly hatched modern nation-state should have a single national language in which people could communicate with each other anywhere throughout the Japanese archipelago. As Okamoto Shigeko and Janet Shibamoto-Smith have argued, 'A critical factor for Japanese policymakers, then, was to unify the country under the umbrella of a single language with the aim both to extend the Meiji regime's control and to promote economic growth by producing a literate population' (2016: 37). Consequently, the standardization of language accelerated the eradication of regional dialects, which have

---

[8] The Ainu are an indigenous people in Hokkaido, with their own traditional culture and language quite different from those of the Japanese. This production was co-directed by Ainu director Akibe Debo, and contained traditional performances by the Ainu dance group Pirikap. For the performance at the Tara Theatre, see the detailed review written by Sarah Olive (2019) and also that by Howard Loxton (2019).

historically been deemed inferior compared to standardized Japanese. Shimodate believes that such dialects have seldom had the chance to be refined as a language through use in works of art, particularly as a dramatic language, whereas standardized Japanese has been refined throughout the long history of Japanese literature. Therefore, following the pioneering use of dialects for the stage by Kinoshita Junji (1914–2006), a playwright and translator of Shakespeare, Shimodate has been attempting to transform the Tohoku dialect into a theatrical language. When Kinoshita wrote *Yūzuru* (*Twilight Crane* 1949), he adapted the Sado Island dialect, blending it with various regional dialects of Eastern and Western Japan, and thus, the characters in the plays converse 'not in any particular dialect' but in 'a fabricated dialect composed of mixed expressions that sound particularly rural' (Kinsui 2017: 34). Kinoshita successfully created a theatrical language by mixing various dialects and standardized Japanese, which he referred to as a 'universal dialect' or a mixed dialect for the stage. He believed this was a language audiences in any area of the country could understand. Likewise, Shimodate mixes standardized Japanese with the Tohoku dialect in order to create a sophisticated theatrical language style which is comprehensible for the audience.[9]

The Great East Japan Earthquake and tsunami of 2011 and the 'Hot Spring Trilogy'

An earthquake with a magnitude of 9.0 struck the East Japan region at 2:46 pm on 11 March 2011, and the devastating tsunami triggered by the quake engulfed a wide extent of the coastal areas in Tohoku. The National Police Agency of Japan has reported 15,898 deaths, 2,531 people missing and 6,157 people injured in the 2011 Great East Japan Earthquake and tsunami as of 10 September 2019. Moreover, the calamity

---

[9] For a comprehensive analysis of dialect use in television dramas, particularly in the NHK television drama series, see Tanaka Yukari (2014).

caused another disaster, the meltdown at the Fukushima Daiichi Nuclear Power Plant, which led to the evacuation of a considerable number of residents from the surrounding areas. Many survivors and evacuees have suffered from psychological distress and, according to the Ministry of Health, Labour and Welfare of Japan, the total number of the suicides connected to the earthquake reached 239 as of May 2020 ('Statistics of Suicide of Japan' 2020).

Most members of the SCJ were living in the Tohoku region when the earthquake occurred, and therefore they were themselves victims of 3.11. Some of them lost their jobs due to the severe damage to their workplaces, others had their homes washed away by the tsunami, and still others searched for their missing friends and relatives (Shimodate 2017: 127). In the aftermath of this unprecedented disaster the SCJ faced the possibility of disbandment, and even with the support they gave to one another, they were still in the depths of despair. The best they could do was to get through each day despite such despair. They were not in a state of mind to attempt to stage Shakespeare for the Tohoku people who had similarly lost hope.

For a while, Shimodate wondered whether it would be appropriate for the company to continue. However, two encounters stirred him to resume his work with the SCJ: an encounter with a woman and an encounter with 'Shakespeare'. While walking on a street in Sendai, Shimodate was approached by a retired woman who had seen performances by the SCJ before, and she implored him to continue and to produce Tohoku versions of Shakespeare that were neither 'sad nor long' and in which no one dies (Shimodate 2016: 74). At that time, he realized that the SCJ owed its existence to the many audience members who had been loyal to them over the past sixteen years.

Moreover, in the summer of 2011, Shimodate revisited British Hills, a resort in Fukushima that offers a 'British experience', on business; this was where his company had staged its first production of *Romeo and Juliet* in 1995. He was astounded that the hotel which had once been full and extremely busy was so empty in the aftermath of 3.11. While he reminisced about the last scene of *Romeo and Juliet* once produced there, he came across the statue of Shakespeare, which was placed in front of the manor house when British Hills opened in 1994, and felt as if it were talking to him. It was a moment of inspiration in which Shimodate decided once again to stage Shakespeare, particularly *The New Romeo and Juliet*, and to repay the Tohoku people for all their support.

The SCJ decided to produce the 'Hot Spring Trilogy', three shortened adaptations of Shakespeare's plays, with happy endings, which aimed to inspire a sense of hope in local people still in the depths of despair. They got the idea of setting these adaptations in a hot spring (*onsen*) when they went to Oiwake Onsen near Onagawa in Miyagi, one of the hardest hit towns, and saw the dispirited people refreshed with smiles and laughter after enjoying a bath. The company wanted to help revive the local audience as the *onsen* did and therefore located the trilogy in a hot spring modelled on Naruko Onsen, a famous hot spring resort in Miyagi. *The New Romeo and Juliet* was the first of the three adaptations, *The New King Lear* the second and *The New Merchant of Venice* the last.

The New Romeo and Juliet was created in the wake of the earthquake and toured some of the hardest hit areas: Osaki, Ishinomaki, Sendai, the Onagawa Dai-ni Elementary School, the Yamamotocho Central Community Center and Fukushima. Furthermore, workshops of *The New Romeo and Juliet* were held at schools in the disaster-hit area between 2013 and 2015, and students of Furukawa Gakuen junior high school staged the SCJ's *A Midsummer Night's Dream in Matsushima Bay* and *The New Romeo and Juliet* at their school in 2017 and 2018 as a part of an educational programme to enhance understanding of the local culture and encourage self-expression.

The SCJ started staging regular performances of its plays at the Michinoku Joseki Hanaza theatre in Sendai in November 2019, with a shortened version of *Romeo and Juliet*, *Juliet of Tohoku*. The second performance in January 2020 was also an abridged version of *The New King Lear* from the 'Hot Spring Trilogy', *Lear Sushi*.

INTRODUCTION TO *THE THREE DAUGHTERS OF LEAR*[1]

Tetsuhito Motoyama

The primary concern of the Tokyo Shakespeare Company (TSC) is the text, and this is as evident in *The Three Daughters of Lear* as it is in their more straightforward productions of Shakespeare. Edo explains in the interview at the end of this introduction that she started the TSC from a wish to engage directly with Shakespeare's text instead of through a ready-made translation. In describing their rehearsal process, she mentions the importance of the table read and the care she takes to ensure that the actors' physical performance does not detract from the delivery of the lines. In other interviews, she has stated:

> I feel the appeal of Shakespeare lies in his lines ... I like to see the lines handled in a way that brings the characters to life; the allure of the lines can be found in, among other things, how they convey emotional and psychological shifts or in the rhythms they form, so I would like to see these things brought to the forefront instead of glossed over.
>
> (Edo 2017: 156–57)

This attitude carries over into the company's original works and can be seen in the sheer number and length of the monologues that constitute *The Three Daughters*. Okuizumi, who had to cut lines from the play at the request of the director for the 1995

---

[1] Part of this introduction is based on Motoyama and Edo, 'Strange Oeillades No More' (2013).

production, admits to finding it difficult to be sparse with words ('Lear Ō *o shin-kaishaku*' 1995: 8). The impressive flow of words has struck both audiences and critics alike. One audience member of the 1997 production in Mikawa was amazed at how the actors 'delivered those long speeches effortlessly' (Sasaki 1997: 2). Literary critic Konno Kaoru writes,

> ... more than anything, there were the lines which were nothing short of a torrent. They would probably not be considered the lines of a play in any ordinary sense. Okuizumi Hikaru believes, 'Only that which is pursued to the extreme is interesting', and it is this pursuit of the extreme that has completely done away with the policy of *gembun itchi*.
>
> (1996: n.p.)[2]

Edo herself has stated, when speaking about this play, that she wanted to 'create a grandiose tale, not through stage sets but through a deluge of words' ('*Engeki: Lear*' 1997: 5).

What is interesting about this 'deluge of words' and *The Three Daughters* is the similarities they share with *rakugo*, a form of oral storytelling. To begin, the play's structure closely mirrors that of rakugo stories. The stories generally open with the *makura*, or prelude, during which the storyteller acknowledges the audience, offers a self-introduction, and leads into the main tale with an anecdote (Yamamoto 2007: 16–17). In the play, the Fool begins by directly addressing the audience. The original script included a long anecdote about the walk from Shibuya station to the theatre; though this is now lost, the Fool still introduces himself and reminds the audience that they have entered Hell of their own accord, despite the warning sign in the theatre lobby. This allows for a smooth transition into the plot of the play, starting with the explanation of how the Fool

---

[2] *Gembun itchi* was a movement in the nineteenth century that led to the use of colloquial Japanese for written texts.

Introduction

found himself in Hell. In rakugo, the actual story, or *hombun*, is told primarily through a re-enactment of the conversation of the characters, with the only props being a fan and a towel (ibid.: 4); this is also true of the play, which relies on very few props and stage sets. Finally, the last part of a rakugo performance is the *ochi* or *sage*, a witty twist that serves as the conclusion. At the very end of *The Three Daughters*, a single stage direction reveals that the Hell Wag is actually Cordelia and the audience realizes that she, among all the characters, has the least hope for salvation: 'It is then that he [the Fool] realizes the ring has been in his pocket all along; he takes the ring out into the palm of his hand and with a puzzled look, stares at it.' While this is not comical, as twists often are in rakugo, it packs great irony, which can also be found in the *ochi*.

The structure of *The Three Daughters of Lear* is not the only thing that ties the play to rakugo. The two main features of rakugo are *kaigyaku*, which can be translated as wit or humour, and *ugachi*, which is 'the ability to convey subtle points effectively' (Yamamoto 2007: 3). There is no lack of humour in *The Three Daughters*, which one reviewer has described as a work that 'builds upon layer after layer of erudite lines filled with wit and kaigyaku' (Takadō 1995: 4) and another as 'a tense straight play scattered throughout with humour' (*'Zuisho'* 1995: 9). The moments of humour also often contain the element of ugachi in that they reveal the dynamics of the characters as well as their personalities. For example, in the following exchange, the Fool starts out disparaging the Hell Wag, only to discover that the Wag has actually made him out to be the dim-witted character.

WAG ... they say the good Lord dislikes those who lend money. Don't be surprised if you find yourself in Hell.

FOOL Marry, I have a question for you. Where do you think we are? What exactly do you think this place of darkness is?

> WAG　Guv'nor, don't you know where we are? How now. Guv'nor, could you be an idiot? With that face of yours and the intellect of an idiot, how unfortunate . . .

These lines convey the Fool's sense of superiority and the Wag's ability to turn the situation to his advantage while appearing to be a simpleton. Many rakugo stories involve similar situations in which the dynamics of two characters are cleverly proven to be the reverse of what they initially seemed. Moreover, the epitome of ugachi is the ochi, which should be conveyed as succinctly as possible. The aforementioned short stage direction at the end of *The Three Daughters* presents the shocking twist of the play as effectively as the best examples of ugachi.

The most important similarity, however, is that both rakugo and the play depend predominantly on the spoken word to create a specific world and to form distinct characters. In rakugo, the conversation of the characters not only shapes the plot but also conveys their psychological states and establishes a tangible sense of their world. With no set but a well on the stage, the Hell of *The Three Daughters* becomes a real place also through the words of the characters. For example, the Fool's complaints at the beginning of the play transport the audience into a world of stenches and eerie sounds. Likewise, in scene three, Goneril makes the darkness and interminable despair of Hell palpable as she complains:

> No moon, no stars; no one, of course, has seen the sun. Owls hooting all the time . . . I can't stand that it's always the same undefined moment. The only thing that signals the hour is the skull bell suspended there, from the crucifix of the castle of Dite. Even that is unreliable. It constantly rings then is silent for a hundred years. And more than anything, the sound it

makes is execrable. It grates on my delicate nerves. Boon, boon, boon, it is maddening.

In order to make concrete the setting of the story, the rakugo storyteller will often describe the manners, customs, and trends of the time. *The Three Daughters* sets up the world of the play through references to the reality the Japanese faced during the time it was written at the end of the bubble economy. Hell is a ruthless corporate world driven by capitalism. It is no place for those without the drive and acumen to survive, as is seen in the fate of Virgil.

> WAG Me master's been completely listless. All he does now's hug the bed and keep as still as a dried slug. He now lives frugally off Hell's pension system.
>
> FOOL Is that so? What a plight. With this inflation, it must be impossible to live on nothing but his pension. If he finds himself in need, let me know.
>
> WAG Guv'nor, you also lend money?
>
> FOOL At ten per cent interest for ten days. I also deal in various insurances. ... Money makes Hell go around. The first step for peace of mind in Hell, insurance. We have been approved by the proper authorities. Check this for more details.

Even the Hell Wag, who initially seems to reject the pursuit of fame and fortune, is actually very much part of this world. In the beginning, he declares, 'I've never had nothing as important as a name or fame or a sack of gold.' It turns out, however, that he is no less susceptible to their charms than the other inhabitants of Hell. When the Fool attempts to procure his services, the Wag explains, 'I ain't got no sack of gold, but that don't mean

I ain't got the gold for the sack. There's nothing like gold fully on display.' This is a world founded on money, power and success, for as the Fool says, 'Money makes Hell go around.'

Greed and ambition not only rule Hell but they were also at the heart of Lear's world when the characters were all still alive. Goneril and Regan hint at rumours about Lear's shady past, from which he rose when he joined the mercenary army. In Regan's words:

> Grandfather gave Mother to him. This was how Father founded his foothold for ruling over Britain. But he was at that time no more than a lowly son-in-law. There were no prospects. After all, Father was a scoundrel whose origins could not be traced.

Lear then proceeds to murder his brothers-in-law to ascend to the throne. An even more shocking revelation is that it was his

1 Naratani Yūki (Goneril), Sakō Yoshi (Fool), Edo Kaoru (Regan) and Makino Kumiko (Hell Wag) from the 1995 production of *The Three Daughters of Lear*.

wife who desired status and power and urged him to carry out the murders, for as Regan says, 'she was the one who abused his ear, saying that he should kill her three brothers'. This obsession with power and wealth is at the heart of the tragedy of Lear's family.

Likewise, the decisive factor in the unravelling of the family is also compulsive excess, not of power or wealth, but of love. Critics have argued that Shakespeare's *King Lear* associates salvation with love, rather than morality or justice. For example, Enid Welsford argues that there is no 'justice or gratitude either from Gods or men', but hope lies in 'the power to choose love when love is synonymous with suffering' (1935: 266). For C.J. Sisson, justice in *King Lear* can be sought in the 'love that moves the sun and all the stars' (1961: 98). The world of *The Three Daughters*, however, transforms this love into another form of excess. First, it was Edmund's infatuation with Cordelia that drove him to evil. The Fool explains:

> Love and hate are two sides of the same coin. Edmund had always been infatuated with Mistress Cordelia.... Mistress Cordelia was not unmoved by his ardour, but they were unmeet in their titles.... Yet, Edmund, undeterred, insistently pursued her until her rebuff struck him as a common cur is struck on the muzzle. It was then that love became hate.[3]

---

[3] Although Nahum Tate's 1681 adaptation of *King Lear* was not a direct inspiration for the TSC, this scene brings to mind how Tate's Edmund, drawn to Cordelia, decides he must 'quench this hopeless Fire i'th' Kindling' (Tate 2000: 79). Tate focused on 'the exposure of the good characters' inner being (which) encourages identification not only through sympathy but also through the voyeuristic pleasure of the onlooker' (Massai 2000: 446). Edmund's obsession with Cordelia in *The Three Daughters*, on the other hand, reveals Lear's youngest daughter to be a problematic figure, who encourages the audience to recognize similar excesses in their own world.

Also of interest is Cordelia's obsession with social status, which ultimately dashed Edmund's hopes and drove him to commit his wicked acts. Similarly, Goneril and Regan's rejection of Lear is a result of their blind love for their mother. They believed he had murdered her for her infidelities. The most destructive love, however, is Cordelia's uncompromising love for Lear. At the end of the play, it becomes clear that it was she, not Lear, who took the life of their adulterous mother. Goneril remembers, 'It was not Father, I saw. It was clearly not him. It was smaller and white . . . a ghost'; then the truth dawns on Regan as she replies, 'No, it was human.' The Cordelia of the afterlife bombards Lear with hyperbolic declarations of her love for him. Lear remains deaf to these words; he proclaims his devotion to her as he strangles her. In this penultimate scene blind, excessive love literally destroys the dysfunctional family. As suggested earlier, this study of power, ambition and excess can be perceived as a response to Japanese society during the early 1990s.[4] The play, true to the series title, 'Shakespeare through the Looking-Glass', holds up a mirror to the audience and forces them to question their values; it is also a mirror held up to Japanese society during the economic bubble. In the words of Rustom Bharucha, the play 'introject[s] the present into the past' (2010: 275) by responding to the issues that face the contemporary social and cultural setting and makes Hell part of the world in which the audience belongs. The monologues and conversations presented on the near empty stage transform it into a reality that the audience recognizes, while the struggles

---

[4] In 1987, the Women's Theatre Group and Eileen Feinstein created *Lear's Daughters*. This is a prequel that questions Thatcherite consumerism and its effect on the arts and gender identity. In Stephanie Gearhart's description of the play, 'the Fool calls attention to the intersection between artists and women in a culture where both have become goods to be sold on the market' (2013: n.p.). The TSC had not known of Feinstein's *Lear's Daughters* when they created their sequel to *King Lear*, yet both works can be seen as a response to consumerism and capitalism.

2 Tange Makoto (Fool) and Tsukasa Mari (Hell Wag) from the 2004 production of *The Three Daughters of Lear*.

of the characters force them to re-examine their own values and actions.[5]

As it thus urges the audience to reflect upon their own lives, the play also engages with issues explored in the source text and challenges existing readings of the play. For example, critics such as Janet Adelman and Coppélia Kahn have examined the absence of the mother in *King Lear*. Adelman argues that Lear suspects she is 'an adulteress' (2.2.304), which fuels his fears concerning his 'sexuality and masculine identity'

---

[5] The TSC brings together the text with the world of the audience in some of their productions of Shakespeare as well. For a discussion of how they did this in their 2016 production of *Measure for Measure*, a play that holds special importance for Edo, see Motoyama (2017), 'Theatre Review: *Meja Meja*' (*Measure for Measure*).

(1992: 108); Kahn attributes the tragedies that take place to the 'patriarchal conception of the family in which children owe their existence to their father alone' (1986: 35). In *The Three Daughters*, Goneril and Regan's conviction that Lear killed their mother because of her infidelities brings to mind these arguments. The play, however, undermines such readings of the play by identifying Cordelia, driven by her own excesses to condemn excess in others, as the murderer. As theatre critic Yūki Masahide argues, the play 'presents profound philosophical ruminations along with fresh readings of Shakespeare's works' (1997: 72). It engages with issues that Shakespeare's play explores, through the perspective of late twentieth-century Japanese society. The play serves to transform the audience's understanding of *King Lear* while, at the same time, transporting them into a world in which they are confronted with their own reality. The distinctions between the original text and adaptation, in the words of M.J. Kidnie, 'continually shift over time . . . in response to textual and theatrical production' and 'authenticity in the context of Shakespearean text and performance is continually redefined over time by activity and debates that take place at the work's constantly shifting edges' (2009: 7–8). While *The Three Daughters* contributes to this shifting of boundaries by having a twentieth-century Japanese audience engage with *King Lear*, this act of redefining *King Lear* also leads to a re-evaluation of the audience's own world. *The Three Daughters* is an important work for the 'politics of reception' for Shakespeare's play in that it transforms both *King Lear* in the eyes of the audience and the audience themselves by making them part of the world of the play.

The Three Daughters neither overtly appropriates the styles and conventions of Japanese theatre nor resituates the play in a Japanese setting. Nonetheless, with the focus being on the spoken word, the play shares features with rakugo storytelling, one of which is the acknowledgement of Japanese life at the time. It is interesting to note that many of TSC's early productions, including the first production of *The Three Daughters*, were staged in Jean-Jean, one of the theatres closely tied to the shōgekijō movement of the 1960s. This movement rejected 'the fourth wall and the dominant role of the play text' in accordance with its anti-establishment agenda. It also took to heart the words of director Senda Koreya: 'it truly feels to us that Shakespeare is our contemporary' (Joubin 2013: 92). Edo, in a personal correspondence with the author on 18 September 2019, writes that shortly after she entered university she saw a production by Jōkyō Gekijō, one of the leading angura theatre companies. The actors continually screamed unintelligible words, which she found off-putting. She would, however, go on to work with angura troupes. This ambiguous stance towards the movement perhaps helps explain why her work both rejects yet is rooted in it. Anzai Tetsuo writes that Deguchi's Shakespeare Theatre Company, which Edo joined at the beginning of her theatrical career, 'while being anti-modernist, at the same time rejected the stance that perceived the West as the norm; though it could perhaps not be called indigenous, the company attempted a thorough rereading of Shakespeare that was obdurately rooted in the sensitivity and physicality of contemporary Japanese youths' and was thus part of the angura movement (1989: 11). Edo's approach towards the text and exploration of the audience's reality in her work can also be tied to this. *The Three Daughters* provides an example of one of the directions in which the shōgekijō movement evolved. It explores contemporary issues through Shakespeare's play, by reverting to the text and reclaiming the conventions of traditional forms of performance. This is not so much out of a need to reshape the plays into something with which the audience is familiar, as with shinpa, or to recreate something that is 'authentic' as with shingeki; it is instead acknowledgement that Shakespeare has very much become part of contemporary Japanese culture and society.

INTERVIEW: EDO KAORU

What was the motivation for starting your theatre company, and how do you see your company in relation to the many other companies in Japan that stage Shakespeare?

Early on in my stage career, I joined Deguchi Norio's Shakespeare Theatre, which has always used Odashima Yūshi's translation of Shakespeare. I had been reading Shakespeare in English, and this made me realize that if I wanted to give expression to my understanding of the plays, I would need to translate the text myself. Otherwise, the performance would be dictated by the translator's choices; as a feature of the Japanese language, the word-choice and register often determine the identity of the character. So when directing Shakespeare, I would have to consult with the translator and get approval to make changes, which is troublesome. Because of this, I decided to start my own theatre company and not rely on others' translations. For a while after Anzai Tetsuo passed away, the TSC was the only theatre company with a director using his or her own translation.[1] One of the advantages of creating my own translation is that I can choose language that suits what we want to do in the production. For example, we might set a play in the present day or in a particular historical period; the language can be of that specific period. Also, when it's a history play focused on political issues, we can use formal language; when it's a play like *Pericles*, we can make the decision to use colloquial expressions. The same goes for the characters. *Twelfth Night*'s Maria is often portrayed as a middle-aged woman, but I see her as a coquettish imp; she can be transformed from one to the other simply by changing the kind of language she uses.

---

[1] Shimodate has been staging his translations since 1995 and Kawai began his Kawai Project in 2014.

With regards to the other Japanese theatre companies that stage Shakespeare, most of the companies with commercial backing are, in the words of Deguchi, 'part-time Shakespeare' companies. And even the smaller companies that are more committed to performing Shakespeare seem, in my eyes, to be approaching the plays with the stance that the text is difficult or tedious because it is a classic. I find that to be a shame. If you trust the text instead of changing, for example, the jokes that might seem archaic or even difficult to understand, the audience will surprise you by responding well to that. The TSC holds to the belief that Shakespeare's text appeals to people today and continues to dedicate itself to keeping its focus on the text.

With regards to the Saitama Arts Theater, they have plenty of funding and tend to go for large-scale spectacles. The TSC is at the other extreme, with barely any funding. We will have only the simplest of props like a chair and, with the help of the audience's imagination, have them transformed into any number of things. So, in a sense, we get the audience involved in staging the plays. I enjoy the challenge of trying to figure out how to put together a production with limited resources and in a very small space.

What kind of process do you follow when preparing your translations of Shakespeare? Do you have a policy when choosing editions? Do you translate the entire text, then decide which parts to cut/change, or do you make those decisions before you start the translation?

I choose an academic edition of Shakespeare as the source text – in the case of *Hamlet* (1998), we used Philip Edwards' edition and in most other cases we have used the latest Arden edition – and don't go beyond that in deciding the source text. In cutting the text, the first thing I keep in mind is to make sure the plot still makes sense. But it is also important not to destroy the world of the play. For instance, some productions of *The Merchant of Venice* cut so much of what is not directly relevant to the plot that you no longer get a sense of what a complex world Venice is; it is the scenes that are not part of the main plot, the scenes with Lancelot Gobbo, which Michael Radford's film version cut, that make Venice such an enchanting world.

Because most of the theatres in which we perform do not have a proper lobby, we cannot have an interval, which means the entire play must be kept to just over two hours. I usually have a general idea of which parts or lines I will cut before I start translating the text. If the text ends up taking much longer to perform than I had expected, I will make further cuts after finishing the translation. Also, there have been occasions when I realized during rehearsals that an actor was unable to perform a particular line and ended up cutting that line.

How much is created during the writing process and how much is created or changed through the rehearsals?

When it's an original play inspired by Shakespeare, I have a pretty clear idea of what it will be like when the script is being written. We also have actors in mind for each of the roles at that point, so we know their strengths and weaknesses when preparing the script. Also, these plays are generally short, so there is very little need for changes to be made during rehearsals. With the writing of the script, I've already started the process of directing, so there are only minor changes made during the rehearsals.

This was not, however, necessarily the case with the first production of *The Three Daughters of Lear*. When we first staged the play, we didn't have a clear idea of what to expect. It was Okuizumi's very first play; the text gave each actor a phenomenal number of lines to deliver. The entire play was much longer than what it is now, so we weren't sure if the actors would be able to get through the entire performance. Once we started rehearsals, we realized that we were demanding too much of both the actors and the audience. In the end it was Maekawa, the director, who chose what to cut. But because we did this after rehearsals had begun, the actors kept mistakenly saying lines that had been removed. Because of this experience, I make it a policy to go over the text numerous times and decide what to cut before rehearsals. This was a production in which we learned what works and does not work through the actual process of staging the play.

The second play in the series, *The Trial of Macbeth* (1996), also underwent drastic changes after rehearsals and the first production, which was also directed by Maekawa. In the first production, it was not clear why Macbeth was able to bring down the wall of Hell. So we added a few lines that would explain this more clearly. Also in the later productions, we had the demons play the supporting characters, which brought them more into the limelight.

With regards to rehearsals, it is often necessary to prevent actors from engaging in too much stage business when they deliver their lines. Since Okuizumi's plays often have characters speak long monologues, actors instinctively want to move around the stage. This distracts the audience from the lines that are inviting them to use their imagination. This is especially true of the actors who are used to performing in avant-garde shows since they are trained to entertain the audience through physical movement. For example, when an actor who belonged to the theatre company Jiyū Gekijō played the Fool, he would try to bring in props and pace around the stage, which made things very confusing. So the director had to tell him to speak his lines standing in one spot and concentrate on his delivery skills to stimulate the audience's imagination. Directing these plays is a balancing act since the actors need scenes that allow them to give vent to their desire to give a physical performance. We always try to find moments when the actors can be physical to their hearts' content. When I direct the plays, I have the actors try what they want as much as they want in rehearsals, and as the opening night approaches, I rein them in.

Because we place such importance on the script, the initial table read takes much more time than in other companies. Usually, we spend at least ten days doing the read-through, and it is during this process that we establish the rhythm with which the actors speak their lines. After that, we immediately move on to run-throughs during which the actors will be completely off-book. Sometimes, the actors try different kinds of stage business but end up disrupting the rhythm of the lines because of that; so I tell them that the lines must always come first and ask them not to sacrifice the delivery of the lines for the sake of stage business. That's something I learned from working with Deguchi. In my view, this is true not only for Okuizumi's original plays, but also for Shakespeare's plays even in translation. A translation that is sensitive to the sound as well as the meaning of the words, such as Tsubouchi's, deserves the beauty of the lines to be conveyed through the delivery. I once performed a one-woman show called *Giulietta* (1992) using Tsubouchi's translation; an editor from a publishing house came to see the show and afterwards commented on how he was impressed with the beauty of Tsubouchi's lines. This made me realize that in preparing the translation, I myself have to be attuned to the beauty of the Japanese language, and so I read writers like Tanizaki Jun'ichirō[2] (1886–1965) before working on a translation.

In some cases, the personality and the persona of the actor can affect the way the play turns out. A good example is the production of *A Comedy: Romeo and Juliet* (2019). Marco was supposed to be a privileged, happy-go-lucky fool who is interested in Rosaline while she is drawn to the dashing devil who approaches her. But the actor who played Marco was hard-working and endearingly earnest, and by the end of the rehearsals he conveyed his affection for Rosaline so convincingly that the actress playing Rosaline started to think her character should be attracted to him instead of to the devil and even felt that she should eventually marry Marco.

---

[2] Tanizaki is a novelist known as one of the masters of Japanese literary style. Among his many important works are *Shisei* (*The Tattooer*, 1910), *Manji* (*Quicksand*, 1928–30) and *Sasameyuki* (*The Makioka Sisters*, 1943–48).

Could you talk about how you collaborate with Okuizumi?

With *The Three Daughters of Lear*, I created the main outline of the plot and the central question, is Cordelia really faultless or is she the root of all evil in the play? And based on this, Okuizumi wrote the entire script in about two weeks. While he was writing the script, he started becoming interested in the absence of the mother and explored that. Also, humour is very important for Okuizumi, so it was his idea to shape the exchange between Goneril and Regan into something that resembles the skit of a *manzai* stand-up comic duo. The appearance of Edmund was also his idea, to show how Goneril and Regan are not as completely heartless and malicious as they may first seem. Furthermore, he was responsible for the explanation of how the mother killed off her siblings one by one. We would discuss ideas while he wrote the script. There were no changes made to the script after it was completed other than cuts, which were necessary since it ended up being close to four hours when performed. Maekawa, the director, wanted to remove all the jokes and laughs from the script, which did not sit well with Okuizumi. In the revival productions, many of the laughs were put back into the script. The published text is based on this reconstructed version, but since the very first version was written on a word processor that can no longer be used, there are things that have been lost.

The Trial of Macbeth was a great pain to create. We started with the idea of Macbeth in Hell, and Yoshida Kōtarō agreed to play the protagonist. His persona gave us the idea of Macbeth as a womanizer who spends all his time seducing women and witches instead of suffering. The director Maekawa insisted that Macbeth must be lauded as a hero at the end of the play. This led to Mephistopheles and Beelzebub being tormented with the task of making Macbeth suffer; and through this process, they become more and more human. In the first production, it was not entirely clear why Macbeth was able to destroy the wall of Hell and why Beelzebub decided to save

Macbeth. The ending was too abstract. So with the revival production, we had to add a little more explanation to clarify these two points. One of the problems with the first production was that Maekawa insisted on Macbeth's heroism and kept demanding that Okuizumi rewrite the script over and over again. Then once rehearsals began, the actors who were ex-members of Deguchi's Shakespeare Theatre had different ideas from Maekawa. And eventually, the actors from the Shakespeare Theatre took over Maekawa's role as director, which was very much in the tradition of the avant-garde 'underground' theatre. There were differences of opinion about the sets, and we ended up having to redo the costumes. We learned from this experience that we must start rehearsals with a clear idea of the staging and with no intention of changing the script.

Of all of Shakespeare's works, why did you decide to start the 'Shakespeare through the Looking-Glass' series with a play based on King Lear?

We needed to choose a play that most Japanese know well. That's why the line-up for the series includes *King Lear*, *Macbeth* and *Romeo and Juliet*. We wanted to make sure the audience would understand how we were playing with and at times challenging the original play. With regards to *Lear*, I heard that there was a primary school textbook that had reading material based on the play; the textbook described Cordelia as a virtuous daughter, King Lear as being tormented by his older two daughters, and the father and daughter dying in the end. So the audience would come to the play expecting a story about how the pure, innocent daughter loved her father. Because of this, we could get the audience to think about the problem of whether Cordelia really was innocent or just in love with the idea of her own upright, virtuous nature.

And since we set it in Hell, we had to think about what kind of place Hell was, which led us to Dante's *Divine Comedy*. We wanted it to be a Western, Christian idea of Hell.

What are your thoughts on the reception of Shakespeare in Japan today, and where would you place your theatre company and its works in relation to that?

There are many theatre companies today, both large and small, that stage Shakespeare. And there are productions at the National Theatre, the New National Theatre,[3] as well as shows produced by large production companies. I think this shows that the people realize the appeal of Shakespeare, on the one hand; on the other, since large-scale commercial productions cast well-known stars, they are instrumental in further educating a part of the general public that would otherwise not be interested in Shakespeare. With regards to education, Meiji University is also doing an amazing job promoting Shakespeare among young people with their Shakespeare Project. They start their productions by first translating the plays. It's fascinating since the students use the Japanese that they themselves speak, which often produces fresh, unexpected translations.

The TSC is focused on conveying the richness of Shakespeare's text. That's one of the reasons we also have regular stage readings of the works as well as staged performances. For the stage readings, we explain the different interpretations and staging possibilities after each scene. The aim of the 'Shakespeare through the Looking-Glass' series is also to get the audience to engage more directly with Shakespeare's text, without feeling that it is something antiquated.

---

[3] The main purpose of the National Theatre, inaugurated in 1966, was 'to preserve and hand down the traditional arts'. In the same year, when approving a bill for the National Theatre, the House of Representatives also made a supplementary resolution that called for 'the promotion of arts other than traditional arts' (Umehara 2009: 16). This led to the opening of the New National Theatre (NNT) in 1997. Though the government had sought to exclude from the National Theatre works of the shingeki movement with its radical politics, shingeki had lost its political proclivities by the 1980s, and shingeki drama, along with music and dance, became the three pillars of the NNT, whose purpose was 'to promote the presence of Japan throughout the international community' (ibid.: 20–21).

What do you envision for the future of your theatre company?

In 2012, we staged *The Merchant of Venice* and its sequel, *Portia's Garden*, together. So sometime in the next five years, I would like to stage *King Lear* and *The Three Daughters of Lear* together. Other than that, I think we will continue as we have, staging both Shakespeare and original plays inspired by Shakespeare, as well as holding stage readings. I've also become more flexible in my stance towards staging Shakespeare, so collaborating with some of the many companies that perform Shakespeare might also be a possibility. I could, for example, translate or adapt the text, and have someone from another company direct the performance. It would be interesting to see what another director would do with my adaptations.

THE THREE DAUGHTERS OF LEAR

(1995)

THE TOKYO SHAKESPEARE COMPANY

LIST OF CHARACTERS

FOOL (EDMUND/KING LEAR)
WAG (CORDELIA)
GONERIL
REGAN

THE THREE DAUGHTERS OF LEAR

Prologue

GONERIL, REGAN, CORDELIA.

They each hold the gemstone their father, LEAR, *bestowed upon them.*

GONERIL
    Sir, I do love you more than words can wield the matter,
    Dearer than eyesight, space, or liberty,
    Beyond what can be valued, rich or rare,
    No less than life; with grace, health, beauty, honour,
    As much as child e'er loved or father found,
    A love that makes breath poor and speech unable.
    Beyond all manner of so much I love you.
    Sir, I do love you!

REGAN
    Sir, I am made
    Of the self-same mettle that my sister is,
    And prize me at her worth. In my true heart
    I find she names my very deed of love –
    Only she came short, that I profess
    Myself an enemy to all other joys
    Which the most precious square of sense possesses,
    And find I am alone felicitate
    In your dear highness' love.
    Sir, I do love you!

From the castle of Dite, the bell formed from skulls begins to toll.

CORDELIA
    Sir, it is you that I . . .

The gradually increasing clamour erases CORDELIA*'s voice.*

Black out.

Scene One: Enter the Fool

Hell.

Enter the FOOL.

FOOL Good evening, ladies and gents. Welcome to Hell. I am the Fool, at your service. Very pleased to make your acquaintance. Alack, what a stench. It is as if the entrails of pigs and toads had been pickled in sulphur and blood and pus, then left out in the sun for three years and three months. And this noise. So ghoulish, I must say. Even if you had gathered a thousand and one ailing cormorants, it could not compare to this dreadful cacophony. It is like despair trapped within agony, then plastered over with misery and raucous laughter. Is it any wonder it is so jarring? After all, the deceased, not finding relief merely by releasing groans from their gobs, project their voices from all orifices of their bodies. These orifices consist not only of their mouths, ears, eyes, nostrils and anus. Maggots fester on the rotting flesh. Not merely the head, or the thorax, or the abdomen. They eat through the skin and create new orifices. From there, the groans that the soul releases spill forth with the sanies. The deceased, their entire body wailing, writhe like a caterpillar assaulted by ants. No wonder the noise. It has been a while since I descended here, yet not a whit have I become accustomed to this heinous noise and stench. Nay, it is truly unbearable.

A dark shadow passes over the FOOL*'s head.*

FOOL Zounds! Watch it! O, pardon me. As you have just seen, torn fragments of souls, at times, get caught in the wind and fly by. The souls of those who have fallen into Hell are

Scene One

hard, and so we must take heed not to be hurt by them. I pride myself on having a thick skull, but even I would not survive clashing into one of them. I urge you to mind your head. By the by, since I am handing out advice, it would do you well to remember who I am, now that you have fallen into Hell. Not that I am trying to sway you with a display of bureaucratic power, but though it may come as a surprise, yours truly wields certain authority in this here dark place that seethes with blood and sulphur. It is the way of the world: knowing authority figures has its benefits. For I feed bones to the three-headed Cerberus, the watchdog of Hell; I make certain the cruel judge Minos never needs for sinus medicine. And, when it comes to the lowly demons, I am in such standing with them that we idle away the time together throwing dice and making a racket, finding ourselves all together sleep-deprived as the dawn breaks. Having said that, there is no morning or night in this world ruled by eternal darkness. – How now, what is the matter? Why the long face? Was it something I said? By my troth, it seems you are ignorant of your circumstances. Therefore, let me take this opportunity to make them clear to you. Indeed, you have fallen into Hell. What? That was not what you wanted? Well, too late now.

Those who pass through me arrive in the land of torments.
Those who pass through me arrive at eternal pain.
Those who pass through me become citizens of despair.
Those who pass through me need abandon all hope.

So read the sign up front, did it not? Was there not a sign at the top of the stairs that descended into this hell hole? No use telling me you missed it. After all, what rises above us? Immediately above us. Indeed, a church. And it is common knowledge that below a church lies Hell! Not that I should be criticizing others. I am yet another example of someone who is ruined because of a temporary lapse in good sense.

Just like you all, I, too, belong in this hell hole. I do not wish to toot my own horn, but despite how I come across now I used to be one of the most virtuous of the countless fools in service. The state even awarded me for excelling in my duties as a fool. In the past, I served Lear, the king of Britain – you may at least have heard of him. Yes, that obdurate old man. And I, when that pitiful old geezer was betrayed by his very own daughters and exiled – though, of course, it was partly his own doing – anyway, even on that evening of the billowing tempest, when the old man roamed the moors, I was by his side and was loyal enough to share in his sufferings. My word, that was a tumultuous tempest: thunder tearing through eardrums, raindrops like pellets of lead, gusts mixed with sand scratching eyeballs so that they could not be kept open even for a moment. And on top of all this, the old man by my side, he continued to wail. 'Blow, wind, and crack your cheeks! Rage, blow', he would howl at the tempest and try my patience. When the thunder calms, the king cries out; when the king quiets down, thunder crackles. And so it goes that the commotion was tantamount to the roar of a thousand lions. Alas, it was in no way possible to keep one's wits about. Nonetheless, being single-mindedly loyal, I spouted nonsense after nonsense, and constantly tried to distract the king in some way. So sang I,

He that has a little tiny wit,
With hey-ho, the wind and the rain,
Must make content with his fortunes fits,
For the rain it raineth every day.

Had we remained on the windswept plains for two hours longer, the body would have been divested of all warmth and, I must say, death would have been inevitable. But God had not abandoned this poor fool. He took pity even on such a useless runt as I. He had sent Master Kent. A most

Scene One

gracious man. A great hero. In the far corners of Britain there was not a single warrior as honest and dauntless. The old man was blessed to have had such an excellent vassal. Though the old man had not a single redeeming feature, his vassal was peerless. As Master Kent guided us to a hovel on the moors, the old man and I escaped death by the skin of our teeth. But it was then that my troubles began. Shivering like a cur, I wrung the sleeves of my drenched garment, gathered wood for a fire, took the opportunity also to search for food and drink – and lo, there was a hole in one corner of the land. That hovel seems to have been the remains of an ancient monastery. I must profess, I am a man with an unfathomable fondness for holes. Like all of you, I have a predilection for holes. I am a sucker for holes. In I went. And behold. It led to a tavern with a fireplace burning bright. Needless to say, the best remedy for a body chilled to the marrow is a shot of a spirit that will light your insides on fire. I settled myself onto a stool and was about to take a shot; to down in a single swill, a shot glass filled to the brim – but to my dismay, I had no gold. In my purse, only dust. Dust does not buy drink. And the tavern owner is not so generous that he would let a stranger start a tab. But what mattered to me was my circumstance; the circumstance that my stomach craved for a drink. Just half a shot glass, just one mouthful, nay just one drop. Short-sighted though it may be, my entire body, craving for a drink, had turned into a ravenous wolf. Once the craving takes hold, the stomach cries for the drink, and it is out of my hands. It was at that moment. A man perched on a stool offered me a drink. The devil. That dark villain with a tail. In such situations, the devil is expected to appear. Of course, ordinarily I would not jump at such an offer. I would make the sign of a cross and send him on his way. But at the time, I had even prayed to God that I would happily give my life for one drink. What an inane thing to pray for. The insidious devil must have been waiting for me to let down my guard. I had no choice. Delirious, I took him up on the offer. Of course, in exchange for my soul. Three days and three nights followed, or rather, since sunlight did not reach this hole, I have no idea how many days had passed. I continued drinking. The devil said, why stop at one drink; why not all the drink in the tavern, nay he would give me all the drink in the world. There is truly no one in this world as generous as the devil. I held, in this way, a bottle of scotch in each hand, and took a swill, in turn, from each. How I had always wanted, if only just once, to drink like that. And when I came to, here I was. The servant of the devil, slaving away for him. Having said that, all that has changed is that I now serve, instead of a human king, the subterranean sovereign; other than that, there is not much difference in my life as a fool. And the human king – I mean that obstinate old man – died without any warning, while I was drowning in drink. I was going to have to look for new employment anyway, and this was not such a bad option. Even so, this stench is a totally different matter. By my word, it is thoroughly revolting. Truth be told, this is my first visit to this area. Though in Hell, I am usually a little further up where the air is a little better. I would never descend this deep unless I had a reason. Even demons detest this area. Well, there is no time to lose. There should be a guide somewhere near. I am afraid this is my first time here and I have no sense of the place. I must make haste or I will really suffocate. Now, what was the name of that guide? Why, yes, it was something like Vir or Vi.

The FOOL *searches his surroundings and steps upon something.*

FOOL   O fie, what is this? Fie. It is a corpse. No wonder the ground is slippery. Rotting bodies of the dead are piled in a heap. What they say is true: bodies devoid of souls create a thick stratum here. I will be hanged, that was close. Who would have known there would be an active fault line in this place. Truly terrible. It is not even possible to walk properly. Accidentally trip and you will find yourself spooning a corpse. (*Calling out.*) Lo, Vir. Prithee, make haste. If I stand still, the maggots will start feeding on me. My eyes have begun to sting. (*Calling out.*) How now, Vir, Vir.

Scene Two: The Hell Wag

Enter the WAG.

WAG   Guv'nor, did you call?
FOOL   O, you startled me. Are you Vir?
WAG   No, that ain't me. Vir ain't who I am.
FOOL   Then who are you?
WAG   No one. I think of myself as me, but people call me the Hell Wag. Guv'nor, you'd best call me that, too.
FOOL   The Hell Wag? You must have a name. The name you were born with, what is it?
WAG   I've never had nothing as important as a name or fame or a sack of gold.
FOOL   But you were born of someone, and so you must have a mother. Only dung beetles that infest a dung heap are born motherless.
WAG   I don't know what this dung beetle is, but I guess I'm of that species.
FOOL   So you are saying that you were bred in a dung heap?
WAG   Not a dung heap, but in the mud by the Hell's Pond of Blood.
FOOL   Quite the monster, aren't you? Having said that, monsters are a dime a dozen around here.
WAG   But sir, you can't call yourself normal, neither. You claim to be a fool, but you're much too morose; unnaturally tall you are, but look at that face of yours; a lizard's eyes, a

shark's mouth, a boar's nose and a pig's ears. And the sight of you walking, an emaciated rat. How can you be human? And, lo, look at that tail.

The WAG *slaps the* FOOL*'s rear end.*

FOOL   Sirrah, stop that. You deserve a blow from my knuckle.

WAG   (*Fleeing.*)   And guv'nor if all things bred from mud are monsters, all men are monsters. In the Good Book, don't it say the Lord Almighty moulded men from mud?

FOOL   What quibble from a mere wag. Not that I dispute the theory that man is a monster. Anyway, Wag, I have no time to waste on you. Do you know Vir?

WAG   What is this Vir? Is it your pet dog?

FOOL   He is not a dog. Vir is a man. And it seems an important poet of yonder years. He usually lives in a castle in Limbo, but at times descends deeper and offers tours through Hell. One could say he is a Hell fanatic. There are certainly some crazy forms of fanaticism. Well, seeing that he willingly comes to this fetid, foul place, he must be an oddball. Once, when a man visited from Firenze, I hear he offered to be his guide.

WAG   Guv'nor, could it be this Vir is Master Virgilius?

FOOL   Indeed, that's the Vir, that Vir. What did you call him?

WAG   Virgilius.

FOOL   Yes, him. I am not good with long names.

WAG   I declare I hate long things, too. Can't stand snakes or noodles.

FOOL   And this Vir, you know him?

WAG   Do I know him? He's me master, he is.

FOOL   Is he now? I am in luck. Go call him for me, will you?

WAG   No can do.

FOOL   Why?

WAG   These days Master Virgilius won't leave his castle. Won't leave his bed, let alone his castle. He might as well be a barnacle stuck to a stone. Ain't no reason for him to walk all this way.

Scene Two

FOOL But I was told he would be my guide if I came here.

WAG That was in the past. Master is retired from being a guide. The bloke from Firenze you just mentioned, no matter how you look at it, he was a scoundrel. He threatened me reluctant master with force and had me master show him Hell from one end to the other. To top things off, he went on his way without paying a single farthing. Since then, me master's been completely listless. All he does now's hug the bed and keep as still as a dried slug. He now lives frugally off Hell's pension system.

FOOL Is that so? What a plight. With this inflation it must be impossible to live on nothing but his pension. If he finds himself in need, let me know.

WAG Guv'nor, you also lend money?

FOOL At ten per cent interest for ten days. I also deal in various insurances.

The FOOL *takes out brochures from his bag.*

FOOL Money makes Hell go around. The first step for peace of mind in Hell, insurance. We have been approved by the proper authorities. Check this for more details.

The FOOL *hands a brochure to the* WAG.

WAG Guv'nor, you been in Venice in the past?

FOOL You are well informed. I was a usurer there, as well, but became a fool after facing failure. How did you guess?

WAG Call it a wag's intuition. Anyway, they say the good Lord dislikes those who lend money. Don't be surprised if you find yourself in Hell.

FOOL Marry, I have a question for you. Where do you think we are? What exactly do you think this place of darkness is?

WAG Guv'nor, don't you know where we are? How now. Guv'nor, could you be an idiot? With that face of yours and the intellect of an idiot, how unfortunate; you won't never need to worry about being in demand among the ladies.

The Three Daughters of Lear

FOOL Talking with you would truly turn me into an idiot. Anyway, we, or rather this place in its entirety, has long been out of God's good graces. An act or two of usury makes little difference to the pickle we're in.

WAG This pickle, is it, you know, smoked?

FOOL (*Ignoring him.*) I cannot be dealing with this imbecile. I must procure a guide. After all, I don't know this region at all. I would prefer not to end up lost and finding myself masticated by the Minotaur headfirst. They also say there is a cave of vampire bats and a forest of cannibalistic arrowroots. Those creatures with names are preferable, though. Running into one without a name will scare you out of your wits, and there will be no going back up. Alack, what to do.

The WAG *munches on something.*

WAG So, you're looking for a guide, are you, guv'nor?

FOOL Indeed. If Vir is not available, is there anyone else? – What are you eating?

WAG A smoked snack. Since you mentioned a pickle, I had a sudden craving. Want one, guv?

The WAG *hands the* FOOL *a smoked snack.*

FOOL What cursed thing is this?

WAG A toad. It was pickled in bubbling sulphur and smoked with burning corpses. We don't get no sunlight down here, so it ain't got much vitamin D, but it's nice and salty.

FOOL Absolutely not.

WAG How about this?

FOOL What is it?

WAG Egg soft-boiled in a hot spring.

FOOL Away with it. To get back to what I was saying, do you know anyone? That is, to guide me.

WAG (*Eating the egg.*) There is one person.

FOOL Indeed? Thank God. And where is he?

Scene Two

WAG The thing is, I knew up till a moment ago, but I'm quickly forgetting.

FOOL What?

WAG O, now I've completely forgotten.

FOOL Forget it. I was an idiot to have asked an imbecile.

WAG I can't disagree that you're an idiot, guv'nor. But my memory, my good guv, seems to be of the sort that serves that piece with a golden shine.

FOOL What, money? How surprisingly avaricious.

The FOOL *hands over a coin.*

FOOL Did you not say you carry no sack of gold just a moment ago?

WAG I ain't got no sack of gold, but that don't mean I ain't got the gold for the sack. There's nothing like gold fully on display.

FOOL Now, where is this man who will be my guide?

WAG Ay, he ain't got no name. Nor parent.

FOOL So, he is a monster.

WAG Ay, he's none of woman born. He was bred from the mud by Hell's Pond of Blood. He likes corpse-smoked snacks and loves soft-boiled eggs. He carries gold but no sack. His memory returns at the sight of that which shines. The one they call the Hell Wag is . . .

FOOL You, of course!

WAG How'd you guess? Guv'nor, look like an idiot you might, but you're surprisingly astute.

FOOL Enough. Show me the way.

WAG Where is it you want to go, guv'nor? You've got to tell me where or I can't be taking you there even if I wanted to.

FOOL Are you truly reliable? I do not want to find myself in quicksand.

WAG Trust me. After all, I am Master Virgilius's best disciple. I possess all the necessary know-how when it comes to touring Hell.

The Three Daughters of Lear

FOOL   You do not inspire confidence, but I suppose I must put myself in your hands. The fact of the matter is, I wish to visit the daughters of King Lear. Their names are the Mistresses Goneril and Regan.

WAG   ... the Mistresses Goneril and Regan.

FOOL   What, you know not of them?

WAG   Nay, I do know them. There ain't no one in these parts that don't. They're the only ones that, even after being here for thousands of years, refuse to give up their gaudy outfits and overdone make-up. Rumour has it, they compiled quite a list of evil deeds in the other world.

FOOL   Indeed so. They took advantage of their thoughtful father's kind deed. They betrayed, berated and booted him out. In the end, they vied over an adulterous lover and in a fit of animosity, murdered each other.

WAG   They killed their actual father?

FOOL   They did not commit the actual deed, but they might as well have. Having borne repeated abuse from his two daughters, the poor king lost his wits, and in the end passed away with Mistress Cordelia in his arms.

WAG   Who's this Cordelia? I ain't never heard that name.

FOOL   Of course you haven't. What makes you think she would even be known by the likes of you?

WAG   Are we talking about a dog?

FOOL   Imbecile! Mistress Cordelia is the King's third daughter. She is the absolute opposite of the elder two: innately kind, inimitably loving and with such purity that would put the moon to shame. At present, she must be elevated to the distant heights and picking flowers while keeping God company.

WAG   That must mean she's dead.

FOOL   Sadly so. A villain plotted her death and had a captain of the mercenaries strangle her. Nothing could be as senseless as this: such atrocity claiming the innocent as a victim.

Scene Two

WAG And, what makes you think this Mistress Cordelia be picking flowers?

FOOL Why? Because it is said that in heaven there is a garden of flowers that never wither. Well, I suppose – it's an image, just an image.

WAG A maiden picking flowers in paradise. Clichéd, ain't it, for something imagined.

FOOL Peace. Naught can be done, for the devil himself is a clichéd existence. Just look at my appearance. From head to toe it screams of one serving under the devil. I am not being clichéd out of choice.

WAG Nay guv'nor, you are considerably unusual. Especially with your unnaturally long limbs and disproportionate build.

FOOL Enough of this. You know what I require, so quickly lead the way. Do we descend that cliff or climb this mountain? Which is it?

WAG Pray, why do you, guv'nor, want to see King Lear's daughters?

FOOL What does it matter? It is none of your concern. All that is required of a guide is to wave a flag and show the way. Do you know of any butcher who would ask each customer, why, sir, are you buying meat? Now, mind your own business.

WAG I'd like to mind my own business, but the law prohibits giving tours without asking for the purpose of the visit.

FOOL There is such a law?

WAG Ay. 'Thou shalt not guide humans or devils without good reason'. It's Article 49 Clause 3 of Hell's Criminal Law. Break this law, and you're subject to a fine.

FOOL Is that so. If it is the law, I will have to comply. This may come as a surprise to you, but I am a law-abiding civic fool.

WAG So, your purpose?

FOOL Truth be told, this is a matter that calls for discretion. I cannot speak of this openly. By my troth, Wag, tell no one about this.

WAG   I won't never do so.
FOOL   Never?
WAG   Never.
FOOL   Then, lend me your ear.
WAG   Ay.

The FOOL *moves his mouth towards the* WAG*'s ear,
then bites the ear.*

WAG   To the devil with you. What's the meaning of this? Guv'nor, are you a pervert?
FOOL   It was to check how firm and tight your ear is. Things could become difficult for me if you leaked the secret.
WAG   Tight-lipped is what you mean.
FOOL   Nay, it all comes down to the ear. Those with a firmly tight ear are trustworthy. So goes the old proverb from Hell. Anyway, there has never been a man with a firmly shut mouth in this world. No matter how firm his determination, man is plagued by a loose tongue and yaks yaks yaks yaks away; truly, the worst combination imaginable. On the other hand, those with firmly tight ears are a safe bet. After all, having a firmly tight ear means that what is spoken will not reach the brain. Wag, rejoice. Your ear is as firm as a three-year-old piece of bread.
WAG   That don't make me happy.
FOOL   Nonsense. Having a firmly tight ear is an innate blessing. A sign of God's grace. My ear, on the other hand, is softer than butter left out in the sun. Take a bite.
WAG   I'd rather bite into a rotten rat. Enough of this. Come now, let us know the purpose of your visit. But remember, there's no place for lies here. As you know, guv'nor, lies are banned here. The moment you lie, winged pliers will come flying your way and immediately yank out your tongue.
FOOL   So be it. Pray, pay attention. Hell is now embarking on a grand project. The initiator of this project is none other than the Head of Hell and the Emperor of Evil, Lord Lucifer. It is

Scene Two

well known that Lord Lucifer once occupied the seat of archangel and served by God's side. God showered this very Lord Lucifer with all His favours and blessings. Nonetheless, there came a day before the birth of man into the world, that Lord Lucifer, plagued by envy towards God, rashly revolted against Him and as a result was banished to this place without light. However, Lord Lucifer, being by nature brave and having suffered subjugation for a millennium, rallied together the devils of Hell and attempted another coup. But his adversary, unfortunately, being God, he had to retreat in defeat; this time as punishment he was trapped for eternity in the world of absolute zero degrees and darkness, in the deepest reaches of Hell. And it has been several millennia since then. For a time, he killed time tempting God's favourites, the men who roam the earth, but he is not one to find contentment in such pastimes. Clandestinely, he has begun to plot his third revolt. Naturally, a battle requires warriors. Hence, he plans to select the exceptionally evil among men and add them to his battalion.

The WAG *is eating an egg.*

FOOL Wag, do you attend me?

WAG Ay, I do. I do, but you speak so seamlessly that I'm overcome with drowsiness.

FOOL Do you eat eggs when you are drowsy?

WAG It ain't just any egg, but eggs soft-boiled in a hot spring. Want one, guv'nor?

FOOL Nay. Now you know the circumstances, so promptly lead the way.

WAG What circumstances?

FOOL I have just explained them. In short, Lord Lucifer plans to choose either Mistress Goneril or Mistress Regan to become a witch. And not just any lowly witch, but the cold-blooded Charmed One.

WAG Why don't he make them both into witches?

FOOL That is not possible. For they loathe each other too much. Internal strife is detrimental to success in a battle. Enmity among friends is an even greater threat than the enemy. One needs to be selected.
WAG You'll be testing them?
FOOL Ay, that is the plan. For I have known those two from the past. Lord Lucifer commanded me to carry out this task.
WAG How are you going to make the decision?
FOOL It is obvious, choose the more evil of the two.
WAG That makes sense. And can Lord Lucifer triumph over God this time?
FOOL You do understand, Wag, it is God that he will be battling.
WAG Ay, that's true.
FOOL . . . so there you go.
WAG . . . indeed.
FOOL By my faith, I have offered Lord Lucifer my services; the way of the devil demands that I comply with the master's wishes and do my best.
WAG Or rather do your worst.
FOOL Wag, excellent use of wit. Now, lead me to the two. If we tarry any longer, the cormorants will start their clamour again. They indiscriminately assault anyone not moving.
WAG Right you are.

The WAG *and the* FOOL *leave.*

Scene Three: Goneril and Regan's Punishment

In the deep reaches of Hell.

GONERIL *and* REGAN. *They are both collecting rusted nails in buckets.*

GONERIL How now.
REGAN . . .

Scene Three

GONERIL How many do you have?
REGAN ...
GONERIL How now, how many?
REGAN ...
GONERIL How now, how goes it?
REGAN ...
GONERIL How many do you have now? You could at least answer me.
REGAN ...
GONERIL Well, how many?
REGAN Quiet!

For a while, they both collect in silence.

GONERIL How now.
REGAN Peace.

They collect in silence again.

GONERIL Alack, my shoulders are stiff. What time could it be? More to the point, what a nuisance not to have a clock here. No moon, no stars; no one, of course, has seen the sun. Owls hooting all the time. So no way to know what time it is. Eternity may rule here, but couldn't there be some way of telling time, like two or three, or at the very least, like morning or night or evening? I can't stand that it's always the same undefined moment. The only thing that signals the hour is the skull bell suspended there, from the crucifix of the castle of Dite. Even that is unreliable. It constantly rings then is silent for a hundred years. And more than anything, the sound it makes is execrable. It grates on my delicate nerves. Boon, boon, boon, it is maddening. Don't you agree? That sound, does it not bother you? Boon, boon, boon, boon, boon . . .
REGAN Peace! You've made me lose my count. It's such a hassle to recount everything from the start. It's all your fault.

The Three Daughters of Lear

GONERIL So sorry. This makes 456 for me. (*Continues picking.*) 457, 458, 459 . . .

REGAN (*Agitatedly stirring the contents of her bucket.*) I have completely lost my count.

GONERIL How unfortunate. 460, 461 . . .

> REGAN, *sulking, starts to smoke.*

GONERIL How now? What are you doing? You will run out of time.

REGAN There's not enough time, anyway. In less than ten minutes, that ghastly bell will ring, and the supervising demon will appear. I cannot hope to reach 666.

GONERIL So you say, but unless you carry out the task to the letter, you'll be fed 666 nails.

REGAN We will be fed them, anyway. Do tell me, dear sister, has there been even one instance since we arrived here that we didn't have to swallow nails?

GONERIL Admittedly, there has not.

REGAN See? This whole thing is a farce, to begin with. The demon tells us we will not have to swallow the nails if we collect exactly 666 within the given time, but the bell always tolls when there's only one or two left. Don't you think that's strange?

GONERIL Well, put that way, it could be seen as strange.

REGAN How long has it been since we have had to collect nails?

GONERIL Let's see, at least a millennium?

REGAN Every single day throughout that millennium, we have collected nails, yet not once collected exactly 666. We have not once avoided having to swallow the nails. Don't you think that's strange? Don't you think we could have succeeded at least once? Why do we have to continue this absurdity?

GONERIL It's our punishment; naught can be done.

REGAN I understand it's our punishment, but do tell, what does this all mean?

GONERIL How should I know?

Scene Three

REGAN If the objective is to inflict the pain of swallowing nails, why not do so from the beginning? I don't know whose idea this is, but it's simply absurd.

GONERIL Naught can be done. Hell is absurd. You must have realized long ago that demons and devils are all dunces. Dim-witted simpletons. But when it comes to executing ludicrous orders to the letter, they are moronically earnest. It's best to resign yourself to this.

REGAN Since arriving here, I've resigned myself to many things myriad times over. But I cannot bear this absurdity on top of that. I am not as stolid as you, dear sister.

GONERIL Fie, you're one to talk. Anyway I witnessed a punishment the other day, having dried snot rolled into a ball and stuffed down the throat to cause suffocation. And there was also synchronized swimming in a dung heap all day long. This was without earplugs. Our punishment isn't as bad as those.

REGAN It's equally ghastly. Yesterday, I thought for once I had collected exactly 666 nails and with great confidence took them to the demon. The demon carefully counted each nail and when he reached the 666th one, it suddenly broke in half. What the cursed demon then said was that it was 667 and so I hadn't fulfilled the task. It needs to be exactly 666, but how close you were, he smirked as he filled my mouth with nails. I can't be bothered anymore.

GONERIL What are you going to do?

REGAN As I said, nothing. Collect the nails or not, the result is the same, and so there is no sense in struggling studiously.

GONERIL My, you really have decided not to care. What gall. You do live up to your childhood name, half-hearted Regan. But aren't you afraid? Who knows what will be done to you for slacking off like this?

REGAN What more can they do? I would very much like to know. I swallow 666 nails, and that's not even the worst part. Boiling lava is the chaser for these nails. Then I'm placed in ice seven times, burned seven times, and buried alive. After three sets of that, another three sets of being devoured alive by dogs, pigs, alligators, lions, rats, cormorants, and then snakes.

GONERIL   You still have it easy. On top of all that, I'm decapitated with a saw ten times every day.

REGAN   Instead, I have my eyes gouged out twenty times. It's no better.

GONERIL   Hear this. There's a new demon in charge of the decapitation, but this one's a novice and cursedly incompetent. He says to me, if it hurts, let me know; but since he goes about it gingerly, it's excruciating.

REGAN   It's not easy being a demon; you have such a thick neck, sister dear. It's easier decapitating a boar.

GONERIL   Hang you. The demon in charge of gouging out your eyes was rejoicing at how easy his task is. Apparently, your eyes fall out with a simple blow to the back of your head.

REGAN   Let me be.

GONERIL   Really.

GONERIL *begins collecting nails again.*

REGAN *watches in silence.*

REGAN   By the way, dear sister.

GONERIL   What?

REGAN   How many is that?

GONERIL *is alarmed.*

GONERIL   Lo, how many was that? It was 456, then seven following that. O . . .

REGAN   It's 470.

GONERIL   Of course, that's right, 470. (*Collecting nails.*) 471, 472, 473, 474 . . .

REGAN   I was just joking.

GONERIL   Don't speak to me. I'll lose track . . . what did you just say?

Scene Three

REGAN   I was just jesting. I made up the number.
GONERIL   How dare you.
REGAN   I blurted out a random number. You've now lost track. How unfortunate for you.
GONERIL   What a deplorable human being you are.
REGAN   I've stopped being human long ago. I'm a dissolving piece of flesh, worth less than worms and crawling at the bottom of a bog. Now, I'm going back to collecting the nails.

REGAN *begins collecting nails.*

GONERIL   What is this? Didn't you quit? What are you doing?
REGAN (*Ignoring this.*)   So, I had exactly 500, and this is 501, 502 . . .
GONERIL   How now, you've kept count.
REGAN   What did you think? I'm not going to be fed rusted nails.
GONERIL   . . .
REGAN   504, 505 . . . don't speak to me. Otherwise, I'll lose count. I must collect exactly 666 nails. 506, 507 . . .

GONERIL *throws in a fist-full of nails into* REGAN*'s bucket.*

REGAN *is dumbfounded.*

The two glare at each other.

GONERIL   A pox on it, I give up, I'm giving up. Give me a fag, won't you.
REGAN   Absolutely not. Smoke one of your own.
GONERIL   You wretch.

GONERIL *takes out her own cigarette and smokes.*

REGAN *also smokes.*

GONERIL   Look at that, dear, you're smoking the Golden Bat brand. How outdated.

REGAN What can I do, this is all that they sell. What about you, dear sister?
GONERIL Mine are Echo.

Silence.

GONERIL Look here, I've been thinking. Since coming here, I've faced all manner of frightful things.
REGAN . . .
GONERIL Are you listening?
REGAN Even if I wanted to ignore you, you're so loud that I can't help but hear you.
GONERIL Is that so?
REGAN And what is it you want to say?
GONERIL Nothing.
REGAN You were trying to say something.
GONERIL Are you curious?
REGAN I am not.
GONERIL Indeed? I'll tell you, anyway. I've faced plenty of frightful things, but by far, the worst has been the presence of your company.
REGAN Is that so? I don't feel the same way. Your presence grants me the greatest joy.
GONERIL Truly? What a sweet thing to say.
REGAN It's true. When I'm with you, I'm constantly given confirmation that there's someone worse off than myself. When I see you I'm reminded that in this world, there's always someone less fortunate. I even begin to feel that I might be relatively blessed. You are truly a blessing.
GONERIL Pshaw.
REGAN But I'm afraid we shall have to part presently.
GONERIL Do you plan on becoming a witch?
REGAN I do. And you must rejoice, dear sister, since once I become a witch, I will shower upon you torments a thousandfold greater.

Scene Three

GONERIL But shouldn't you think this through? Things which seem too good to be true often are so.

REGAN It doesn't matter, so long as I can escape this situation. I won't mind jumping from the frying pan into the fire.

GONERIL The fire is definitely what awaits you. True, if you become a witch, you join the demons in tormenting humans. But you pay for it later. Have you thought of what will happen when the horns of the heavens sound and the last day of judgment arrives?

REGAN As we stand, we burn in eternal flames anyway. Can it get any worse?

GONERIL It most certainly will. You will be tortured by the most vicious, violent means possible, beyond the imagination of any human being, even a thousand fanciful poets. It is bound to be a hundredfold, a thousandfold more excruciating than now.

REGAN Do you think so?

GONERIL Absolutely. So do drop this nonsense. I'll speak with the devil in charge, on your behalf. I'll tell him my dear sister is withdrawing. I'll go do that now.

GONERIL starts to leave.

REGAN Wait.

GONERIL It's really no trouble. I understand it'll be awkward for you to do this yourself at this point.

REGAN Sister, dear, do you remember?

GONERIL What?

REGAN When we would eat watermelons as a child, you had me eat only the seeds. You told me that only the seeds of watermelons are meant to be eaten, that the red flesh of the fruit contains the blood of beasts and it's best to avoid it. So, until recently, I would pick out the seeds and discard the flesh. Imagine my shock when seedless watermelons were introduced.

The Three Daughters of Lear

GONERIL There was no damage done. After all, it gave you very strong teeth. You used to pride yourself on your fangs of steel, on not needing a can-opener.

REGAN Sister dear, you've prepared your CV, haven't you?

GONERIL Fine, so you know. Ha, ha.

REGAN What gall you have to talk about the day of the final judgment.

GONERIL Having to swallow 666 nails. To have swallowed 665, and to be told I won't have to swallow the last one. For that, I would do anything. Even if I knew that the eternal damnation I would be subjected to the following day would be even more wretched than that which Judas Iscariot suffered. That's simply human nature.

REGAN Are you calling yourself human?

GONERIL At any rate, I feel sorry for you, but I will be the one to serve at Lord Lucifer's side. Oh dear, that would mean that demon in charge of decapitation will be out of work. That's most unfortunate; why don't you offer him your head?

REGAN You jest. I'm the one meant to be a witch.

GONERIL That would be quite impossible.

REGAN Why?

GONERIL Because I excel at being evil. You are admittedly quite the villain. You're cunning, like a weasel. I give you that. But you're not accomplished enough yet.

REGAN That may be so.

GONERIL That is so. Admit it this time. Respect your sister's seniority.

REGAN But, sister dear, what did you include in your CV?

GONERIL What else? My address, name, age and a list of the numerous evil deeds I committed while alive.

REGAN Approximately how many?

GONERIL Three.

REGAN So few. That's surprising for the villainess Goneril, reputed to drive even Satan to avert his eyes. I traced back my memories to list every single sin I committed and ended

Scene Three

with a thousand and one. The list didn't fit onto a single sheet. I had to continue onto separate sheets which became yea long. So, three. How surprisingly few.

GONERIL Quality over quantity, I would say. Or rather it's about, how should I put it, how incendiary the sins are. Their explosiveness. There's no point in fastidiously scraping together all those trivial deeds.

REGAN Sister, dear, I wonder if you remember?

GONERIL What?

REGAN Our mother.

GONERIL What about her?

REGAN When we were children, we would often visit that holiday home.

GONERIL So we did. The one in Bath. It was a mansion built on a hill known as the remains of Romans. In the backyard there was an old well, said to have been dug by the Romans.

REGAN Our mother fell into that well and died.

GONERIL I know. So what of it? You're not going to tell me you killed her, are you?

REGAN I am.

GONERIL Ha, ha. Jest not.

REGAN It's true.

GONERIL You lie. It was an accident. When Mother went to the holiday home, she used to sit on the ledge of the well and enjoy the cool of the evening. Under that large oak tree. The marble stonework of the well was cool and comforting. She must have fallen asleep or had a sudden bout of anaemia and . . .

REGAN You're wrong. It was suicide. And I was the cause. So I might as well have indirectly murdered her.

GONERIL What do you mean?

REGAN You must remember the gems Father gave us. He gave one to each of us.

GONERIL I do. Mine was a sapphire, the colour of the deep sea. Yours was. . .

The Three Daughters of Lear

REGAN   An emerald, the purest green of a kingfisher's feather. Cordelia, a blood-red ruby. And Mother, a diamond the size of a quail's egg.

GONERIL   It was truly enormous. Larger than the droppings of the deer we had at home.

REGAN   What an odd thing to compare it to.

GONERIL   I'll make whatever comparison I choose.

REGAN   I stole it.

GONERIL   . . .

REGAN   I stole it and threw it in the well. I can't remember why I did such a thing. But that has to be why Mother threw herself into the well. Father gave all of us the gems, saying it was proof of his love for his family and telling us to treasure it for the rest of our lives. It's no wonder Mother became sick with worry, thinking she had lost it. That's why it's my fault. When Mother died, I was terrified, and I continued to suffer long after that. But as things stand, I'm glad through and through that I killed Mother. I must say, it pays to commit murder no matter the cost.

GONERIL   You have it all wrong.

REGAN   What do I have wrong?

GONERIL   I was the one who had you steal the diamond from Mother's jewellery box. I was the one who inveigled you into doing this.

REGAN   You lie. That can't be true.

GONERIL   You've just forgotten. You were still young so I'm not surprised. I planned it all and had my little sister carry out the plan. If it had all come to light, I would have been able to put the blame on you. Being older means being that much more cunning, wouldn't you say?

REGAN   Then tell me this. Why did you have me do this?

GONERIL   Why . . . I don't remember. It must just have been to amuse myself. Anyway, to kill for amusement the mother

who gave birth to you; you have to admit it's impressive. Evil incarnate.
REGAN   I was the one who actually stole the gem. Don't forget that.
GONERIL   Well, well, we shall eventually learn which one of us makes the worse impression.
REGAN   Humph.

Silence.

GONERIL   How now.
REGAN   What?
GONERIL   The bell hasn't tolled yet.
REGAN   . . .
GONERIL   . . .

The two hurriedly start collecting nails.

From the castle of Dite, the bell formed from skulls begins to toll.

Exeunt with the buckets.

Scene Four: The Way to Hell and the Fool's Plan

The FOOL *and the* WAG *in medias res on their journey through Hell.*

The WAG *is mounted on the back of the* FOOL.

WAG   Guv'nor, stop. Halt, I prithee.
FOOL   What is the matter? Is anything wrong? Do you need to make water?
WAG   No. Me legs are so sore, I can't go no step further.
FOOL   Indeed so? We did traverse a great deal. Could we have been walking a hundred years – wait, you have not walked at all!
WAG   I did walk a little.

FOOL Just the first hundred steps. I have carried you the rest of the way.
WAG Guv'nor, you've got two humps on your back. It's camel-like and quite comfortable.
FOOL Really!

The FOOL lets the WAG down from his back.

WAG Guv'nor, anything wrong?
FOOL I am also tired. Rest, I need to rest.
WAG Guv'nor, you must be ravenous.
FOOL Come to think of it, I am hungry. It feels like my stomach is so hollow that a wind is blowing through it.

The WAG reaches into his inside pocket.

FOOL Do not take out your soft-boiled eggs. I do not want your smoked toads, either.
WAG Well, there ain't nothing I can offer you, then.
FOOL I generally don't eat anything without scales. Just sit there and dine on your own in silence.
WAG As you wish.

The WAG eats the smoked snack.

FOOL So, how much longer?
WAG . . .
FOOL How much longer till we get there?
WAG . . .
FOOL Hey, I am speaking to you.
WAG . . .
FOOL Do not provoke me.

The FOOL pokes the WAG.

WAG Guv'nor, you're so querulous. You told me to eat in silence, and so that's what I was doing.
FOOL Why is it that you only listen to others when there is no need? Pray, tell.

Scene Four

The WAG *weeps.*

FOOL Okay, okay. I am sorry. Now, answer my question.
WAG Guv'nor?
FOOL How much longer till we get there?
WAG Can't say.
FOOL You cannot say? Why? You . . ., who was it, that knave?
WAG Virgilius.
FOOL Indeed so. Did you not boast that you were this Vir's top disciple and when it came to the geography of Hell, your knowledge extended to all corners?
WAG So I did.
FOOL Then why can you not tell me?
WAG Guv'nor, you have it wrong. This is a place with no time. Infinity and an instant are interchangeable. Time's long yet short, short yet long. It takes as long for the dew from the tip of a leaf to leave a hole in a rock as it does for a drop of dew to disappear in the desert. While you and I thus speak, a million eternities may be passing by. And if you, guv'nor, presently stare into the eyes of the Gorgon and turn into stone, you won't never reach the daughters of Lear.
FOOL A Gorgon, here? That abominable creature with snakes for hair?
WAG That red light that you've been eyeing.
FOOL What about the light?
WAG That's a lantern the Gorgon's swinging to signal you.
FOOL (*Quickly covering his eyes.*)   Warn me at the start, before all else.
WAG Thus I can't say when you'll reach them. Anyway, we'll cross that river where the dead are drowning; go by the Gorgon's castle through Hydra's Forest; venture into the cave of the single-eyed giant and cross seven mountains of skeletons; descend into seven valleys of cannibalistic lions and on the way step onto the tail of the fire-breathing dragon; and walk through the sandstorm in the desert. From there we turn south, then east, next west, and finally head

north where there is a field of ice as far as the eye can see. A blizzard that will freeze you to the bone. By the tenth crevasse we fall into, we'll be at sea with sharks, so we can collect bones to build a raft, and with luck we'll brave the vicious waves and arrive in a terrifying town. There, we jostle through a crowd of villains to find a cat with a split tail. By the name of Tama.

FOOL   Why do we look for a cat?

WAG   A magical cat, it is. Without it, we ain't moving on to the next stage.

FOOL   A knave that's into Nintendo games?

WAG   What's this Nintendo? If it has anything to do with nandinas, I'm partial to them.

FOOL   Enough, enough, never mind.

WAG   Ain't you going to ask what follows? After we find Tama?

FOOL   I have had enough. Snack on your nandinas or whatever.

The WAG *eats.*

The FOOL *takes a crown from his bag and tries it on.*

WAG   Guv'nor, what's that?

FOOL   This? (*Solemnly.*) What do you think?

WAG   What do you mean?

FOOL   What does it look like?

WAG   A dimwit donning a daft headpiece.

FOOL   That is not what this is. (*Standing and posing.*) How about now? Eh?

WAG   A standing simpleton.

FOOL   Wrong. This is a king. A king. Do I not appear as a king exuding courage and compassion?

WAG   Well, with a stretch of the imagination.

FOOL   Yes?

WAG   Not a bit.

FOOL   Lo, you are a queer creature, so that's to be expected of you. You probably don't even know what a king is.

Scene Four

WAG   Right you are. A lord's about the only thing I know that comes with a title.

FOOL   . . . you could say the two are similar.

The FOOL *removes the crown.*

WAG   So, guv'nor, when you wear that weird headpiece, you become a lord?

FOOL   A king. I become a king.

WAG   Just by wearing it.

FOOL   Indeed.

WAG   By my troth, what an uncomplicated thing this king is. It's not so with lords.

FOOL   Hear me, forget the lords. Is that clear?

WAG   Aye. And so, what will you do after becoming king?

FOOL   I am not actually becoming king. In no way could a fool like myself ever become king. I will only appear to be one.

WAG   So it's a sham?

FOOL (*Nodding.*)   I suppose I should tell you. Now Wag, never speak of this to others.

WAG   I don't want me ear bit again.

FOOL   Not to worry. I know already your ear is firm and tight. Now, attend closely. This hat is not just any hat.

WAG   I understand.

FOOL   What is it that you understand?

WAG   It's a magic hat, ain't it?

FOOL   You are surprisingly sharp. And that saves me trouble.

WAG   And what'll you do with the magic?

FOOL   In short, when I wear this hat, I will appear as King Lear to Goneril and Regan.

WAG   And what'll come from appearing so? Does deceiving others amuse you?

FOOL   Why would it amuse me? This is at Lord Lucifer's behest. He desires to observe again how despicably they will abuse their father, the king.

WAG   Then he should summon the king himself.
FOOL I would prefer that, too, but as things stand, it's not known where the king is.
WAG   Is he, as expected, up high, acting out the cliché of picking flowers?
FOOL No, the king probably remains in this darkness. From ancient times, it has been rare for those who wield secular power, whether they are royalty or noblemen, to ascend to those heights.
WAG   If he's here, why not swiftly search for him?
FOOL So much weight would be lifted off my shoulders were that possible. As you know, the sectionalism here knows no bounds. Everyone single-mindedly desires to gather large numbers of the deceased. I had to hand out huge sums of gold to track Goneril and Regan. The search itself results in abruptly getting the cold shoulder. Were I to announce that I would whisk King Lear away, who knows what treatment I would be subjected to.
WAG   Then, why not appeal directly to Lord Lucifer?
FOOL Such nonsense. Lord Lucifer is an infinitely formidable being. He presides in a place where all gravity converges; he does no more than issue commands. He would never exchange words with someone like myself. Were I to eye him, let alone speak with him, it would induce gut-wrenching terror.
WAG   Indeed so?

The FOOL *produces a ring from his bag.*

FOOL Try this on.
WAG   Guv'nor, what is this? This hoop?
FOOL Just put it on.

The WAG *attempts to place it onto his nose.*

FOOL Why are you putting it through your nose? It is for your finger.

Scene Four

The WAG *puts it on. The* FOOL *observes him.*

FOOL   Well, it will have to do.
WAG   It might have to do for you, but it's not doing nothing for me.
FOOL   Do not move. Do not speak. If possible, cease breathing, too.
WAG   I can't do all three at once.
FOOL   The deuce, Wag. Attend me well.
WAG   What more do you want me to do? Give me my due for what I already do.
FOOL   Be quiet and listen, or I will bite your ear again. Now, with this ring, you become Mistress Cordelia.

The WAG *points to himself.*

FOOL   Indeed. Or rather, as with the headpiece, when you wear the ring you simply take on Mistress Cordelia's appearance.
WAG   I don't want to take on an appearance.
FOOL   I do not want you taking on her appearance either. But this is Lord Lucifer's bidding, so there is naught to be done.
WAG   Does this mean I'll be abused, too?
FOOL   Deem this as your fate. There is no going against Lord Lucifer's command. And, Wag, you have been pegged as someone fated to be abused.
WAG   Who's been pegging me?
FOOL   I have. I have just pegged you as the abused.
WAG   I ain't amused.

The WAG *removes the ring.*

The FOOL *produces a gold coin.*

FOOL   Wag, with this gold coin, how many soft-boiled eggs can you buy?
WAG   With one that size, I could buy me all the eggs in Hell and still have change left.

FOOL Do you not want all the soft-boiled eggs in Hell?
WAG Would I ever.
FOOL You could even buy smoked toads with the change.
WAG That I could.
FOOL And buy the fruit of nandinas.
WAG That I could.
FOOL So, are we good?
WAG We're good.
FOOL Then we are set. When we arrive, and I give you a signal, you will wear the ring. Is that clear?
WAG Aye, wear it I will.
FOOL Good, we have a deal.

The FOOL *puts away the gold coin.*

WAG I don't get it now?
FOOL After all is done. Carry it out well or you will not get the gold coin.
WAG Guv'nor?
FOOL What?
WAG Guv'nor, you ain't going to trick this honest, law-abiding Wag, are you?
FOOL Rest assured. Nothing in this world is as watertight as a contract with a devil. It is like crossing Styx in a large casket.
WAG I ain't completely certain what it is you're saying.
FOOL So long as you are not completely uncertain, you are fine. After all, I am not completely certain what it is I am saying.

The FOOL *places the hat and the other things into the bag.*

WAG But guv'nor, I am, who was it?
FOOL Mistress Cordelia. At least try to remember her name.
WAG This Cordelia is a woman, ain't she? That would mean that I'm to be a woman, don't it?
FOOL Indeed.

Scene Four

WAG   No can do, guv'nor. The two things I can't be are women and snails.

FOOL   What has snails to do with anything?

WAG   It's just a fact.

FOOL   All you need to do is to stand there like a wooden puppet. After all, Mistress Cordelia is a person of few words. If she had been a little more forthcoming with her words, we might have avoided this tragedy. Anyway, you do not need to speak.

WAG   I may not need to speak, but I have a mouth and might want to speak.

FOOL   In such cases, let me see, say the opposite of what you mean to say. Now, Mistress Cordelia is unrivalled when it comes to the pureness of her heart. She is a paragon of virtue. You, on the other hand, are a Hell-wag, bred from the mud of Hell.

WAG   Guv'nor, you remember!

FOOL   If we were to compare Mistress Cordelia to a lotus flower.

WAG   If so.

FOOL   We could say you were a lotus root.

WAG   I'm a lotus root . . . why?

FOOL   You are covered in mud and completely hollow.

WAG   Guv'nor, an admirable conceit.

FOOL   Thus, it would be about right if you spoke the opposite of what you thought.

WAG   Right, speak the opposite.

FOOL   Yes. If it is black, it is white; up is down, right is left, yes is no, fair is foul and foul is fair.

WAG   That sounds familiar. But that will make me a dunce.

FOOL   Exactly, like that.

WAG   Like I just did?

FOOL   If it is likely to work, I like it.

WAG   But guv'nor, I have to say, Lord Lucifer must have serious issues to get pleasure out of tormenting others even though he's the Emperor of Hell . . .

The FOOL *hastily places his hand over the* WAG*'s mouth.*

FOOL   You idiot. Why would you speak ill of Lord Lucifer here? There will be consequences, yes, consequences. Now, we must go.

The FOOL *leads the* WAG *away.*

Scene Five: The Witch Test

In a deep part of Hell.

GONERIL *and* REGAN.

GONERIL
>Sir, I do hate you more than words can wield the matter;
>Drearier than rheum, restricted jail space,
>Or rats that roam there,
>Beyond what is vulgar, dreadful, or dreary,
>No more than a roadside beggar; with cowardice, conceit, coarseness, cruelty,
>As little as child e'er rebelled or father found,
>Malice that makes breath poor and speech unable.
>Beyond all manner of so much I mistreat you.
>Sir, I do hate you!

REGAN
>Sir, I am made
>Of the self-same mettle that my sister is,
>And prize me at her worth. In my true heart
>I find she names my very deed of hate –
>Only she came short, that I profess
>Myself an enemy to all other joys
>Which the most sordid square of sense possesses,
>And find I am alone felicitate
>In your dear highness' pain.
>Sir, I do hate you!

Scene Five

The FOOL *enters.*

FOOL (*Clapping.*) My, my, my, my, mind-blowing. No one can quite voice their viciousness with such eloquence as you two. I am sure Lord Lucifer will be immensely pleased.

GONERIL Why, you must be a messenger from that noble being from the deepest reaches of this land, the dark-winged Lord Lucifer. It is an honour to have you come all this way.

REGAN Your journey here must have been fraught with tribulations.

FOOL I travelled with this wag who calls himself a guide, but who proved to be incredibly incompetent. And there were some hairy moments. Nonetheless, we have arrived safely.

REGAN I am so pleased you have. I have been sick with worry. And where is this guiding wag?

FOOL We were separated. He should arrive by and by. But it is no great loss if he fails to do so.

GONERIL You must be exhausted. Would you not like to have some tea and rest a while?

FOOL Unfortunately, I cannot allow myself that luxury. I am here on a mission. (*Solemnly.*) I am a law-abiding fool who has ventured here under the orders of Lord Lucifer.

GONERIL Law-abiding?

FOOL Indeed. A law-abiding fool.

REGAN I cannot help but feel we have met before.

GONERIL Truth be told, neither can I.

FOOL It is of the greatest honour to know that someone such as myself managed to leave an impression in some corner of your minds. Indeed, I was acquainted with you both in that other world. I am King Lear's fool.

GONERIL *and* REGAN, *in private.*

GONERIL Really, why is he Lord Lucifer's messenger? It's that fool from Father's train.

REGAN How should I know? He's here and there's nothing we can do.

GONERIL   I can't be expected to speak to that.

REGAN   I feel the same way. (*To the* FOOL.) At any rate, please make yourself at home. My dear sister insists that, how shall I put it, she does not wish to speak to you. She declares that her mouth and ears are intended for things better than to converse with such an unsightly, base fool. Now, let us go forth. There is an exquisite field of poisonous mushrooms yonder. Hand in hand, let us two speak to our hearts' content in a peaceful place.

GONERIL   How absolutely absurd to say I do not wish to speak with you. After all, all I usually have about me are unlettered demons and speechless ravens. And this crass, good-for-nothing sister. I have been long awaiting your arrival. In this bottomless pit, Lord Lucifer's messenger is a figure of great distinction. Pray, do let me bathe in the resplendent words that gush forth from that mouth of yours. Please shower your grace upon this miserable woman who has sunk to the depths of despair.

REGAN   Unlike my sister, I do not thoughtlessly entreat for grace. Grace is not becoming for such a place as this. Rather, I ache to hear you speak. About that almighty being, Lord Lucifer. His hobbies, preferred food and drink, and whatever else there is to know about him. I am slated to serve by his side. You must understand how a woman would wish to do the utmost to ready herself for that day. As the court fool, you were by far Father's favourite. You must be able to convey these things with unfettered eloquence.

FOOL   As one whose livelihood lies in language, I do pride myself to a degree on my eloquence. Also, who could resist passing away time in sophisticated conversation with two such learned ladies as yourselves and sharing in the sublime spiritual bliss that would follow. However, I am merely here as an envoy. Uncouth though it may be, I must immediately get down to business.

Scene Five

The FOOL *retrieves documents from his bag.*

GONERIL (*Aside.*) Sophisticated conversation my ass. How repulsive even having to breathe the same air as this knave. I would much prefer breathing in the belch of swine.

REGAN (*Aside.*) What sublime spiritual bliss? You must be joking. If this knave possesses a spirit, worms would grow limbs.

With documents in hand, the FOOL *approaches* GONERIL *and* REGAN.

FOOL So, as you have hitherto heard, the great emperor of the underworld, the miscreant of darkness, Lord Lucifer, plans to select from among humans one who excels in evil and place this figure directly under him. In doing so, he has taken notice of you two.

GONERIL I am humbled by this honour.

REGAN Obliged am I for such consideration that far exceeds kind words.

FOOL However, only one of you will be appointed. The decision is mine to make.

GONERIL *and* REGAN *stand to attention.*

FOOL Now, you have both submitted documents listing the numerous villainous deeds you have committed throughout your lives. I have conducted inquiries and have examined in detail how evil you are. And my, you are both splendidly sinful. Few among the active demons and witches are as villainous as you. I am in complete awe.

GONERIL I feel undeserving of such praise.

REGAN I have much to learn. But I have great potential, so I hope you put your faith in my future.

FOOL And so, my conclusion.

GONERIL What have you concluded?

REGAN Pray, do tell us.

FOOL   I shall do just that. At the moment, you are both neck to neck. If one of you is a tiger, the other is a bear. A bald-headed eagle here, a hyena there.

GONERIL   A moment, please. There must be a mistake.

FOOL   Which would be?

REGAN   Sister, dear, are you questioning this gentleman's judgment?

GONERIL   I am not. But though I know not how many evil deeds this incompetent sister of mine has scraped together, compared to the deadly sin I committed they are all trivial.

REGAN   Well, what a horrid thing to say. What proof have you of this?

GONERIL   My sin looms as a mountain range that pierces through the clouds and casts a deep shadow over other petty vices.

FOOL (*Flipping through the documents.*)   Let us see, what sin was this?

GONERIL   If the magnitude of our sins is being compared, that one crime would exceed all else combined. Needless to say, I refer to murdering this sister of mine with my own two hands. I killed her by poisoning her wine. The murdered and the murderer, surely there is no need to consider which of the two is more sinful.

FOOL   Indeed, there is truth in that.

GONERIL   Is there not? Compared to me, this sister of mine is merely good-natured. And a little dim-witted. After all, the good-natured have always tended to be dim-witted. My point is that my sister is nothing more than a victim. If I were a magnificent poisonous flower thriving in a jungle, my sister would be a weed on the side of the road.

REGAN (*Guffawing.*)   My dear sister, you are completely in the dark.

GONERIL   What do you mean?

REGAN   You seem to take great pride in having murdered me, but should you not consider why you did so?

Scene Five

GONERIL It is not obvious? With you gone, things would be in my favour. Of course, we could add revulsion to that. Should there have been any other motive?

REGAN Faith, you did the deed when you and I were facing each other in your chamber in the Duke of Albany's castle, in order to discuss a secret matter.

FOOL It was, I believe, about Edmund.

REGAN Indeed.

FOOL That villain who connived as a viper, illegitimate though he was, to oust the legitimate heir, Edgar, and his own father the Earl of Gloucester, to incarcerate King Lear, and even to order the murder of Mistress Cordelia; you both had exchanged vows with that Edmund.

GONERIL Yes. Of course, I was a married woman. Lo, that also makes me the greater sinner. For my sister was already a widow when she became acquainted with Edmund. No matter how bestial, the pleasures of the unwedded cannot be adulterous. Ha ha ha, how unfortunate. I, on the other hand, immediately don the depraved cloak of sin, simply with the brushing of the lips. Even more so with what Edmund and I did in bed.

FOOL What did you do?

GONERIL This and that that make even a devil blush.

FOOL Details, please provide details. I desire to blush.

GONERIL This is not for all to hear. But fine, lend me your ear.

GONERIL *whispers in the* FOOL*'s ear.*

FOOL Zounds. What perversion, what obscenity; licentiousness that makes even Emperor Caligula pale in comparison.

GONERIL What is more, while I abandoned myself to such acts with Edmund, I surreptitiously schemed to murder my husband. My design was to send my husband to his demise, welcome Edmund as my spouse, exile my sister, and rule over the whole of Britain. Now, is that not villainous?

FOOL You are such a villain. Truly remarkable.

REGAN You are still wet behind the ears.
GONERIL How? How could I be wet behind the ears?
REGAN Sister dear, you are so trusting. I could even say you are good-natured.
GONERIL Stop with this slander. Which part of this is good-natured?
FOOL What are you saying? Pray, explain.
GONERIL Yes, pray. Do not think you can get away with lies.
REGAN Very well. You are aware that, just like you, Edmund and I had agreed to marry.
FOOL I am. In short, Edmund was two-timing you.
REGAN That is correct. But it was I who persuaded Edmund to do so.
GONERIL What?
REGAN Even if Edmund and I had married, we would have had no peace of mind so long as your husband, the Duke of Albany, lived. We needed to send that obstinate thorn in our side to his grave by any means possible. But Albany was renowned for his valour and so dear was the love the people bore him; a head-on battle would not yield us victory. Hence, my ploy.
FOOL Which was?
REGAN To have Edmund seduce my sister. After all, my dear sister has a weakness for such apparently shallow lotharios, smooth as peeled fava beans.
GONERIL You are the one with such a weakness. Who was it that first made a fuss about Edmund this and Edmund that?
FOOL My, you are both not only vile but also exhibit the utmost lack of taste in men. I wonder if genetics has anything to do with you both being thus. I have taken the liberty to check the history of your affairs with men. (*Checking his documents.*) First, the king of Naples, whose only interest was to hypnotize chickens, then the prince of Saxony, who would eat a manger full of potatoes, followed

Scene Five

by the Duke of Banquo with congenital inebriation, and of course, the Prince of Morocco, who claiming to be a human pump, would swallow then spit out goldfish. And this is just to name a few. How could I put it, they were a selection of scum or a reservoir of rejects. And just to be thorough, you would, without fail, both become involved with each of them. I was deeply impressed at how you were able to gather together so many inconsequential men.

     GONERIL *and* REGAN *are offended.*

FOOL (*A little flustered.*) Well, let us put all that aside. And what of your plan?

REGAN As expected, my dear sister fell prey to Edmund. Being, at heart, gullible and good-natured, she would become infatuated with Edmund and blind to all else. To marry Edmund, she would eventually murder her husband, the Duke of Albany. At that point, Edmund and I would officially marry. With Albany gone, it would be an easy matter to crush my sister on her own. And the whole of Britain would be ours. That was the plan.

GONERIL Such lies. Stop with the lies.

REGAN I am afraid it is all true. You must find it mortifying for two reasons. First, the evil design you devised with your limited intelligence turned out to be exploited for my dirty little plan. Second, Edmund was in cahoots with me all this time.

GONERIL Nonsense. This is all nonsense. True, Edmund was friendly with my sister in the beginning. But once his heart shifted towards me, there cannot be any doubt that he was completely mine.

REGAN My poor sister. Not only were you blinded by a false love, but you also still have not realized that you were deceived.

GONERIL What proof have you? You could be the one that Edmund was deceiving.

REGAN   I have plenty of proof. Now I know all, of what tears of servility you shed, what gifts you gave, how pathetically you carried on, crawling before that man, all to win his love. Dear sister, I heard at Edmund's behest you got on all fours like a cur and licked his toe; the one with athlete's foot. I wonder how it must have tasted? The athlete's foot of the man you love must taste of honey.

GONERIL   How do you . . .

REGAN   Well, you seem to be singing a different tune now. That change in tune is my proof. Edmund told me. While we were in bed. It was actually my idea to have you lick his foot. Our pillow talk was always about you. Gossiping about my kind-hearted sister. Discussing how next to torment you, between kisses. Nothing is more heavenly than the clandestine pleasure of cooking up villainy. Edmund and I devoured each other as we guffawed at the way you bewailed or bristled or begged in response to man's cold-hearted caprice.

GONERIL   How dare you . . .

GONERIL *lunges at* REGAN, *but* REGAN *repels her.*

REGAN (*To the* FOOL.)   So you know now which of the two sisters is more gifted in evil, which of us is more suited to serve by Lord Lucifer's side.

FOOL (*As he writes.*)   Indeed. Well, how truly vicious. Absolutely abominable.

GONERIL   But the fact that it was I who murdered you cannot be undone. The thousands, nay the tens of thousands, of tales you weave out cannot outweigh this single fact. The murderer and the murdered are as distinct as light and darkness.

FOOL   There is reason in that, too.

GONERIL   My sister's tales are, in the end, merely illusions created through words. I remember; that thrilling moment when the white powdered wolfsbane began melting into

the wine. The dissolved poison did not discolour the wine. But I knew; the taste of hate hidden in that semi-translucent liquid. My sister guzzled down my hate with repulsive gulping sounds. In the end, I emerged on top.
FOOL   I see, so you did.
REGAN   But sister dear, who do you think is more evil, the one who murders or the one who incites a murder?
GONERIL   What do you mean?
FOOL   What could she mean?
REGAN   For instance, you boasted that you had me steal Mother's diamond and drove her to suicide.
GONERIL   Yes, I did. (*To the* FOOL.) You have taken that into consideration, haven't you? That I am a matricidal superlative sinner.
FOOL   Well, in a way I have.
GONERIL   And what does that have to do with anything?
REGAN   In that case, who do you think is more evil? I actually stole the gem while you tricked me into stealing it.
GONERIL   Of course, I am.
REGAN   To give another example, it was the Captain that strangled Cordelia to death, but on the other hand, Edmund inveigled him into doing so. (*To the* FOOL.) In this case, who is the more malicious?
FOOL   Faith, it is a difficult choice, but I would have to say Edmund.
REGAN   Which means, I am the more villainous.
GONERIL   How can that be?
REGAN   How can it not? I had you murder me.
GONERIL   You are not making any sense.
REGAN   See here, that day, we faced each other in your chamber. We were to discuss Edmund. With your crude words, you urged me to withdraw from our rivalry. Or rather you embarrassed yourself by throwing a fit. The infatuation of an over-the-hill woman is truly appalling. However, I laughed and did not comply. After all, I had the

assurance that Edmund's heart belonged to me. How could I not sit back and enjoy it all? It was then that murderous thoughts began to cross your mind.
GONERIL   It was. I decided to do away with you.
REGAN   Why?
GONERIL   Why else, because of hate.
REGAN   Why did you hate me? What caused the dark flames of enmity to start in your heart?
GONERIL   I detested your eyes, ears, mouth, hair, voice, everything about you. The only thing I did not hate was that flat nose and flat chest.
REGAN   My, how insulting. But I understand why you wished to murder me. You wanted Edmund, the man you loved, for yourself. You sensed that in no way would you be able to separate Edmund and myself. That is why you decided to murder me at that moment. To see me laugh and enjoy the situation drove you to kill me. In other words, the one who moved you to murder me was actually me. I am so sorry. Your sister, Regan, was all to blame.
FOOL   This is not completely convincing.
GONERIL   This convinces completely no one. This is gibberish that does not even amount to a quibble.
REGAN   It is not. No use trying to hide it. You live for love. A fountain of limitless love flows in your soul, forever gushing forth and glistening. Dear sister, how bounteous and benevolent you are. The light of your love has shone upon me as spring sunlight ever since I was a child.
GONERIL   Cease speaking in this manner.
REGAN   I cannot, for your radiant love forces my words to flourish. Dear sister, you are a paragon of virtue. After all, you have loved even this hateful sister who stole your lover.
GONERIL   To whom are you referring?
REGAN   Me.
GONERIL   Do not mock me. I would rather love Penia, possessed by the god of pestilence.

REGAN   How splendid that you never lose your sense of humour. Though I must say you are devoid of wit. And to see you as demure as ever. Of course, expressing your love openly embarrasses you.
GONERIL   Cease with this nonsense.
REGAN   Then let me ask you, why did you, dear sister, kill yourself after killing me?
GONERIL   That is . . .
REGAN   You must be holding your tongue out of humility, so I shall explain on your behalf. The moment you killed me, you trembled out of fear for the sin you committed. No longer in the throes of passion, you notice the corpse of your exquisite sister. Your own two hands took the life of none other than the sister you loved. You could not forgive yourself. And so you stabbed your own chest. It was love, an outpouring of love for your kin that drove you to do so.
GONERIL   What drivel. The corpse of what exquisite sister? My main concern was that you might spew blood and stain the carpet. Anyway, what is crucial is why I chose death. (*To the* FOOL.) From antiquity, the greatest sin of all has been that of killing oneself. It has been said that no sin is worse than destroying what God has bestowed upon us.
FOOL   Indeed. Suicide is, as it were, a renouncing of the Gospel, a revolt against the Creator. Of all human sins, it would have to rank at the top.
REGAN   But motivation must be important.
FOOL   That is also true. Not all suicides bear the same weight. For example, particularly notable is a man in Russia who recently hanged himself with a cord rubbed with soap. There was no reason whatsoever for the suicide. Nor was he mad. He killed himself simply out of spite, sheer scorn for life, and the satisfaction of sabotaging God's order. Taken to this extreme, human suicide becomes the admirable apotheosis of vice.

REGAN   No such existential quality can be sought in my dear sister's suicide. Her motivation was much more sentimental and human. In other words, it was the act of a soul seeking salvation after having committed a sin. Acknowledgement of the horrors of sin is surely proof of an unadulterated soul. In short, she is rooted in love and infallible faith.

GONERIL   Well, try to tarnish my reputation as much as you like with your words, for they cannot change the weight of my sins.

REGAN   In comparison, I am a barren desert. My parched soul has long been dead; it has become withered and mummified. I have not once, since birth, loved. Nor have I cherished what God has created. Unfortunate am I never to have known what love is.

FOOL   Which would mean that you had not loved even Edmund.

REGAN   Of course.

GONERIL   What facile two-facedness. You were ready to die for that man.

REGAN   I did not dislike him. He was adorable.

GONERIL   There you go. You loved him.

REGAN   But it was affection one feels for a stray cat that has by chance wandered in. Love is a totally unsuitable word for what I felt. It was a simple passing fancy.

The FOOL *uses magic to transform into* EDMUND.

An illusion of EDMUND *appears.*

GONERIL   Edmund!
REGAN   Edmund!
GONERIL   When did . . . is it really you, Edmund?

EDMUND *nods.*

GONERIL   Edmund, my love. Where have you been? How I have searched for you, ever since arriving here. Pray, say something.

Scene Five

EDMUND Forgive me. How thick-skinned am I to have insouciantly shown my face here. Having tormented you both with false love and acted sinfully, I have completely lost face.

REGAN And yet here you are.

GONERIL Where have you been since then?

EDMUND In this world without light. At the bottom of an abyss much further down than here, a hole where traitors and recalcitrants are gathered, is my present abode. Tamora, queen of the Goths, Iago, the Moor's ensign, that Richard, the Duke of Gloucester who made the whole of Britain bleed; with these, I am crushed in a stone mortar, day after day.

GONERIL Why, how horrid that you must endure such pain.

EDMUND Nay, far worse should I face for the sins I have committed. But what weighs heavy on my heart is the thought of you both. Victims of my shameless ploys and the playthings of fate, you were brought here to receive countless, atrocious punishments. Every time the two of you scream in pain it renders my heart asunder. Though I might close my ears, your voices reach my soul and crush my heart to pieces. The tears with which I fill a bucket every day are not for myself.

GONERIL Kind Edmund. Your words alone console me. What is most unbearable here is that no one offers sympathy. No one lends an ear. There is not even contempt, only interminable indifference. Only the cogwheels of fate, a sturdy and precise machine, that rotates ad infinitum. To know that my voice had reached you! Prithee, Edmund, you will at times address your gait to me hereafter, won't you?

EDMUND If I could, I would do so every day. But nay, I have come to bid you farewell.

GONERIL Why? Are you going away?

EDMUND I heard that you are both to grace Lord Lucifer with your company. That would mean eternal separation. One day, the angels will sound their glorious horns and all sinners will be thrust into the blazing flames; the glimmer of hope I held of how, from that day onwards, our fates would converge, allowing us to share in our agony and comfort one another, now dissipated. Those who serve Lord Lucifer and those who do not must go separate paths. Never more to meet. Perhaps this wisp of hope I held was meant to be shattered. It must have been intended as punishment. After all, there is no hope here. This is the final and eternally unrelieved damnation that I am to receive. Farewell, my love.

GONERIL Take comfort, Edmund. Your hope has not yet dissipated.

EDMUND How can that be?

GONERIL We are not both going. Only one will descend to Lord Lucifer.

EDMUND Can this be true?

GONERIL You need not worry anymore. I am here for you. Edmund, I will remain with you forever more.

EDMUND I do not deserve this.

GONERIL Dear Edmund.

The two embrace.

REGAN Dear sister, are you certain about this?

GONERIL About what?

REGAN What, you say? About becoming a witch. Are you certain about not becoming a witch?

GONERIL Oh, that. The position is yours. Go to Lucifer or whatever. (*Embracing* EDMUND.) Oh, Edmund, my darling.

REGAN Off I go, then. . . . Farewell.

There is no reply. EDMUND *behaves as a cat.*

REGAN I cannot watch this. Sister, I say, sister.

GONERIL What? Still here?

REGAN Still obtuse. The wool is being thrown over your eyes. That man, in faith, does not love you in the least.

Scene Five

GONERIL   Avaunt! Out of our sight. Do not attempt to undo our bond.
REGAN   Bond? What bond?
GONERIL   Here, now, we are hand in hand. This steadfast bond.
REGAN   Edmund. I say, Edmund. Answer me.
EDMUND   What is your bidding?
REGAN   Is it your intention to continue tormenting my dear sister even in this world?
EDMUND   I just . . .
REGAN   Speak honestly. You do not love my dear sister.
EDMUND   But that is . . .
REGAN   Then answer me. Do you love my dear sister? Be truthful in your reply.
EDMUND   I love her . . . am I not permitted to say so?
REGAN   No lies. Lies are not permitted in this place of darkness. Speak the truth.
EDMUND   I . . . have lied.
REGAN   Well, now you know.
GONERIL   Know what?
REGAN   How this man truly feels.
GONERIL   I do. Edmund has declared his love for me.
REGAN   But that was a lie. You, too, heard what he just said. It was all a lie. His heart lies elsewhere.
GONERIL   His heart? What is the heart? An individual's thoughts? Then the heart cannot be trusted. Thoughts now, thoughts next in line, thoughts to follow and thoughts not yet formed. They are never the same. There is no end to how they might change with the tide. They are more fickle than windswept clouds. Instead, it is words that are constant. All that can be trusted are the words of heartfelt love that this beautiful mouth uttered. And this arm, cheek, chin, hair, lips; what these eyes see, these ears hear, this skin feels; only they can be trusted. After having fallen thus far, I reflected on all that happened while I was alive and came to this conclusion. What heart? It is but a flickering shadow.

An apparition that wanders with the purpose to frighten others. But I do not fear apparitions. I love you, I love you, I love you. I chant words of love as if they were a spell which instantaneously dissipates. I will repeat these words over and over. Repeatedly for a thousand, nay two thousand, times each day; until the words solidify in the air and can be touched.

REGAN   Enough, dear sister. I will remain here.

GONERIL   You are on your way to Lord Lucifer.

REGAN   It cannot be helped, for I am the one Edmund loves. I do not desire it, but I shall have to remain behind.

GONERIL   There is no need to do what you do not desire.

REGAN   Dear sister, stop being unreasonable. For your happiness, I sacrifice my own. My, little did I know that being loved brings such sorrow.

GONERIL   Mock me not. I am to remain behind.

REGAN   Be rational. She who is loved has the right to remain behind. And to do so would be for the good of Edmund, the one you so love. Prithee, for poor Edmund's sake, you must go to Lord Lucifer.

GONERIL   I will not. You go.

REGAN   Enough of this.

GONERIL   Edmund is mine for eternity. I yield him to no one.

GONERIL *and* REGAN *fight as they hurl abuse at each other.*

The FOOL *lifts the magic.*

EDMUND *disappears.*

GONERIL   Edmund, where are you?

REGAN   Where, Edmund?

The FOOL *writes something.*

FOOL   Neither of you seem meant to serve by Lord Lucifer's side.

Scene Five

GONERIL *and* REGAN *are dumbfounded.*

REGAN   Was that . . .?

FOOL   Indeed, it was an illusion. You both witnessed an illusion.

REGAN   Illu . . .

GONERIL   (*With hysterical laughter.*) I should have known. Edmund would never come here. And what love? How could love exist in such a dark place?

REGAN   Where is Edmund? He is with us in this subterranean world, is he not?

FOOL   He is. An infinite distance, the distance between one corner of the universe and another, separates you. You will probably never encounter him. (*Preparing to leave.*) Might I add, Edmund seems not to have loved either of you. Well, perhaps that knowledge was superfluous.

GONERIL   So superfluous.

REGAN   That is a lie. That cannot be true. After all, how could you know this?

FOOL   Well, I have intelligence for general facts. And there is Judge Minos' deposition.

REGAN   This cannot be. Edmund's eyes were the eyes of someone in love. His love could only have been for me or my sister. (*Looking at* GONERIL.) It could not have been for her. Thus, I conclude through this process of elimination, that it was for me.

FOOL   The one Edmund loved was Mistress Cordelia.

REGAN   Such drivel. Edmund ordered the mercenary captain to kill Cordelia. Why kill someone he loves?

FOOL   He loves to hate.

REGAN   . . .?

GONERIL   . . .?

FOOL   Wrong expression. Love and hate are two sides of the same coin. Edmund had always been infatuated with Mistress Cordelia. He wrote her hundreds of letters; he spent countless nights by his window just for a glimpse of her face. Mistress

Cordelia was not unmoved by his ardour, but they were unmeet in their titles. One, the daughter of he who ruled Britain, the most peerless country in the world; the other, though son of an earl, from the quarters of a mistress. From the start it was a doomed love. Yet Edmund, undeterred, insistently pursued her until her rebuff struck him as a common cur is struck on the muzzle. It was then that love became hate.

REGAN   That cannot be.

GONERIL   Ha, ha, so the truth is finally out.

REGAN   Did you know?

GONERIL   I did not know, but it does not surprise me. It explains perfectly why Edmund conspired to such extent and mounded evil upon evil to rise in power. It was to win Cordelia.

FOOL   Indeed.

REGAN   In the end, it is Cordelia. In a word, it is Cordelia. Cordelia, Cordelia. Always enjoying good fortune. Always having to be the good one.

FOOL   Well, in that life Mistress Cordelia did meet a dreadful end.

GONERIL   But I suppose now, in exchange for that, she is in the light enjoying herself.

FOOL   It must be so. Now, I must take leave of you.

Scene Six: Cordelia's Resolution

CORDELIA *enters, bathed in heaven's blinding light.*

REGAN   Cordelia. Why it really is you, Cordelia.

CORDELIA   How I have missed you, dear sister. I did not see you again after I departed for France.

FOOL (*Aside.*)   That Wag, such inopportune timing to make his entrance. And what an ostentatious entrance at that.

CORDELIA   Dear sister, have you been well?

GONERIL   How could I be well? Where do you think this is?

Scene Six

CORDELIA Alas, you have been unwell? How most unfortunate. Have you consulted a physician? Are you on medication?

GONERIL Yes, yes, everyday. I swallow rusty nails.

CORDELIA Is that some folk remedy?

GONERIL You could say so. I also have my neck cut half a score times with a saw.

CORDELIA My word, to require such surgery must mean what ails you is most serious.

GONERIL What a dimwit.

FOOL Forgive me for interrupting. Please continue with this later. (*Taking* CORDELIA's *arm.*) All is ended. Off we go. Now promptly remove the ring.

CORDELIA What is the meaning of this?

FOOL You have earned the gold coin. Now make haste.

The FOOL *tries to remove* CORDELIA's *ring.*

CORDELIA (*Fleeing.*) Stop. Thief. Dear sister, this man is a thief!

REGAN This man is Father's fool. You must remember him.

CORDELIA Now that you mention it.

GONERIL More importantly, Cordelia, why are you here?

FOOL Not to worry, for she will be gone presently.

GONERIL (*To the* FOOL.) You were not addressed. If your business is complete, be on your way. The sight of you is odious to my eyes.

FOOL What a change in tune.

GONERIL There's no surprise there. I've realized that there's no reason to curry favour from the likes of you anymore. Pox on Lucifer. Enough with this farce.

GONERIL *kicks the* FOOL.

FOOL Ow, how cruel. Ladies have slapped me without warning, but never have I been kicked.

GONERIL Is that so? You shall be introduced to so much more that's new to you.

CORDELIA   Dear sister, please stop. Violence is wrong.
GONERIL   Why must you always be the good girl. In the end, Cordelia, you are always to blame. Even with Edmund. If you had been decisive in rejecting his advances from the start, Edmund would have been able to forget you and not have turned to the path he did. It's always the elusiveness of your words that invites disaster.
CORDELIA   No more, dear sister. If Cordelia is at fault, please punish Cordelia. This man has committed neither sin nor wrong.
GONERIL (*Continuing to abuse the* FOOL.)   Why do you have to be the voice of reason?
CORDELIA   I beseech you, cease. It is Cordelia, Cordelia that you should strike.
REGAN   Enough, sister. Surely, you have had enough.

GONERIL *stops the abuse.*

CORDELIA (*Comforting the* FOOL.)   How do you feel? Have you been injured?
GONERIL   This knave's fine. He holds onto life more steadfastly than the lowest forms of life. He's akin to the tardigrade that is said to withstand exposure to ten thousand roentgen of radiation.
REGAN   Never mind that. Cordelia, why did you come here?
CORDELIA   Ah, yes. I am here in search of our father. Might you know where he is?
REGAN   Father? But you, for sooth, must have been high above, by God's side.
CORDELIA   Yes, I have.
GONERIL   What do you do every day? Here we keep busy swallowing nails and so forth.
CORDELIA   I have been picking flowers.
GONERIL   Well, the garden of heaven really does exist. But isn't it tedious with nothing to do but pick flowers? I often hear rumours that it's dull there.

Scene Six

CORDELIA Not in the least. There is not a dull moment in a day spent simply listening to birds chirping; and looking at rainbows and auroras that create luminous patterns. And at times dancing with angels or singing in chorus to the music Apollo plays on his harp.

GONERIL How delightful. Here we chant poems to the devil's belching. Come, there is something I have wanted to ask for a long time. What kind of man is Christ? Is he bearded?

CORDELIA Yes, he sports a splendid beard.

GONERIL How about that piece of flesh?

CORDELIA Which piece of flesh would that be?

GONERIL There, down there; in brief, down under.

CORDELIA . . .?

GONERIL Is he circumcised down there?

CORDELIA My!

REGAN Enough, sister. You want decency. More to the point, Cordelia, you said you've come looking for Father. What do you mean?

CORDELIA Alas, Father is not in the other place. This is, of course, what God, the Creator of all things, has decided. It cannot be a mistake. Nay, it would be presumptuous even to think it a mistake. I do not in the least doubt Father's honour. Yet I realize that even a just and benevolent lord cannot rule his land by observing principles alone. I was once a daughter in Britain's royal family. I am familiar with politics. Philosophy and ideals alone will not suffice. Be God's word as it may, one may need to sacrifice one lamb to save another ninety-nine. Father must have had no choice but to commit a minor, insignificant sin. Though it may not have been an act of avarice or arrogance or atrocity, in the eyes of God a sin is a sin. While I understand that, the thought of poor Father in a place of darkness where no light reaches clouds my face.

GONERIL What filial piety. The thought of someone's misfortunes would not cloud my face but illuminate it with joy.

REGAN   Hold your tongue, sister. And so what did you do?

CORDELIA   Archangel Gabriel noticed my distress. I mustered the courage to explain the situation to him, and Gabriel, feeling my pain, spoke with God on my behalf. God, giving ear to my story, was moved by my words and sent me into these depths.

REGAN   Amazing that Lord Lucifer allowed this. Above all else, Hell loathes light. It would never allow entry to one so copiously embraced in Heaven's light. (*To the* FOOL.) I'm not mistaken, am I?

FOOL   No, it is quite so. But I see no need to ponder over this.

GONERIL   What, sirrah, still dallying here?

FOOL   Forbearance. I wish to depart presently, but the Wag acts erratically; if I do not take back the magic ring, trouble will ensue.

GONERIL   How now, still prating on, are we?

FOOL   Sorry. Forgive me.

GONERIL   Come, the gates of Hell are closed, aren't they?

FOOL   Indeed, they are. Ever since Christ was mistakenly allowed entry, causing havoc for all here, there has been strict border control. But I suppose exceptions are not unknown.

GONERIL   What an evasive response. Come, a clear answer.

FOOL   Yes, they are.

REGAN (*To* CORDELIA.)   So God allowed you here with His special blessing.

CORDELIA   That is correct.

REGAN   And you are searching for Father.

CORDELIA   Yes.

REGAN   What will you do when you encounter him?

CORDELIA   In faith, I intend to save Father from the depths of this darkness.

GONERIL   Ha, ha, why, however omnipotent God may be, there are rules here. God cannot interfere with them. No precedent exists of a deceased in Hell being removed without leave. (*To the* FOOL.) Isn't that so?

Scene Six

FOOL   It is. God has recognized Lord Lucifer's rights. The number of the deceased cannot be reduced at will. After all, the precision required when dealing with numbers down here borders on the insane. A thousand lashings will never be 999 or 1001.

GONERIL   I can physically vouch for that.

CORDELIA   I am well aware of this. To reduce one, one must add one. Hence, I intend on remaining here instead of Father.

GONERIL   What?

REGAN   So you plan on being Father's replacement?

CORDELIA   Yes.

GONERIL   Really, you are . . . Do you realize where you are? Remaining here doesn't simply mean to be here physically. The demons will torment you every day, pulling out your tongue, gouging out your eyes, decapitating you; it's beyond words. And day after day, wet sulphur turns into rain, destroying the skin and creating rashes that become boils. The word unpleasant doesn't even begin to convey our suffering. No matter how much manicure we apply to our nails, they continue cracking.

CORDELIA   I am aware of this. And I accept it all.

GONERIL   Really!

REGAN   But why is it that you must go so far?

CORDELIA   I wonder if you remember.

CORDELIA *removes the ring.*

CORDELIA   This is one of the gems Father gave to Mother and the three of us, as a token of his love for his family. This is what father said at the time. It is the cruel fate of those who are born into royalty, consanguineous as parent and child or as siblings though they may be, to become, at times, enemies and engage in battle. The father may kill his child, siblings may strike at one other, and the child may exile the father. This family may one day face such a fate. But no matter how cruel the fate that awaits us, let us, with our hearts as one, always love one another. He also said this. Even though we may come face to face across the blades of swords or have no choice but to take one another's lives, let this family never hate one another. Never shall we harbour resentment. Let us quietly accept the fate God has imposed upon us and as much as it is humanly possible, forever in our hearts, love one another. With those words, Father bestowed upon us the gems as tokens of our vow to love our family. Looking back, I wonder if Father already had an apprehension of the tragedy that awaited us at the end of our lives. Dear sisters, you each have one gem, do you not?

REGAN   I threw away that trifle long ago.

GONERIL   I lost mine, in an all-night poker game with a demon. They are such cheats. Whenever I attempted a bluff, they would torture my hand out of me. It was such a scam.

CORDELIA   But you both kissed your gems and made a vow.

GONERIL   That I did. So bombastically, grandiloquence upon grandiloquence. Any gift, even from one's father, deserves something in return. I recall that even then you exasperated father with the sparsity of your words.

REGAN   Forsooth, Father was infuriated because Cordelia alone was bizarrely brusque.

CORDELIA   I simply spoke my vows from my heart.

GONERIL   That is your problem. In faith, you are mistaken. Without words, no one would know what lies in your heart. Even an infant conveys hunger by wailing. A child who does not cry receives no dug. Famine is your fate if all you have are thoughts in your heart.

CORDELIA   Even with a tearless infant, a mother will know what the child desires. Thoughts that remain in the heart may be shrouded in darkness now, but one day God will illuminate them.

Scene Six

REGAN There is no God here. This is Hell. Nay, not just here. There is no place in the entire universe that is not part of Hell. Even by God's side. So long as man has a heart.

CORDELIA But if true feelings cannot be communicated, all that remains is despair.

REGAN Exactly. But become accustomed to despair and it won't seem so dreadful. Or rather, without true despair, there is no hope for a new start.

CORDELIA I do not wish to despair.

REGAN You exasperated Father. What lay in your heart failed to reach him. And what ensued? You must remember how miserable Father was at the end of his life.

CORDELIA Which is why I have descended to the depths of this subterranean world to save Father's soul. Upon the truth in my heart, upon this gem of my vow, I intend to save Father.

GONERIL What determination. We understand what thoughts lie in your heart, but . . .

REGAN I do not understand. Pray, tell me, what thoughts did you share with Edmund to ensnare him? The truth of your heart, could it be to tease men?

CORDELIA Not once did I share my true thoughts with Edmund.

REGAN Then what of Edmund, of his thoughts?

CORDELIA There is no truth in his thoughts. Only evil schemes.

REGAN How can you be sure? He may have been in love with you. That might have been the one true thought that came from his heart.

CORDELIA It is not so. If he had had truth in his heart, it would invariably have made itself known to me. All that my heart sensed were the murky umbrages of hunger.

REGAN True thoughts for you are simply those agreeable to you. The only mirror you cherish is the one with your own reflection. You do not understand what true thoughts are.

GONERIL   Come, let her be; it is what she believes. There is no sense in turning over what has passed. More importantly, Cordelia, why do you obsess only with Father?
CORDELIA   It is because I love him deeply.
GONERIL   But those precious gems were tokens of a vow for our entire family to love one another.
CORDELIA   Indeed.
GONERIL   Our family does not solely consist of Father. There is Mother and your two lovely sisters.
CORDELIA   That is . . .
REGAN (*Aside.*)   Dear sister, you are not completely wanting in useful arguments. And here I thought you were just a simpleton. So true that Father is not Cordelia's only family.
GONERIL   I would save Mother rather than Father.
REGAN (*Aside.*)   She is a simpleton after all.
CORDELIA   But Mother is not here.
GONERIL   That is not true. Mother has to be in this place of darkness.
CORDELIA   That cannot be. Our Mother was incapable of committing even the slightest sin. You know well she was as the Virgin Mary, more virtuous than the angels.
GONERIL   You are simply ignorant, so let me enlighten you.
CORDELIA   Please, no. I do not wish to listen to this. I cannot bear to witness you continue the sin of lying in this way.
GONERIL   Do you accuse me of being a liar?
CORDELIA   That is not exactly what I said.
GONERIL   No, it's exactly so. But I'm not lying about Mother.
CORDELIA   It cannot be true. Not our mother.
GONERIL   So intractable. So much like Father. Pray, tell me, have you seen Mother up there? Have you picked flowers with her? And danced with her?
CORDELIA   That . . .
GONERIL   There, you haven't. Mother is also here. Here where there's no light.

Scene Six

CORDELIA   That cannot be.
GONERIL   (*To the* FOOL.)
You, all this is true, isn't it?
FOOL   I am relieved. I thought that I was forgotten. That no one would address me ever again.
GONERIL   Well?
FOOL   Indeed. The mistress is here.
GONERIL   There. Now you know.
CORDELIA   It must be some mistake.
FOOL   There is no mistake in God's judgment.
CORDELIA   Then I will also save Mother.
GONERIL   Impossible. As you just said, to remove one, one must be added.
FOOL   That is so. The devil is devilishly precise with numbers.
CORDELIA   I am with child.

Silence.

FOOL   Reduce two, add two. The accounts are balanced.
GONERIL   Tush, so you are going to sacrifice an innocent child.
CORDELIA   . . .
GONERIL   How exactly like Father.
CORDELIA   (*To the* FOOL.)   Pray, Father is here today, is he not? That is what I heard. Prithee, tell me where Father is.
FOOL   It is not totally untrue to say he is here.
CORDELIA   He is, is he not? Please bring him to me. Bring him here now.
GONERIL   Hasn't she begged enough? Fetch him here.
FOOL   Aye, or nay, or rather, I could call him forth if you wish; what I wish to say is that all this attention embarrasses me and makes it difficult for him to appear.
GONERIL   What's this prattle? Shall I strike you again?
FOOL   Please, spare me.
REGAN   A moment, please. Cordelia, your father will appear.
CORDELIA   Truly, dear sister?
REGAN   Truly. I promise you.

GONERIL   How can you guarantee that?

REGAN   Peace, dear sister. Cordelia, your tale has moved me deeply; in a way I have never been moved. Your love is marvellous. More spacious than the sea, more purely resplendent than the morning dew, it can transport the soul far away, more swiftly than a bird in the sky. You may not believe this, but the truth in your heart has, for the first time, finally made me rue my sins. I am put to shame. No wonder God has granted you so much. The truth in your heart has reached directly into my heart.

CORDELIA   Dear sister.

GONERIL   Well, what a change in tune.

REGAN   Please, let me see your ring once again.

CORDELIA   Yes, dear sister.

REGAN (*With the ring in her hand.*)   How beautifully it shines. Gems catch the light and shine. Why is it that this gem shines alone in this place of no light? It must be that the unclouded truth in your heart inspires it to shine from within.

CORDELIA   No, it is not only the truth in my heart. It also reflects the heart of you who holds the stone in your hand.

REGAN   Thank you. But that cannot be. I no longer have a heart. What I have is dark and sullied.

CORDELIA   That is not so. This change of heart is proof that it is not so.

REGAN   It is too late. Do not mind me. Do not console me. I have lost the gem Father gave me.

CORDELIA   It is of no consequence. However lovely or valuable, a stone is no more than a stone. What is important is the vow you made; what you felt when we swore that we would love one another as family forever more and not forget we are bound to one another as parent and child, as siblings.

REGAN   You still love me even as I am.

CORDELIA   How can I not? We are sisters that share the same blood. Who would I love if not you.

Scene Six

REGAN   That gives me joy. More than all the flowers in the world. But you have chosen to save Father and Mother from this place, not me.

CORDELIA   Dear sister, that is . . .

REGAN   No need to worry. It is expected. I would most likely do the same. An objectionable, vile sister, such as I, does not merit saving.

CORDELIA   Forgive me.

REGAN   You are not at fault.

CORDELIA   But.

GONERIL   A moment. Suppose Cordelia is carrying twins. Would that not mean that three can be saved? (*To the* FOOL.) Is that not so?

FOOL   It is. Triplets would save four; quadruplets, five.

GONERIL   So it is. Why, you are finally displaying traits fit for a fool.

FOOL   Quintuplets, six; sextuplets, seven; and centuplets would mean a swooping hundred and one.

GONERIL   Enough of this overkill. (*To* CORDELIA.) Well, since it is so Cordelia, you will bear twins.

CORDELIA   I am afraid this is not something that can be suddenly willed.

REGAN   Dear sister, cease with this foolishness. Have you no shame? Your presence itself is insufferable.

GONERIL   You're one to talk. Isn't there a way to split the child in her womb in half? (*To the* FOOL.) Come, tell us.

FOOL   Well now, it's not like dividing a watermelon.

GONERIL   So it is not feasible.

REGAN (*Enraged.*)   Sister, do you realize what Cordelia must feel being down here? Have you given any thought to that?

GONERIL   Why this outburst?

REGAN   Can you not appreciate your sister's admirable desire to sacrifice herself to save the souls of Father and Mother? Do you not perceive the truth in Cordelia's heart? You know what kind of place this is. You know the pain of punishment. Cordelia is willing to leave behind the world of light and sink into this place of darkness for eternity. Could you do the same? I could not. Not everyone could do this.

GONERIL What are you plotting?

REGAN My heart goes to Cordelia. I feel sorry for her.

CORDELIA Dear sister.

REGAN To think that you are willing to sacrifice yourself for people such as they. It is as if a fragrant lily is to wither to give way to a poisonous thistle.

CORDELIA What do you mean?

GONERIL Of course. That makes sense . . . indeed Cordelia, you say you have come to save Father, but he is not such an honourable man.

REGAN (*Interrupting.*) Peace, sister. Pay no attention to her, Cordelia. Do not mind what she says. She understands nothing. You must act as you will. To love to the extent of sacrificing oneself, regardless of who it is that will benefit, is admirable. There is such beauty in your readiness to hold to the truth in your heart; even if it is for the cold-hearted who would reject truth and the relief truth brings.

CORDELIA What are you saying?

REGAN Nothing. I shed tears, simply being moved by the depth of your love.

CORDELIA Forsooth, there is something you wish to say.

REGAN There is nothing. And even if there is something, nothing can be done.

GONERIL There is much I wish to say. Look, my belly is bloated with all that I wish to say.

FOOL Is it not simply corpulence?

GONERIL How dare you!

FOOL It was nothing, a slip of the tongue.

REGAN I realize there is much you wish to say, but please refrain from doing so. Simply silently watch over Cordelia.

CORDELIA Dear sister, please speak what you hide.

Scene Six

REGAN   What now. Cordelia is now troubled. It is because the two of you could not hold your peace. No, Cordelia, do not mind what they say. Do not lend your ear to the murmurings of the devil.

FOOL (*Aside.*)   Who is truly a devil?

CORDELIA   I would like to hear. Dear sister, do tell.

REGAN   It is best that you do not ask.

CORDELIA   That is not so. No knowledge should be forbidden to man. God granted man wisdom to obtain knowledge.

FOOL (*Aside.*)   Marry, should Adam have eaten the fruit from the tree of knowledge?

CORDELIA   Please, speak.

REGAN   If you insist. But do promise not to waver in your resolution because of what I say.

CORDELIA   Of course.

REGAN   Then swear once again on your ruby ring.

CORDELIA   I swear.

REGAN   By my faith, I will speak. Our father is a murderer.

CORDELIA   It cannot be. Please do not jest.

REGAN   I am not surprised that you do not wish to believe this, but it is true.

CORDELIA   It is not. If you are referring to Father's feats on the battlefield, I do not deny them. After all, Father was known for his inimitable prowess and valour and his ability to take down a hundred enemies on his own. But his exploits in battle should not be known as murders. It is a misuse of the word.

REGAN   I speak not of such exploits. You know that Father, as a young man, drifted into Britain from the cold north.

CORDELIA   Yes, I have heard the story.

REGAN   The preceding king of Britain, our grandfather, took in our father. Father rose in rank until he became the captain of the king's mercenary army. (*To the* FOOL.) Is this not so?

FOOL   It is indeed. In his youth, King Lear was a hero unrivalled in Britain and known as the wild eagle of the

Northern Sea. He was a warrior reputed to be the reincarnation of King David, who could defeat not a hundred but a thousand, nay ten thousand, enemies on his own. It was because of King Lear's prowess that Britain succeeded in expanding its territory into what it is today.

REGAN Father received recognition for his feats in the form of the youngest daughter of the British royal family; Grandfather gave Mother to him. This was how Father founded his foothold for ruling over Britain. But he was at that time no more than a lowly son-in-law. There were no prospects. After all, Father was a scoundrel whose origins could not be traced.

FOOL Forgive my presumption in contradicting you. King Lear descended from the royal family of a northern kingdom that was frozen in snow and ice for more than half the year.

REGAN The genealogical tree can be fabricated at will in later years. I know what Father did before drifting into Britain.

FOOL Strictly speaking, they are simply rumours. It is true that various rumours existed of King Lear's origins. But they were all unfounded, negligible nonsense.

REGAN What were the rumours? I am not familiar with the details. Prithee, let us know. What was being said?

FOOL Why, well, much was said.

REGAN Pray, tell.

FOOL Ay, forsooth.

GONERIL Come, speak.

FOOL Ay. Well, for example, some said King Lear had been a pirate that terrorized the Northern Sea, while others said he had been the leader of bandits that raided towns and set them on fire.

REGAN What others?

GONERIL The others. Come now, the others. Do you refuse to speak?

Scene Six

FOOL   I will speak. I will. Some believed he spirited away village maidens to sell in Arabia, or counterfeited money, or was a swindler, or preached a heathen religion.

CORDELIA   Lies! Father would not engage in such acts.

FOOL   Of course, they are all strictly rumours.

REGAN   But there are no means to verify if they are truly just rumours anymore.

CORDELIA   Such stories cannot be true. Dear sister, you know how noble and abounding with compassion he was; how he was as a saint in the desert in the purity of his heart.

REGAN   Once one ascends to the throne, the mask of nobility fits the face with ease. Polish a clod of mud and it will shine.

CORDELIA   I refuse to believe this.

REGAN   None of this is important. It does not matter what kind of man Father was in his youth; a bandit or not, it does not concern us. All that matters is what he did after his betrothal to Mother. You know Mother had three brothers.

CORDELIA   Yes.

REGAN   They were the Lords Suffolk, Stanley and Hastings. We had three uncles. It has been said that all three, of Grandfather's blood, combined great intelligence with valour.

FOOL   Very much so indeed. As the names of these three have been mentioned, this must be said. They were each meet to inherit the throne, with their wisdom and courage. And they were remarkably close to one another. Always together in all that they did, they would make even their father, the king of Britain, jealous. Eventually the three matured into adults. The people invariably spoke of how prosperity awaited the kingdom and not a single cloud hung over its future. What good memories. Lords Suffolk, Stanley and Hastings; how many thousands of years has it been since I last heard those three sweet names. The mere sound of their names projects before my eyes recollections of so many happy episodes.

GONERIL   What, have you been a fool from such antiquity? It does not show.

FOOL   I had been kept in the court since the previous king. I have seen more years than my appearance would suggest.

REGAN   So you have. You seem well versed in history, so in your own words, tell Cordelia the fate of those three uncles.

FOOL   Why, yes. The sensation of having scorching metal chopsticks forced into my mouth accompanies the mere thought of their fate; there is a weight upon my chest, a miserable constriction in my stomach and lungs, feverish liquid pours forth from my eyes and nose. Alas, how wanting in mercy was God's plan. In succession, tragedy befell the three. All three died.

REGAN   Do describe in detail how they died.

FOOL   So I shall. Lord Suffolk was the eldest; he fell ill after he sustained a dog bite while fox hunting in the forest of Arden. Lord Stanley, the second son, was a dauntless, hot-blooded hero; he lost his life to a crossbow arrow the enemy shot through his heart in the battle against the king of Denmark. The remaining son, Lord Hastings, was a born poet and daydreamer; he, along with his father, the king of Britain, ate wild rabbit stuffed with caviar and abruptly died from food poisoning. Could it have been someone's curse? All three tragedies occurred successively, in less than a year. The dark clouds that suddenly hung over Britain withered every tree, every blade of grass, even the weeds that grew by the side of the road; it was believed the skies would nevermore be clear. But at no point did God completely uproot the seeds of hope. He deserves our gratitude for this. Praise be to the omnipotent one. It was fortunate that there was Lear. The son-in-law betrothed to the king's only daughter assumed control over the kingdom and brought further glory to Britain.

REGAN   You ask if it was someone's curse, but is not the answer clear from what you have just related?

Scene Six

FOOL   What do you mean?

REGAN   With the deaths of the three brothers, who stood to gain?

FOOL   That is malicious slander! That must not be. Even to suggest this is deplorable.

REGAN   But if even one of the three uncles had lived, Father would not have ascended to the throne. Surely the natural thing to do is to question the course of events.

FOOL   Natural? What is natural?

REGAN   It is God's will. You have mentioned God's merciless plan. God could not take, all at once, the lives of those who were elevated in virtue and who deeply loved God.

FOOL   God's will eludes human understanding.

REGAN   To blame everything on God is a sign of cowardice or apathy.

FOOL   Proof, that is what is lacking, proof.

REGAN   There is plenty. Let me ask you, whose dog bit our eldest uncle?

FOOL   It was . . . King Lear's dog. But it was an accident. Lord Suffolk was hunting with King Lear and had the misfortune of being bit by a vicious dog.

REGAN   In the battle with the king of Denmark, our late uncle was in the same troupe as Father. Was it not so?

FOOL   It was.

REGAN   Uncle was not shot with an enemy's arrow. It was from his side of the battle. The arrow pierced not his heart, but his back.

FOOL   That is not so. I swear it is not so.

REGAN   But you did not witness the death. The most irrefutable is the third death. The dining table where Uncle and Grandfather died was in Father's castle!

CORDELIA   You cannot be saying that Father eliminated our uncles.

REGAN   That is exactly what happened. I am convinced it is so.

CORDELIA   No. Only madness could make our Father seem a murderer. (*To the ring.*) No matter what others say, I know Father was a man of virtue and he was innocent.

REGAN   You know only what you wish to know.

FOOL   They are all unsubstantiated rumours. There is no proof for any of these stories. True, immediately after King Lear's inauguration, there were those who spread such malicious stories. Jealousy consorts with suspicion to spread, as the plague, from mouth to ear, from ear to mouth. But presently the rumours dissipated. They vanished completely. Why, what more proof do you need of the king's innocence? No one is a more reliable judge than the people.

REGAN   Father executed the opposition. He ruthlessly eliminated entire clans with their women and children. He captured anyone who spoke of the rumours and beheaded them all together. This created a mound of severed heads.

CORDELIA   Please stop, dear sister. I no longer wish to hear such abominable curses being spewed from your mouth. Only Cordelia and, yes, Mother are privy to Father's innocence.

GONERIL   Now, about Mother. Cordelia, I have been silent on the matter since you insisted on not wanting to know, but I do not think Mother was praiseworthy, either. Lo, every disreputable Jack has his disgraceful Jill.

CORDELIA   Respect for each other and a solid bond of love made Father and Mother the ideal pair. Even the most adamant sceptic would not doubt this. If there is anything you wish to say, pray, speak. No cursed words will be able to tarnish their nobility.

REGAN   It is true that Father and Mother were an ideal pair, solidly bound together. How true. No one was as well suited for Father as Mother. It was because of Mother that Father was able to rise in rank. After all, she was the one who abused his ear with words urging him to kill her three brothers.

Scene Six

CORDELIA ...!

FOOL You are a viper! A vicious scorpion! How else could you poison something so beautiful with such frightful conceits. Raising such accusation against that gentle lady is worse than a sin. You are attempting to build a fanciful Sodom with no foundation.

REGAN I know that the caviar stuffed rabbit that Grandfather and our youngest uncle ate was Mother's specialty. And why did Father and Mother, at the same table as the two who died, escape death?

FOOL You are mistaken. I remember the occasion clearly. Sturgeon roe is a valuable delicacy, a costly treat that even royalty are rarely able to taste. The lady, because of her father and brother's visit, secretly sold her jewels to prepare enough for two. Her grief at the outcome would have drawn tears even from the devil. For a month, she refused to eat or drink, she renounced the company of others, and she confined herself to the chapel to pray.

GONERIL What did she do while she confined herself? She must have been dallying with the monks.

CORDELIA No matter what you say, my confidence in Mother's love will not waver.

GONERIL I have confidence in Mother's love, too. She had an overabundance of love. The problem was that the love was showered not on her husband.

REGAN Are you saying that Mother was guilty of infidelity?

GONERIL That very sin. Did you not know?

REGAN I did not. Well, little did I know that Mother was a heinous harlot, wanton with whatever man came her way and adulterous without any compunction.

GONERIL Those were not my words, but I cannot deny it.

CORDELIA I imagine it is once again with trifling gossip that you verify this. I have come across many who delight in spreading such rumours.

REGAN   Was there such a rumour? Indeed. (*To the* FOOL.) Come now, the details.

FOOL   That is nonsense. My lady had no faults to encourage such rumours. Anyone who spoke about my lady would not be able to suppress a kind smile. Even the most execrable of sinners refuse referring to my lady as anything other than an angel. Those who love the most are loved the most; she was known for being loved and admired by all.

REGAN   But the brightest light creates the most impenetrable umbrage. If there were no negative rumours, why did you not challenge my sister when she spoke about Mother's infidelity?

FOOL   Well, now.

GONERIL   How curious.

REGAN   It is strange.

FOOL (*Flustered.*) . . .

GONERIL   You know something.

FOOL   I do not.

REGAN   You do not look well.

GONERIL   Speak forthrightly. Do I have to remind you what to expect if you do not?

FOOL   I know nothing.

GONERIL   Do not lie. No lies. In faith, it is only natural that he should know. You always accompanied us when we spent the summer at the holiday house. Did you not?

FOOL   Indeed.

GONERIL   It was Mother, rather than Father, that was fond of you. That is why, even when Father returned to the castle on business, you remained with us.

CORDELIA   Dear God, please forgive them for speaking so.

GONERIL   Who was Mother's paramour?

FOOL   It . . .

GONERIL   If you do not confess, we shall conclude that it was you.

Scene Six

FOOL   I know nothing. I cannot speak about what I do not know. Let me query you in return. Lady Goneril, what is it that you know?
GONERIL   Me? I know so much.
REGAN   Dear sister, tell us. Explain to Cordelia.
GONERIL   I suppose I could.
CORDELIA   I will not believe such lies.
GONERIL   This is not a lie. It is what I witnessed.
FOOL   For a witnessed account, it seems you place too much thought into it.
GONERIL   Go to. I acquiesce and will tell you what happened. I have never spoken of this before. You must remember, there was an old well in the backyard of the holiday house. It was believed to have been dug by the Romans, under the large oak tree.
REGAN   Where Mother died.
CORDELIA   Mother, why did you die? And leave Cordelia all alone?
REGAN   At night, the well was frightening.
GONERIL   So it was. Even during the day it was dark, and at the hour when crows returned to their nest we children would not approach it out of fear.
REGAN   The oak spread its arms like a golden-web spider, completely enclosing the well; Mother often frightened us by saying ghosts would appear.
GONERIL   That was why we were afraid and always slept at night in Mother's bed.
FOOL   You often quarrelled about who would sleep next to my lady.
GONERIL   So we did. That day – yes, that day Father was not at the house.
FOOL   King Lear was not there?
GONERIL   I am certain. I woke in the middle of the night from a terrifying dream. And Mother was not next to me as she should have been. In desperation, I searched throughout the

house. And Mother was there, at the other end of the north corridor, in profile with a candlestick in her hand. An immense shadow clung to the corridor wall and appeared as a colony of centipedes.

FOOL   Mistress Goneril, you could have been dreaming.

GONERIL   It was not a dream! I called but Mother silently moved on. Mother seemed transformed into something I did not recognize. I was terrified, but unable to return, I chased after her . . . I don't remember what happened then, but I found myself outdoors.

FOOL   With no light?

GONERIL   There was moonlight. A crescent moon like a sickle glowing pale hung between deep blue clouds. The forest treetops shuffled noisily, and I found myself among thickets with a view to the well. There I lowered myself. I saw Mother had placed the candle stand by the side and sat on the stonework of the well. She was not alone. She was with someone.

CORDELIA   It must have been Father!

GONERIL   No, it was not Father.

REGAN   I also saw that moon, the pallid, cruelly thin moon. I remember the thicket, too. It was hawthorn with bramble, and the thorns painfully prickled my fingers. The oak, the well, the flickering candlelight, I remember them all. But why? Hearing you speak of them has suddenly brought them back to me.

GONERIL   Perhaps I was too terrified on my own. I must have woken you. But that may have been a different night. Mother snuck out of bed not just that once.

REGAN   Yes, that is right. When I woke in the middle of the night, you were walking away. Weeping, I followed you. Cordelia must have been with us, as well.

CORDELIA   Mother, please forgive them for continuing with this. They are possessed by the devil. I know better than anyone who you were. Your innocence is safely guarded within Cordelia's heart.

Scene Six

GONERIL   Mother met with someone in the middle of the night. Who was it?

REGAN   I do not know.

GONERIL   He is dark and small and with a strangely large head.

REGAN   It is not human. It is an eerie body of a black shadow. Tiny, yes, like a mud figurine. It is in Mother's arms. Only the eyes are crimson, and it suddenly begins to expand and swallow Mother. It is a ghost, the ghost of the Roman that Mother spoke of. The ghost was about to swallow Mother.

GONERIL   In a panic, I covered your mouth as you began to weep. I understood we must not make a sound. I knew what Mother's actions meant. Then there was an unpleasant dampness around my rear, where I had lowered myself. Blood. It was blood.

REGAN   That mud figurine has repeatedly assaulted me. Even as an adult, countless times. Dreaming, not dreaming.

GONERIL   Shall I tell you why I killed myself after killing you? The black blood hung from your lips – those lips that had just drunk the poison. The moment I saw that black blood, I suddenly remembered that night. I remembered *that*. What I had, until then, forgotten. I remembered it all. And when I turned around, it was there in what should have been an empty room. The tiny, dark, shadow; it was probably less than two-foot tall. It looked this way, its red mouth crooked and smiling menacingly. Suddenly it said, 'The very same lascivious blood that flowed through your mother flows through you'. Then it licked the blood from the corpse's mouth and guffawed that she was also of the same blood.

CORDELIA   Mother could not do what you accuse her of. Her spirit was purer than pristine snow, purer than spring water running through a vale. She was as chaste as a lily, more solidly constant than iron.

GONERIL   Cordelia, the same blood flows through you, as well.

CORDELIA No one can tarnish Mother. No one can break the bond between Father and Mother.

REGAN I remember. The diamond, Mother's gem. We stole it and threw it into the well to foil that creature. To drive away that monster. We desired to help Mother with the help of Father's strength.

GONERIL I wanted Mother to remember that gem. I believed had she but remembered that gem, that she would be stopped from visiting that well. That I could put a stop to it all. That Mother would be as Mother should be. I removed that diamond from her jewellery box time and again and left it where it would catch her eye. So she would notice it. So she would desist. But she did not stop visiting the well. That is why I stole it and threw it away.

CORDELIA Mother, forgive them. Forgive them for their past actions and for continuing as they do now. Cordelia will atone for all their sins. No one knows better than Cordelia that our mother could not do what they say.

REGAN I saw. From among the hawthorns. White flowers bloomed. Their nectar was sweetly fragrant. We threw the gem into the well, yet the creature appeared. From a dark hole. Such a diabolic, dark face. Smiling sardonically. The oak seemed to burn in the candlelight. The dark shadow swayed. And . . . and, what happened? Yes, an owl cried deep in the forest, then the creature disappeared. Mother sat alone on the stonework of the well . . . Mother did not kill herself!

GONERIL Someone appeared from the facing woods. A white shadow ran to Mother and pushed her into the well. Who was that? Who?

REGAN Father. It must have been Father. He punished Mother!

GONERIL No. It was not Father. No, but I also thought it was Father. All this time. That is why I hated him. I loved Mother. For all that she had done, I still loved her. I loved Mother for making jam from the raspberries we picked in the garden. I loved mother for reading to us.

CORDELIA   Dear Mother. Purer than the April moon. As merciful and deserving as the Holy Mary.

REGAN   Why did Mother die? Why did she have to die? What of Father? ... Did I know? Or was I ignorant? Was that why I hated Father? Or what?

GONERIL   It was not Father. I saw. It was clearly not him. It was smaller and white ... a ghost. It must have been the ghost of the Roman that Mother spoke of.

REGAN   No, it was human.

CORDELIA   Mother could not do what you say. Cordelia's Mother is as pure as pristine snow; more virtuous than angels; as austere and clear as spring water running through a vale. Mother, dear Mother, Cordelia loves you.

Scene Seven: King Lear

The FOOL *transforms into* KING LEAR. *Ruined though he may be, he retains the dignity and grace of a king.*

GONERIL   Father!

REGAN   Father!

KING LEAR   Daughters. You there, are you my daughters?

GONERIL   Here stands Goneril, as do my two sisters.

KING LEAR   Is it truly you?

GONERIL   Indeed.

KING LEAR   To see you once again in such a place as this. Eternal solitude, I fear, was the burden placed on Lear. Could this be a hallucination? Could it be a deception meant to mock a miserable old man? Ay, it must be a hallucination. It must be the evil doings of Hell's devils. No longer will I be tricked by such.

GONERIL   We are not hallucinations, Father. We truly stand before you.

KING LEAR   In any case, I cannot see. Hallucination or not, I cannot lay eyes on those faces I have so missed.

GONERIL   Father, what has happened with your eyes?

The Three Daughters of Lear

KING LEAR They have lost their light. For a long time, I have seen naught but the dark. At times, I do see an immense serpentine creature shift in the darkness. But that is all. I attempted to see everything; from one end of the world to the other; from the depths of the human mind to the highest point in the heavens, even that which I should not have laid eyes on. This is my punishment.

GONERIL Father, where are you held? What kind of place?

KING LEAR In the deepest, absolute base of the mortar-shaped pit. In the darkness of the darkness. In the narrow place for traitors who have betrayed the most trusted loyalty. Few are found there. I do not even know who they are. But Judas Iscariot is certainly among them. That abominable traitor. We few there kill one another. No one knows when his turn will come, whether it is today or tomorrow or the next moment. Not even a single moment to breathe a sigh of relief; continuously in fear, crawling while fumbling in the darkness filled with the stench of blood, hoping to kill before being killed. Suspicion and trepidation and dismay and pain; such are our food. Having fed on this food, we feel anguish burning even deeper into our backs like a soldering brand; we chase and struggle to flee from unseen enemies. With no sleep or respite, we kill one another for eternity. We are an intertwined viper.

GONERIL What atrocious punishment.

KING LEAR Punishment well deserved. For the crimes I committed it may even be considered light punishment.

REGAN Father, you killed our uncles, the three brothers.

KING LEAR Kill them I did. I killed them. In a shameful manner, for a shameful motive. Any one of the sins I committed deserves tenfold, nay a hundredfold, the torment I now receive.

GONERIL You do not. You have atoned enough. In this place of darkness. You have paid your debt. In the currency of pain and despair. You must not continue tormenting yourself.

Scene Seven

KING LEAR   O Goneril. Do you forgive me? Sullied with sin and responsible for leaving such cursed seeds though I am?

GONERIL   Yes, Father. For Father, you forgave Mother for betraying you. Did you not?

REGAN   That is a lie. Father killed Mother. Pushed her into the well. Father did not forgive mother's betrayal even at the very end.

KING LEAR   Did I, her? I might have. I no longer know. Did I forgive her? Nay, I must not have. In the distant land of France, I heard she had died. Divine punishment has befallen her. From my twisted lips I spewed these words as I would a curse.

GONERIL   True; of course. It cannot have been Father. Father was in France then. You must remember the earrings he brought back for us. Mine were sapphire and yours . . .

REGAN   Emerald, just like the gem.

GONERIL   Father purchased diamond earrings for Mother, too. Mother wore them as she was sent off in her coffin.

KING LEAR   So it was. I, myself, fixed them onto her ear. For a long time she pained and perturbed me. But as I faced her in the coffin the hate dissipated. For a week after that, I knelt at the altar and continued to cry like an infant.

GONERIL   Father, you did forgive her. There is no doubt you forgave. Then how can I, your daughter, not forgive you?

KING LEAR   Goneril, sweet daughter. You are a kind-hearted child. Rough though your words and manners may be, I know well that gentleness deep in your heart.

GONERIL   Father.

KING LEAR   But Regan, you are punctilious. You will not be able to forgive me.

REGAN   It is not a matter of forgiveness. I simply . . .

KING LEAR   Simply what?

REGAN   Think upon you as my father.

KING LEAR   Who is this Father that you speak of?

REGAN   Who else? It is you, Father, with whom I now speak.

KING LEAR   I am he?

REGAN   Yes. Need you ask after all this time? Father, you are my father.

KING LEAR   You are truly a wise daughter. You have offered me salvation with that single statement. I am grateful to you. I had wanted to hear those words. That the I here is the he who I am. That is the gospel I had been seeking. I feel as if I have ascended to heaven. As if my soul has been cleansed and is levitating.

REGAN   You exaggerate . . . but if it was not you, then who killed Mother?

GONERIL   As I said, a ghost. The ghost of a Roman.

REGAN   It was not. I saw it. It was, without doubt, human. That white shadow ran from deep in the woods. Barefooted. The soft patter of feet moving across the earth. Moonlight on a naked shin. Who was that?

CORDELIA   Mother could not have done what you say. Mother was as pure as pristine snow; more virtuous than angels; as austere and clear as spring water running through a vale.

REGAN   Cordelia . . .

GONERIL   . . .

> GONERIL *and* REGAN *stand motionless as they stare at* CORDELIA.

CORDELIA   My mother could not have done what you say. My mother. My mother. Mother is mine. My beautiful and kind mother. My warm-hearted mother. Mother, I love you truly from the bottom of my heart.

KING LEAR   Cordelia. All that remains is you, Cordelia. Sweet Cordelia, where are you?

CORDELIA (*Without looking at* KING LEAR.)
   Cordelia is always by her father's side.

KING LEAR   You will, needless to say, forgive me, will you not? You, who have constantly loved me from the bottom of your heart and been kind to me. You are the one person on whom I can rely wholeheartedly. Come, Cordelia,

Scene Seven

present me with your words. Let me hear your voice and its rich tone that consoles my soul.

CORDELIA (*To the ring rather than* KING LEAR.)
Sir, I do love you more than words can wield the matter, dearer than eyesight, space, or liberty.

KING LEAR   How? Nothing can come of nothing. Present your words to me here, before your eyes.

From this point onwards, KING LEAR *does not hear* CORDELIA*'s voice. Therefore, their lines overlap.*

CORDELIA   Beyond what can be valued, rich or rare, no less than life; with grace, health, beauty, honour, as much as child e'er loved or father found.

KING LEAR   Cordelia, where are you? Cordelia?

CORDELIA   A love that makes breath poor and speech unable. Beyond all manner of so much I love you. Sir, I do love you!

KING LEAR   Cordelia, where are you? I cannot hear your words. Where can you be?

CORDELIA   I love you with all my heart. Beyond what can be valued, rich or rare.

KING LEAR (*Exasperated.*)   Damn, I hear nothing. Cordelia, where can you be?

KING LEAR *begins to search.*

GONERIL   Father.
REGAN   Father.
CORDELIA (*By this point like an incantation.*)   If I come too short, I profess myself an enemy to all other joys which the most precious square of sense possesses, and I find I am alone felicitate in your dear highness' love. Sir you are my life, my treasure, dearer than my son. Dearer than God. Far reaching oceans, even the unending universe cannot contain my adoration for you, Father. As pouring rain, as an ever-issuing spring, my love knows no arrest.

KING LEAR (*Overlapping with* CORDELIA's *lines.*)
What, Cordelia? What has happened? What has happened to you?

CORDELIA   Even after the end of the world, my love will not disappear. Father, you are a vessel worthy of such, a vast stomach that can drain unlimited love, yet with space to consume more. I will always swell your stomach with love, its food. As a serpent that has swallowed a calf, Father, you will curl up, and I will gently place a blanket over you.

KING LEAR   Once I was wont to brandish a long, sharp-bladed falchion that would make my enemies bolt in terror. But I am now old. After enduring successive hardships, my swordsmanship is no longer what it used to be.

KING LEAR *takes hold of* CORDELIA *and places his hands on her neck.*

CORDELIA   As long as my life endures, nay even after life ends and maggots strip me to my bones, even after all that remains is the spiritual self, I shall continue to present to you the gift that a pure, true heart produces. In my heart, in my true heart, in truth, I adore you, Father. My love for you knows no end. Boundless is my love for you.

KING LEAR *chokes* CORDELIA.

KING LEAR   Who are you!?
GONERIL   Father, please stop.
REGAN   Stop, Father.
CORDELIA (*By this point as an automaton.*)   Father, I love you, Father. Father, I love you, Father. Father, I love you, Father. Father, I love you, Father. Father, I love you, Father . . .

KING LEAR   And my poor fool is hanged. No, no, no life? Why should a dog, a horse, a rat have life, and thou no breath at all? Thou'lt come no more. Never, never, never, never, never. Pray you, undo this button. Thank you, sir. Do you

see this? Look on her. Look, her lips. Look there, look there.
CORDELIA   Father, I love you, Father!

>CORDELIA *dies.*

>*From the castle of Dite, the bell formed from skulls begins to toll.*

>*A deadly silence.*

GONERIL   Let us go. To where we belong.
REGAN   Yes.

>GONERIL *and* REGAN *exit.*

Epilogue

>*The* FOOL *rids himself of* KING LEAR*'s disguise.*

>CORDELIA, *who had supposedly died, abruptly rises. And it is the* WAG.

WAG   Guv'nor, should things have ended so?
FOOL   Very much so. With your help, I have been able to save their souls. Those two will probably never again toy with the inane idea of becoming witches. Devils and witches are not creatures one should aspire to become. After all, Judgment Day could come tomorrow.
WAG   Guv'nor, you're surprisingly perceptive.
FOOL   As I said, I am a virtuous fool. Becoming a devil does not change that.
WAG   Who's heard of a devil being virtuous? It must lead to many hardships.
FOOL   What do you care?
WAG   True, it don't concern me. All I need is what was promised me.
FOOL   I have to say, you give a brilliant performance.
WAG   Guv'nor, you not so much.

FOOL   Tush. It's the magic ring that did most of the work for you, I'm sure. Here! (*Gives him a gold coin.*)

The FOOL *notices the audience and addresses them.*

FOOL   Dear, dear, I forgot to curtsy. Demons make this world go around. To make it through this world of Hell, courtesy is of grave import. (*Solemnly.*) I now bid you farewell. Let us meet again at the end of the world.

The WAG *exits, dressed as* CORDELIA. *The* FOOL *is about to call him back to demand the return of the ring.*

FOOL   Wag, leave the ring. Otherwise, I will be in trouble.

It is then that he realizes the ring has been in his pocket all along; he takes the ring out into the palm of his hand and with a puzzled look, stares at it. Black out.

INTRODUCTION TO *HAMLET X SHIBUYA ~ LIGHT, WAS OUR REVENGE TARNISHED?*

Rosalind Fielding

In the programme for the 2017 production of *Titus Andronicus*, Kimura Ryūnosuke writes that theatre 'serves the role of a *pharmacon* within society', deliberately using the Greek word which means both 'poison' and 'medicine' (Kimura, Ryunosuke. Titus Andronicus [theatre programme, Tokyo, August 2017]). He has also suggested that when staging Shakespeare as a Japanese artist, it is more important for him to think about 'who I am' and to 'pursue modern expressions while keeping contact with one's daily life' rather than rely on 'pre-modern expressions' preferred by traditional Japanese culture (Kimura 2013). As a result Kimura's directorial style is characterized by its merging of high and low culture, its fast pace and its emphasis on the physicality of the actors themselves. The company's website describes Kakushinhan's productions as a clash between 'classic masterpieces' and 'today's society', and its shows are full of references to popular culture and elements of everyday Tokyo life, alongside call-backs to famous Japanese directors (particularly Ninagawa), artists and productions.

Many of the elements that have come to characterize the company's more recent work can be found in an early incarnation in *HAMLET X SHIBUYA*. For example, Kimura's first play localized the story to contemporary Tokyo, and Tokyo is now an essential part of Kakushinhan's concept with the company often 'performing' the city; Kimura has stated that he finds 'little difficulty in transporting the Elizabethan English plays to present-day Tokyo' (Eglinton 2016).

Under the concept of 'Shakespeare Tokyo', Kakushinhan uses 'ubiquitous city products as props' alongside music (both international and domestic), often vividly recreating familiar images of urban life through a clever use of these props and references (Eglinton 2016). Describing this concept of 'Shakespeare Tokyo' as an 'imaginary third world ... which serves as a bridge that connects today's audience with the distant settings of the stories', a recent synopsis of the play also suggested that the setting of the adaptation was this 'imaginary city, Shakespeare Tokyo' ('Project Proposal' 2017).

The cityscape of Tokyo, be it the imaginary third world version or the real city, is essential to the company's performances and often takes on a role as a character in its own right. *HAMLET X SHIBUYA* is an excellent example of this in practice, with the story of *Hamlet* uprooted from Denmark and moved into twenty-first-century Tokyo. The title alone suggests the importance of this move, implying as it does both '*Hamlet* and Shibuya' and '*Hamlet* meets Shibuya'. Shibuya is a large neighbourhood in central Tokyo and it is also the name one of the main characters chooses to go by; the other is named Akihabara after another large district. Kakushinhan often use video and projections onstage, with the word Tokyo (in both *kanji* characters and in the Roman alphabet) regularly projected onto the walls and the stage. For example, their 2017 *Macbeth* at the Tokyo Metropolitan Theatre opened with a video locating the play in both 'Scotland' and 'Tokyo'. At other times actors are filmed offstage and the video shown in the auditorium (with the implication that it is 'live'): in *Macbeth* this happened in 3.3 when Fleance escaped from the assassins onstage and was then shown running through the theatre lobby, bringing the easily recognizable long escalators and glass walls of the Tokyo Metropolitan 'in' to the play.

Impressions of Tokyo are created not only through these references but also through the characters that inhabit the company's theatrical world and the inclusion of features from outside daily life. Kimura has suggested that there are 'strong affinities' between Shakespeare's '"big" narratives and the minutiae of everyday life', and this is borne out in the 'contemporary young people' that populate his work (Eglinton 2016). In the 2019 *Wars of the Roses*, the majority of the cast were dressed in tracksuits (red for Lancaster and white for York), undercutting any sense of medieval historical drama. Similarly, branded items familiar to the audience often appear within the company's shows, particularly food and drink. In *Macbeth* this tactic meant that the banquet scene in 3.4 was held in a convenience store (*combini*), instantly recognizable from its welcome jingle and shelves of crisp packets and beer cans, with the courtiers queuing up to buy snacks and cheap drinks. A characteristic of recent productions has been the use of folding metal chairs, familiar from various everyday situations, as one of the only props or set used in performance. In *Macbeth* these chairs were held up by actors to become a castle wall or Birnam Wood, or laid out to become the shelves of the convenience store. These chairs have become such a common feature of Kimura's style that a mini folding chair even became the seal of state during the *Wars of the Roses* plays in 2019.

The hyper-presence of the city corresponds to Kakushinhan's desire to 'grasp the here and now' of life in contemporary Japan (Eglinton 2016), and its intention to 'make contemporary theater for today's audiences – especially those of my own generation' (Tanaka 2017). That impression of the 'here and now' for Kimura was deeply affected by the 3.11 disaster, with Kimura stating that he uses Shakespeare because in his generation, 'many people's values have changed unexpectedly due to terrorism or disasters, such as 3.11' and that 'Shakespeare – not Greek mythology or Chekhov – is most suitable to reflect the fragile state of that world' (ibid.). As such, disasters, terrorism, violence and other social issues frequently appear in the company's performances, and its recent work has been particularly defined by a questioning of nationalism and contemporary politics: to take *Macbeth* as an example again, the play ended with an image that could have either been read as the audience looking down at the Macbeths in a pool of blood, or as them standing in front of the Japanese flag.

Kakushinhan's style is an evocative example of Yoshihara's statement that contemporary Japanese Shakespeare performance is often characterized by a combination of 'reverence and irreverence' which destabilizes the 'presupposed notion that "Shakespeare" is the dominant, central, hegemonic icon' by juxtaposing it with 'other cultural artefacts, which are presumed to be of minimal capitalist and cultural value' (Yoshihara 2013: 84). The company itself highlights its own irreverent take by, for example, making references to Ninagawa but with a humorous twist that highlights the differences in styles. In *Ninagawa Macbeth*, Ninagawa had cherry blossoms fall to the stage during Macbeth's death; in Kimura's version, scraps of white plastic fill the stage instead, reflecting the company's familiar reference points of consumerism and waste. A more serious reference came in *Titus Andronicus*, with Lavinia pulled onstage after her attack by a chorus of male actors, draped in red electrical cables that mimicked (but with a marked difference) Ninagawa's use of strips of red cloth instead of blood in his own production (2004).

Performance theorist Uchino Tadashi has described contemporary Japanese performance in terms of 'junkness', using the concept '"J" performance', or 'Japan as Junk' (Uchino 2009: 162). He writes that Japanese theatre often takes inspiration from subcultures, including manga and anime, and that much contemporary performance appears to be 'artistic garbage' since the 'notion of 'art' is always-already elusive' (ibid.). Most crucially for the current discussion he also writes that 'J theatre performances have a certain degree of resonance with the sensibilities and psyche of the youth who sometimes withdraw from society to a pathological degree' (ibid.: 163). As will be seen later, many of the characters in *HAMLET X SHIBUYA* correspond to this characteristic of social withdrawal. It is important to note that 'junkness' is not necessarily a negative thing, and as Anan Nobuko suggests it can be a method of resistance: she writes that many contemporary artists reconfigure 'what is available to them in this consumerist society in order to create a subversive space' (Anan 2016: 2).

Thinking in these terms of subversive space, Kakushinhan regularly parody and undermine the idea of 'Cool Japan', a concept adopted by the Japanese government in the early 2000s based on Douglas McGray's 2002 article 'Japan's Gross National Cool' and inspired by the late 1990s 'Cool Britannia' campaign. Based on exporting 'popular culture and youth phenomena', the concept was intended to influence both the domestic and the international image of Japan (Valaskivi 2013: 492). By using elements of popular culture, particularly anime and contemporary domestic music, Kakushinhan has successfully parodied the idea of Cool Japan by deploying it in bizarre and often dystopian situations. For example, the Macbeths' coronation opened with the actors singing the theme tune to the long-running *Sazae-san* (1969–), an anime following the daily life of a housewife and her family. As the actors solemnly sang the theme tune, creating an enormous sense of dislocation and disparity with the content and its current context, the Macbeths were dragged across the stage on an old luggage trolley to celebrate their coronation. This questioning of Cool Japan is particularly pertinent given the widespread belief that since 3.11 it has become clear that 'Cool Japan was at best a flash in the pan and at worst a tall tale' intended to 'make the Japanese feel good about themselves. Now the party is over, and there is nothing left to do but to pick up the pieces and move on' (Brienza 2014: 386–87).

Another technique employed by Kakushinhan to subvert 'Cool Japan' is the use of grotesque bodies and images, and representations that turn standard media imagery on its head. In the 2017 *Titus Andronicus*, for example, male actor Shirakura Yūji was cast as Tamora and throughout the performance largely appeared wearing only a neon-coloured bikini and high-heels. Actors also regularly appear in their underwear across Kakushinhan's performances, leading one viewer to write online that while they do not 'need one hundred per cent elegance in Shakespeare', they thought that seeing the company 'performing in their underpants ... was a bit disgusting' (*Kakushinhan Makubesu* 2017). The same actor who played Tamora was also Banquo in *Macbeth*, and in another grotesque scene Banquo's ghost entered dressed in the uniform of a high-school girl with his face covered in blood, playing with his phone and making joke references to popular films such as *Your Name* (2016) during the rest of the scene. The company's use of everyday items also creates absurd and grotesque imagery, such as the instant noodle packets ('King Noodle') worn as crowns by the procession of kings in *Macbeth* (3.5), which also became a cauldron from which a seemingly infinite amount of toilet paper was pulled and then carried through the auditorium by a procession of witches.

Having briefly glanced at the wider history and performance style of the company, it is time now to move on to a closer look at the play itself. The script of *HAMLET X SHIBUYA* opens with a quote from Franz Kafka: 'If the book we are reading doesn't shake us awake like a blow to the skull, why bother reading it in the first place?' (Dodson 2004). The sentiment reflects Kimura's desire to wake the spectator/reader with a 'blow to the skull' by raising questions about the society the play emerged from. In the adaptation, Kimura takes the story of *Hamlet* and throws it into contemporary Tokyo, namely the Shibuya district, in a play that is self-described as 'being/not being' *Hamlet*. As a play, *Hamlet* is hyper-visible in contemporary Japanese theatre: it was staged eighteen times in 2010 and twelve times in 2014 in the Kanto region alone and often tops annual lists as the most performed Shakespeare play. Ann Thompson has described *Hamlet* as 'an itch we simply cannot stop scratching' (Thompson 2013: 29), and Matsuoka Kazuko has also written that it has particular relevance for contemporary Japanese society since many have been rendered into a state of 'perpetual youth' due to societal changes, meaning that they see themselves in 'Shakespeare's image of a thirty-year-old "eternal" prince' (Matsuoka 1995: 233).

The two main characters, Shibuya and Akihabara, are both young men who divide the role of Hamlet (and Fortinbras) between them. They match Matsuoka's depiction of the 'eternal prince', particularly in terms of their inability to mature or survive in the world in which they find themselves: their meeting at the end of the play is described in the stage directions as a 'possible dialogue between two people who might have been'. Shibuya, the 'good' Hamlet in the play, is losing his memory after his girlfriend, whose name he cannot remember, was killed in a terrorist incident at the large pedestrian crossing in Shibuya. Akihabara, the 'bad' Hamlet, is the one who drives a truck into the crossing. Throughout the play snippets of both characters' lives emerge and are intermingled with the story of *Hamlet*, and between the two of them the characters cover a

3 Maimi (Ophelia) from a scene recreating *HAMLET X SHIBUYA* in the 2018 production of *Hamlet*

wide range of the social issues facing the zero generation today: parental pressure and abuse, entrance exams, isolation, bullying, unemployment and violence, amongst others. In the 2012 production of the play Hamlet also appeared as a character, with a piece of paper tied around an actor's neck naming him as 'Hamlet' (in *katakana*, the alphabet largely used to transcribe foreign words which is a 'graphically distinguished syllabic script' that locks the 'exterior of the Japanese language into a separate space of signs'), wandering dazed across the stage and observing the action, before giving Shibuya a knife in the final scene (Grassmuck 2016).

Japan is often represented as a safe country with a very low crime rate, but at the same time there are regularly debates in the Japanese media about what is seen as a rise of violent crime committed by social 'loners'. Although Japan has one of the 'lowest rates of violent crime in the developed world', mass attacks are a semi-regular occurrence: for example, a 51-year-old man attacked pedestrians in Kawasaki in May 2019, killing two and injuring eighteen, and in July 2019 a 41-year-old man carried out an arson attack on Kyoto Animation studio, killing thirty-five people in one of the worst mass-murders in Japan since the end of the Second World War (McCurry 2019). The terrorist incident at the centre of the play was likewise inspired by a real event often known as the 'Akihabara Massacre'. In 2008, a 25-year-old man drove a rented truck into a busy crossing in Akihabara, before getting out of the vehicle and attacking people with a knife. The attack in *HAMLET X SHIBUYA* is almost identical, except that it has been moved from Akihabara to the even busier 'Scramble' crossing in Shibuya. A further vehicle attack took place early in the morning on 1 January 2019 in Harajuku, Tokyo, with nine injured after the perpetrator drove a rented car down a pedestrian street.

The real attack in Akihabara also took place during 'pedestrian's paradise', a day when some main streets are closed to traffic, killing seven (the same as in the play) and injuring seventeen people. The perpetrator, who was arrested after the attack, was later revealed to have an abusive relationship with his mother and to be working as a 'temp worker', someone hired on short-term contracts rather than on a full-time or lifetime contract. The economic downturn and changing working styles has led to higher levels of employment instability as the previous employment frameworks vanish. One of the reasons why Akihabara's father, who comes back as a ghost during the play, killed himself was his own perception of himself as a temp worker: 'Is there somewhere for trash like me, earning one million yen a year, labour for hire ... is there a place for someone like that to die?'. He asks Akihabara to take revenge 'on this world' for him, so that he can finally rest – directly leading to the attack at the crossing.

In her discussion on nineteenth- to twenty-first-century 'prequels and sequels' to *Hamlet*, Thompson suggests that many of these plays 'reject or question the revenge motif' of Shakespeare's original (2013: 17). In *HAMLET X SHIBUYA*, revenge is a recurring theme. The ghost of Akihabara's father echoes the ghost in *Hamlet* in his demands for revenge, having poisoned himself at a cheap love hotel in Shibuya. But as stated above, the revenge this ghost wants is not against a brother, but against the world that rejected him. It is also never clear whether the ghost is real or a figment of Akihabara's imagination. The line 'taint not thy mind' (1.5.85) is repeated numerous times, with first Akihabara's and then Shibuya's desire for an 'untainted' or 'untarnished' revenge guiding most of their actions. In the process of taking his revenge, however, Akihabara realizes that he is not Hamlet, but Fortinbras, 'who came into another country in his dirty boots and ruined everything'. Fortinbras' entrance is linked in this play to both the Trojan horse and the truck driven by Akihabara into the crossing: 'Since Fortinbras arrives suddenly at the end of *Hamlet*, I'm thinking about styling it after that "revenge of Pyrrhus" ... Fortinbras probably hid in some big vehicle to break into Denmark – and bursting out of it, took his revenge.' It is interesting to note that in several of Ninagawa's productions of *Hamlet* (eight in total), Fortinbras' arrival was staged as a violent military coup, often with the remaining courtiers massacred by Fortinbras himself or his soldiers; similarly here, his arrival is associated with violence and 'taking revenge'.

Perhaps the most crucial line in the play is 'this is and is not *Hamlet*'. There are many lines from Shakespeare's *Hamlet* in the text and scenes that mirror those of the original – including the ghost, the Mousetrap, and the murder of Polonius (here simply known as 'the father' and seen in a scene set in Shibuya's memory, whose stepfather he presumably is), but there are also many moments which do not follow the original. The story of *Hamlet* has been radically adapted for Kimura's purposes, sometimes diverging totally and at other times with whole scenes or speeches inserted from the original. Of the terms suggested by Adaptation Theory critics, such as Matthew Biberman's 'excision', 'addition', 'merging' and 'segmentation', Kimura's approach could probably be best described as the third option, 'merging' (Biberman 2017: 1). Shakespeare's *Hamlet* is neither merely the sourcetext nor a paratext in *HAMLET X SHIBUYA*, and so it would perhaps be fair to describe it, in Hutcheon's terms, as both a 'process' and a 'product' (2006: 16). Within the play itself, *Hamlet* is both an inspiration to the characters (for example, Shibuya is inspired to stage his own Mousetrap to catch Akihabara) and at other times a threat – one stage direction reads 'lines from *Hamlet* violently intervene', and Akihabara is also described as 'reciting' lines from it during his attack.

Many of the characters are known by names from *Hamlet*, but these are always nicknames: Shibuya calls his dead girlfriend Ophelia because after the accident he 'tried to remember her name, but face to face with a girl with no reality, I forgot what I used to call her. So I call her Ophelia.' The girl herself, whose name is revealed at the end to be 'Light', insists

Introduction

to Shibuya that Ophelia is not her name because 'Ophelia doesn't actually exist'. The second Ophelia in the play is the sex worker, whose real name is never revealed, but who uses the nickname of Ophelia because, as she says:

> Those of us who sell our bodies do it to re-tie that open seam in the heart. That's why I call myself Ophelia. Ophelia who was driven mad by this bloodstained *world* and who fell into the water. I think even as she was losing herself, she was praying for the world's recovery.

The other characters, besides Shibuya and Akihabara, are all anonymous or go by generic titles such as 'the Mother'. The only other named character, Light, is called Hikari in the Japanese text, which is both a name and the word for 'light'. In trying to find a corresponding name in English, Kimura and I considered various options – Ellen, Dawn, Faith, Lucy – but since numerous lines such as 'the noise of a truck and light' were intended to use the same word as her name and since there was no obvious elegant alternative, we chose simply to call her 'Light'.

Laera describes 'transculturation' as an adaptation strategy that relocates a 'culturally specific source to another cultural context, often the target one' (2014: 8). As a culturally hybrid drama, other elements of the 'target' context in *HAMLET X SHIBUYA* that may require explaining for a non-Japanese audience include salarymen, love hotels and Shibuya itself. I have already touched on some of the importance of the location to the play, but it is worth expanding on again here: Shibuya, the key location of much of the play, is a central area in Tokyo that sees roughly 2.4 million people passing through every day (Joy 2019). The scramble crossing, an enormous series of crossings at the very centre of Shibuya, is one of the most iconic spots in Tokyo and is thought to have around 2,500 people crossing it each time the traffic lights change, making it the busiest crossing in Tokyo and one of the busiest in the world, if not the busiest (ibid.). A hub for youth fashion and culture, Shibuya is also home to countless bars, shops and cultural facilities. Dogenzaka, a famous street to the north of the scramble crossing, is a centre for bars, love hotels and the red-light district – a love hotel being a hotel that offers by-the-hour rooms for couples. It is in one of these, the Hotel Elsinore, that Akihabara's father kills himself. Another ubiquitous element of Shibuya are salarymen, the Japanese word for white-collar workers. Towards the end of the play, the police officer lists the 'motifs' of Shibuya that will be instantly recognizable to anyone who has spent time there: the 'crossing, the Yamanote line, 109, Dogenzaka, Hachiko, salarymen, prostitutes, students, tissue hawkers, right-wing agitators' – people, places, things. But just as this is and is not *Hamlet*, it also is and is not Tokyo. Rooms in Elsinore overlap with the contemporary city and much of the story occurs within a dream landscape that may be a 'fantasy of *a large crossing in Tokyo*'.

On a final note on translation, there are several stylistic features in the Japanese that I have tried to replicate in the English version that require some explanation. Italics connote the use of katakana in the Japanese (most often used by Kimura to write *world*), which was a deliberate choice by Kimura to make the words stand out. Kimura also played with the different translations of *Hamlet* in Japanese, having Akihabara and Shibuya recite 'to be or not to be' in two different translations (Odashima Yūshi and Kawai Shōichirō's), and so to replicate the difference for English readers I have used the 'bad quarto' version of the line alongside the 'quarto' version. When Akihabara and Shibuya meet at the end of the play, Shibuya's speech is broken into small components that are dependent on the Japanese alphabet. The Japanese alphabet has forty-six letters, written using *hiragana* or katakana, which nearly all contain a singular vowel or a consonant with a vowel (with some differences due to pronunciation). For example, the first few lines of the alphabet read: a, i, u, e, o, ka, ki, ku, ke, ko, sa, shi, su, se, so, ta, chi, tsu, te, to. Shibuya uses these basic components during this scene, most clearly demonstrated in the way he says Akihabara: 'A, ki, ha, ba, ra'. Since it is harder to split English into equivalent sounds (for example, 'was' could be divided into 'w, a, s' or 'wa, s', but neither one is entirely satisfactory), I have opted for splitting the words with commas to suggest Shibuya's disjointed speech and to imply a pause between letters.

INTERVIEW: KIMURA RYŪNOSUKE

What was your motivation for starting your theatre company, and how do you see your company in relation to the many other companies in Japan that stage Shakespeare?

After 3.11, I became convinced that there was an urgent need to create theatre and art with a new sense of imagination. One way people in Japan stage Shakespeare is by merging his plays with some of the qualities, forms or physical expressions of Japan's traditional theatres, but I think ours might be the only company creating Shakespeare productions based on the values of post-1983 Japan and Tokyo, a consumerist city defined by ruin and loss. Why 1983? That was the year I was born.

What was the inspiration for the work translated in this volume, and how much of the work was created during the writing process and how much of it was created or changed through the rehearsals?

Hamlet is one of its parents, and Murakami Haruki's *Kafka on the Shore* is another, with inspiration also coming from the terrorist incident in Akihabara. The work was finished during the writing process, and there weren't any changes during the rehearsals.

What are your thoughts on the reception of Shakespeare in Japan today, and where would you place your theatre company and its works in relation to that?

Shakespeare is the most popular playwright in translation in Japan, something that is taught and studied at university, or whose stories are enjoyed at the theatre. With the exception of some excellent productions, I feel that there are seldom performances that question our society or communities, or that delve into the world, in the same way that Shakespeare was doing in London in his own time. What if Shakespeare's brain had been preserved into the twenty-first century – in some kind of 'culture fluid' – and as a stimulus it was fed the values of current Tokyo society? What questions would he ask of us? I'm interested in whether he would shake us up or rather entertain us. That's a question Kakushinhan is pursuing. The history of modern theatre in Japan only dates back 100 years or so, and moreover Japan has only been a modernized nation for 150 years. Through the 400-year-old plays of Shakespeare, we can reconsider the strengths and weaknesses of Japan more critically in light of the Western sovereign states. In this way, Shakespeare is useful to analyse this country, Japan.

What do you envisage for the future of your theatre company?

There are two parts to this. Firstly, I want to confront Shakespeare from Tokyo and I want foreigners to see this new style of Shakespeare we have created precisely because we are here in Tokyo. I also want people around the world to see our work, and through their feedback and collaboration to make new discoveries. Secondly, there are theatre forms in Japan that have been around for hundreds of years, like kabuki, *noh* and *kyogen*. I want to heighten Kakushinhan's style into something like the universality of these forms, to shine a light on the dignity of human beings through theatrical creativity – connecting modern props with the desires and emotions that are being crushed by contemporary urban life.

What is the Kakushinhan Pocket series? How is it different to the non-Pocket productions?

The difference between our full-scale productions and the Kakushinhan Pocket series is like the difference between a novel and a short story. The interesting part of the Pocket productions is in clarifying our perspective and the concept, and radically changing the composition of Shakespeare's plays and performing them in a spirit of theatrical experimentation in under two hours. For example, a production where all the mechanicals are dream-dwellers called Bottom and their whispers become *A Midsummer Night's Dream*; *The Winter's Tale* within the veils of membranes in the brain; *The Taming of the Shrew* where a herd of horses tame a stupid man and then shoot him.

What is Kakushinhan Studio, what do you do with it and why did you set it up?

To train actors to perform Shakespeare. There are many plays recently that use contemporary colloquial speech or everyday-style conversation, and conversely noisy productions that are propelled forward only by energy. I started this studio out of the urgency I felt about there being very few actors capable of approaching classics and highly poetic literature such as Shakespeare using both their intellectual and physical abilities. We offer vocal training centred on breath control, physical workshops and practical training in actually putting together a Shakespeare production.

Can you talk more about what you mean by 'Shakespeare Tokyo'? How does Tokyo come into your productions and why?

I see Kakushinhan's series of Shakespeare productions as a saga of an imaginary city, Shakespeare Tokyo. Just like Faulkner wrote the Yoknapatawpha saga. An example of the Tokyo factor is that we use items that are consumed in huge quantities in Tokyo such as metal folding chairs, and also consumer products that you can buy in Tokyo like sweets, clothes and paper bags and sometimes the Japanese flag. I feel that there is something in common between the incidents and issues of Tokyo and the plots and metaphors of Shakespeare's plays. That is, the dignity and richness of humanity stands out most prominently in a world of ruin and loss.

Could you expand on the influence 3.11 has had on you?

In any society there are leftover outdated systems and structures that infringe upon the dignity of individuals. With the 3.11 nuclear disaster, I felt that relying on these old values could lead to further calamity. It seemed more important at that time to believe in your own imagination rather than the outdated systems. Witnessing 3.11 made me feel that what I feel now is more important, and that led me to found Kakushinhan.

Why Shakespeare?

First of all, Shakespeare is now a global asset, not the possession of a single nation. The universality of his plays transcends particular countries or cultural communities. He teaches us the potentials of human imagination. He reveals to us the possibilities for a new future and spiritual guidelines to live well in this world of ruin and loss. And I think that is what is most needed for those of us living in Tokyo, or any modern city-dweller across the world.

Why did you choose Hamlet*? What were the themes in it that inspired you? Why* Hamlet *in Tokyo?*

I think the question of whether or not to take revenge if a loved one is killed is extremely important in the modern world. 'If a loved one is killed' means not only someone killed by another person, but also someone killed by the structures, institutions and systems of the city. It's an important theme when discussing issues such as terrorism or murder, about how young men who discover such truths confront the world. I thought *Hamlet* was a suitable topic to use to think about an incident where someone of the same generation as me crashed a vehicle into a crowded street and attacked people in Akihabara.

Could you speak about why you reference other directors and productions in your work?

Art cannot progress or evolve without criticizing the works of the great maestros. Recognizing what Ninagawa Yukio did and did not do, and thinking about what kind of Shakespeare we ourselves will make is one of the crucial things Japanese directors must consider.

And finally, could you speak about using Matsuoka Kazuko's translations in performance?

Poetry is important in Shakespeare, and because of the linguistic structure of Japanese, Shakespeare in translation cannot be poetic through rhythm and rhyme in the same way as in English. Matsuoka's translations have a poetic style that, besides the poetic imagery of the words themselves, allows for a variety of interpretations in what kind of poetic images the actors can create and what spaces and interpretations the director can make. And they are also written with a fresh and energetic sensibility that touches contemporary people. I think it is the most suitable for my ideas of a Shakespeare production.

HAMLET X SHIBUYA ~ LIGHT, WAS OUR REVENGE TARNISHED?

(2012)

KAKUSHINHAN THEATRE COMPANY

LIST OF CHARACTERS

SHIBUYA
AKIHABARA
OPHELIA (LIGHT)
SEX WORKER
GHOST
MOTHER
FATHER
POLICE OFFICER
CHORUS

HAMLET X SHIBUYA ~ LIGHT, WAS OUR REVENGE TARNISHED?

> I think we ought to read only books that bite and sting us. If the book we are reading doesn't shake us awake like a blow to the skull, why bother reading it in the first place? A book must be the axe for the frozen sea within us.
>
> – Franz Kafka, in a letter to Oskar Pollak (1904)

In the darkness . . . I imagine . . . what if I was a killer.

What if . . . I'd taken another course in that moment, then, there, it could have been me who took a knife to someone who had been loved. And I imagine . . . what if my love was killed . . . Would I be able to see that murdered one as a human?

And in my isolation and in my despair, I would roam like a fearful wandering spirit, searching to fill the void. And I imagine . . . what if my family was caught up in an enormous wave. Should I then hate that force? Can my isolation and despair withstand the bonds of morality? Should I, like Hamlet, seek revenge, be defeated and then be silent? I want music and stories. I want music and stories that will light up the darkness.

It shouldn't be a sin for a searching soul, one that has been wounded in this place and lost everything, that screams, that struggles, and is left with the echoes of that struggle, to want music or a song . . .

Scene One

The theatre, the world *metamorphose into the metropolises* SHIBUYA *and* AKIHABARA.

The clamour of SHIBUYA *and* AKIHABARA *echoes through the grey matter in the theatre.*

Actors enter as though in response to the noise. They are contemporary young men and women.

They ask the empty air 'Who's there?'

The following words are projected with a time lag:
Hamlet is the record of events brought about by a young man's insanity.

HAMLET X SHIBUYA is and is not Hamlet.

This is the record of SHIBUYA *and* AKIHABARA*'s story.*

The actor playing SHIBUYA *enters.*

VOICE Hey.
SHIBUYA Hey.
VOICE There's this play.
SHIBUYA That play, right?
VOICE Be quiet and listen.
SHIBUYA I was waiting for you, Akihabara . . .
VOICE This room will be controlled by their voices.
SHIBUYA Yeah.
VOICE And you . . . you're going to go deep, deep.
SHIBUYA Like always, right?
VOICE Be quiet, close your eyes.
SHIBUYA Alright.
VOICE This room will be swallowed by their voices. You can't turn back now.
SHIBUYA (*Aside.*) Secretly, but with a certain boldness, I focus on all the noise.

The world *starts to be filled with the voices of the* CHORUS.

VOICE A wandering ghost, seeking the light.
CHORUS Who's there?

Scene One

VOICE   A father poisoned by an uncle.
CHORUS   Nay, answer me. Stand and unfold yourself.
VOICE   A young man who saw a ghost.
CHORUS   Long live the King!
VOICE   An incestuous mother and uncle.

The sound of his mother and uncle's heavy breathing eats into SHIBUYA*'s heart for all time.*

CHORUS   Barnardo?
VOICE   The ghost says,
CHORUS   'Tis now struck twelve.
VOICE   Kill thy uncle, but taint not thy mind.
CHORUS   That one may smile and smile and be a villain – at least I am sure it may be so here.
VOICE   A play set in Elsinore.

Waves foam, the earth shakes. Sirens.

VOICE   Take revenge on thy uncle.

The lead VOICE *pulls a knife out of his pocket.*

VOICE   Take revenge on that incestuous, that adulterate beast.
CHORUS   A play!
VOICE   The play's the thing wherein I'll catch the conscience of the King.

Waves.

SHIBUYA   And in this harsh world
CHORUS   Oh, that's right – I've heard this before.
SHIBUYA   Draw thy breath in pain
CHORUS   Guilty creatures sitting at a play
SHIBUYA   To tell my story.
CHORUS   Have by the very cunning of the scene
VOICE   Tell my story.
CHORUS   Been struck so to the soul that presently they have proclaimed their malefactions.

VOICE   The play's the thing.

CHORUS   I loved you, forty thousand others could not with all their quantity of love make up my sum!

SHIBUYA   The play's the thing, wherein I'll catch the conscience of the King.

The sound of sirens and waves, gradually getting louder.

CHORUS   Take revenge on that incestuous, adulterate beast.

The waves surge in, swallowing the world.

The CHORUS *continue to say Hamlet's lines.*

The world *is engulfed by the sea.*

The VOICE *and* SHIBUYA *are bound together by the thread of destiny.*

AKIHABARA and SHIBUYA   Tokyo is in ruins. The sad remains of corrupted spirits and the remnants of desire. Blood is necessary to revive this city. We have to go to the amphitheatre.

The 'intervention' begins. Tick tock tick tock.

Time and space slowly advance towards that moment.

Scene Two

Tick tock tick tock. 'Intervention'. The noise of a truck's engine starting. The world gradually transforms into the crossing in Shibuya. Pedestrian's paradise.

SHIBUYA   The 8th of June, just after twelve. I wasn't there.
OPHELIA   Shibuya.

Tick tock tick tock . . .

SHIBUYA   Mid-day of the *world*, the city was an enormous living creature. The crossing breathed out human beings

Scene Two

like a well-regulated, pulsing heart. People flowed to every corner in a healthy rhythm.

Tick tock tick tock...

OPHELIA Shibuya.
SHIBUYA June 8th, gone twelve thirty. A lone man appeared to break that healthy rhythm. Like a virus, a lone man appeared to destroy the stability of that bloodstream.
OPHELIA Hey, Shibuya?
SHIBUYA Yeah?
OPHELIA What's wrong? What are you staring at?
SHIBUYA I was thinking about the past. About long before we ever met. And long before we were separated like we are now.
OPHELIA You weren't dreaming of blowing up your university?
SHIBUYA That era's gone.

Tick tock tick tock...

SHIBUYA Did we have this conversation, or did we not? June 8th, around twelve-thirty. I wasn't at the crossing. But she was there. The intervention of the virus was under way.

Someone who could be AKIHABARA *enters.*

The noise of a truck, and light.

The clock stops.

In hyper-slow-motion, people drop.

SHIBUYA June 8th. Approaching one o'clock. I didn't see the blood there. I didn't see her blood. So, we probably didn't have this conversation either.

In hyper-slow-motion people collapse. In the midst of them is the shape of OPHELIA. *She becomes stained by death and blood...*

SHIBUYA What were you thinking about?
OPHELIA You want to know?
SHIBUYA Yes.
OPHELIA *(Aside.)* I was there. That day. Leaving my body to the rhythm of the city, I was there. The *world* throbbed. The warm midday sun was shining on us. A man appeared. A virus. The city, that huge living organism, began to spasm. No one could have stopped the invasion of that virus. I took a breath and ran to a convulsing man. Then . . .

The sound of congestion, a news report violently interrupts.

There are seven bodies and blood spreading on the crossing. A scene like Picasso's 'Guernica'. In the distance, a news report: 'The perpetrator is on the run'. Ambulances, police cars, the tumult of the city. Police inspectors from the Metropolitan. Crime scene tape. Body bags.

Scene Three

SHIBUYA *(Aside.)* In time with the painful throbbing of my heart, countless ghosts of her have passed before my eyes. It was always the time for remembrance, and holding that ghost that carried with it the smell of blood, I wanted my blood to burst from me so I too could vanish from this world.

The ghosts of OPHELIA *enter.*

I tried to remember her name, but face to face with a girl with no reality, I forgot what I used to call her. So I call her Ophelia. My Ophelia, who was stabbed at the crossing and vanished into the darkness of the city, her blood rushing out.

Blood spreads over the crossing.

OPHELIA'S GHOST Remember that I'll die here, and think about who you should hate.

OPHELIA'S GHOST   Look at my blood, and think about who in this city you should hate.
OPHELIA'S GHOST   Surely you hate the man who killed me.
OPHELIA'S GHOST   Entrust yourself to the truth and hate that man.
OPHELIA'S GHOST   Hate as much as you want.
OPHELIA'S GHOST   But please remember.
OPHELIA'S GHOST   The colour of my blood will stain the crossing and for good or evil it will contaminate this city.
OPHELIA'S GHOST   It will contaminate the hand of the man who spilled my blood and the deep darkness that surrounds him.
OPHELIA'S GHOST   Then the city will swallow that dirty dark mass and grow monstrous.
OPHELIA'S GHOST   Then someone will rise again.
OPHELIA'S GHOST   Someone will rise again to drag the filthy blood from out of someone's heart.
OPHELIA'S GHOST   So put an end to it.
OPHELIA'S GHOST   Change that corrupted blood in the centre of the city into something else.
OPHELIA'S GHOST   Paint over the colour of my blood with something else.
SHIBUYA   I can't do that. I have no idea what to do. Without you. I don't know how to feel sorrow or hatred.
OPHELIA   Hey. Can you remember my name? I'm your illusion. The answer lies within you. Am I wrong? Because Ophelia doesn't actually exist. You should know that better than anyone, Shibuya.

OPHELIA's ghost disappears. A phone rings.

Scene Four

A phone ringing. SHIBUYA*'s room. Night-time.*

AKIHABARA   Hey.
SHIBUYA   . . . Hey.

Silence.

AKIHABARA   I did it. I did it.
SHIBUYA   Yeah . . . Where are you?
AKIHABARA   In the deep, deep forest of the city.
SHIBUYA   Come out . . .
AKIHABARA   Because it's already been done . . .
SHIBUYA   Why . . . did you kill . . . Ophelia?
AKIHABARA   Hamlet's madness did it. Sorry.
SHIBUYA   . . . She didn't have anything to do with it . . .
AKIHABARA   . . . the shadows have disappeared . . .
SHIBUYA   What?
AKIHABARA   My shadow has disappeared.
SHIBUYA   Shadow?
AKIHABARA   Yeah. And so . . . and so . . . and so . . .
SHIBUYA (*Shouting.*)   That didn't mean you could kill her!
AKIHABARA   Save me . . . I don't have – don't have a – have a shadow . . .
SHIBUYA   . . . Come out.
AKIHABARA   . . . I can't. It's gone, gone, gone, gone, gone.
SHIBUYA   Come out.
AKIHABARA   My shadow's gone, gone, gone, gone, my shadow!
SHIBUYA   Come out!
AKIHABARA   . . . I can't . . .

AKIHABARA *wails.*

Silence.

AKIHABARA   Hey, do you remember . . . in high school, we used to act out Hamlet after class . . .
SHIBUYA   Yeah.
AKIHABARA   It was fun because . . . unlike you I didn't have any friends . . . Because our families were bastards . . . so Hamlet . . . Hamlet . . .
SHIBUYA   So we were the shadows of our shit families.
AKIHABARA   Yeah.

Scene Four

Silence.

AKIHABARA Help me . . . I didn't want to do this.
SHIBUYA Give yourself up.
AKIHABARA I can't . . . It was Hamlet's madness that did it.
SHIBUYA Come out . . . I'm begging you, come out.
AKIHABARA Hamlet. Stage Hamlet, get my shadow back.
SHIBUYA Hamlet?
AKIHABARA Like Hamlet says, right? Guilty creatures, sitting at a play
SHIBUYA Have by the very cunning of the scene
AKIHABARA Been struck so to the soul
SHIBUYA That presently they have proclaimed their malefactions.

Silence.

AKIHABARA That's what I did . . .
SHIBUYA You spilt blood! Ophelia's blood!
AKIHABARA The theatre is a mirror. If there's the light, then here's the shadow. If blood can't be shed over there, then it has to be shed over here.
SHIBUYA What the fuck are you saying!
AKIHABARA So, conclude the story without blood. Finish the performance of Hamlet . . .
SHIBUYA Give me back Ophelia!

The phone dies. Beep-beep-beep-beep.

The beeping tone changes into the whispers of the CHORUS.

AKIHABARA And in this harsh *world* draw thy breath in pain, to tell my story.

SHIBUYA *and* AKIHABARA, *as young boys, circle each other. Like courting butterflies, like moths that hate each other.*

AKIHABARA To be or not to be, that is the question.

SHIBUYA   To be or not to be, ay there's the point.

Their turning gradually gets faster. They turn, becoming so fast that it's impossible to distinguish between them.

AKIHABARA   Tokyo is a ruin. The sad remains of corrupted spirits and the remnants of desire.

SHIBUYA   Blood is needed to revive this city.

AKIHABARA   We have to go to the amphitheatre.

AKIHABARA vanishes.

SHIBUYA   (*Aside.*) Grasping my knife in my right hand, I decided to perform that revenge tragedy Hamlet at the crossing in Shibuya. For murder, though it have no tongue, will speak. I'll have these players play something like the actions of Akihabara, and show it to him no matter where in this *world* he is hiding. I thought that if we did that, perhaps his shadow would appear. The play's the thing. That was my entire reason for living. To recover that guy's shadow. To return the light to this out of joint world; to save Ophelia from Akihabara.

Scene Five

The words 'Hotel Elsinore, before the crime' are projected.

Rain. Thunder. A room in 'Hotel Elsinore'. Neon lights.

This scene is a record of AKIHABARA, *and images shot by* AKIHABARA *are projected on the wall.*

AKIHABARA   I've killed seven people. It began here. Elsinore ... 'Tis an unweeded garden, that grows to seed; things rank and gross in nature possess it merely. A cheap love hotel. A filthy place where nobody salarymen and lonely students meet whores. My whole body throbbed when I heard that the ghost of a man had been seen at this hotel here on Shibuya's Dogenzaka. Crowded out by the sound

Scene Five

of my heartbeat, I briefly suppressed the sentimentality I should hate, but I couldn't help but remember that my father had died. In the pocket of my father who had killed himself was the card of a prostitute, with the name 'Elsinore' printed on the back. So I came here. The girl's name is Ophelia. I wanted to talk to her. I wanted to hear the truth of my father's suicide. I wanted to kill the one who drove him to his death with these hands. It was my father who protected me from my mother's abuse.

A knock on the door. AKIHABARA *opens it.*

A blast of wind blows in. Heavy rain.

A woman is suddenly there, she clings to AKIHABARA *and they kiss.*

The two struggle, AKIHABARA *pushes the woman away.*

AKIHABARA   What the fuck are you doing, bitch! I'll kill you!
SEX WORKER   What are *you* doing! Suddenly biting me!
AKIHABARA   Because you were shoving your tongue down my throat! What the fuck!
SEX WORKER   I was called here!
AKIHABARA   But what the hell are you doing?
SEX WORKER   That's the course you picked. You didn't get the explanation about this place?
AKIHABARA   I only want to hear about my father.
SEX WORKER   What?
AKIHABARA   You know there was a suicide in here.
SEX WORKER   Yeah.
AKIHABARA   That was my father. I heard that a ghost has been appearing here since then and so I ran. He had this card in his pocket. I called the office.
SEX WORKER (*Taking the card.*)   'Ophelia'... This is my card.
AKIHABARA   Won't you tell me what you know? Why he killed himself, the truth.
SEX WORKER   Even if I tell the truth...

AKIHABARA   Anything is fine. What was he like when he was here?

SEX WORKER   What was he like?

AKIHABARA   Was there anything different about him? Any sign he was suicidal?

SEX WORKER   'Different'? In comparison to most people, it was all different... He would straddle me and call me 'this bitch, this bitch'. And then when he was done he'd curl up like a kid and cry in my arms, saying 'sorry, sorry'.

AKIHABARA   My father did?

SEX WORKER   He did. Plenty of guys like that come here. He liked being tied up.

AKIHABARA   Tied up?

SEX WORKER   Exactly. That day, once we'd finished round one and taken a little break, he begged me, sweet Ophelia, tie me up. I did it without thinking. If that's what the customer wants. Tightly, tightly, with this rope. But he suddenly started foaming at the mouth and convulsing. I thought he was excited, because he always got worked up when he was bound. But his whole body started to go red, he foamed more than usual and he started to choke, and then he started to shout forgive me, forgive me, forgive me in a voice I hadn't heard before. He didn't stop convulsing and even when I asked him what was wrong he just carried on apologizing, forgive me, forgive me, and when I undid the rope he didn't listen to me, just kept repeating his apologies until he lost his breath. Tied up with the rope, foaming, crying – he died. After investigating later, I got it. I think he took something before he came to me, to poison himself.

AKIHABARA   Father... why...

SEX WORKER   He was a special client for me. Affection can come with this work. I can still see him lying there in agony.

AKIHABARA   Where?

SEX WORKER   In my mind's eye. And ever since then there's been whispers that a ghost has walked this hotel.

Scene Five

AKIHABARA My father's . . . ghost . . .
SEX WORKER Yes, and maybe since we're talking about him now . . .

Thunder. The FATHER'S GHOST *can be faintly seen.*
He seems to be bound.

SEX WORKER . . . What's wrong?
AKIHABARA Over there . . .
SEX WORKER What, what is it . . .

Thunder. Again the GHOST *is faintly visible. He is bound.*

AKIHABARA Over there, there, look!
SEX WORKER What? What?
AKIHABARA My father!
SEX WORKER Huh?
AKIHABARA Why . . . Stop it, please.
SEX WORKER This is a joke, right? Knock it off. Don't make fun of me.

Thunder. It repeats many times. Heavy rain. The bound GHOST
stands up.

AKIHABARA Why, look you there! My father! Can't you see him? My father, bound up as you left him.
SEX WORKER Don't be stupid!
AKIHABARA He beckons me to follow him. I'll call thee King, father . . .
SEX WORKER Enough! Alas, how is't with you, that you do bend your eye on vacancy and with the incorporeal air do hold discourse?
AKIHABARA It waves me still.
SEX WORKER Are you crazy? Stop it already!
AKIHABARA Crazy? You're the crazy one here if you can't see it!

Thunder. AKIHABARA. *He goes to follow after his* FATHER.

SEX WORKER Don't go! Come back!

AKIHABARA My fate cries out! I've been abused by my mother, bullied, made a fool of by everyone, but my father protected me. My directionless emotions scream out that I must follow him. Father! Go on, I'll follow thee!
SEX WORKER Enough!
AKIHABARA I don't care what happens, I'm going after him.

And so saying, AKIHABARA *follows his* FATHER.

Thunder. Rain. She is left alone.

SEX WORKER What the fuck! Did he want to switch to someone else? I don't know if he's the crazy one or I am!

Scene Six

AKIHABARA *and the ghost of his* FATHER *face each other. The* GHOST *is bound and prostrate on the ground.*

The rain is stained with blood, and the world *overflows with blood. The voices of the* CHORUS *intermix with that of the* GHOST. *It is unclear whether it is really* AKIHABARA*'s father, or his delusion. But the form in front of him is unmistakably that of his father.*

AKIHABARA Father . . . What happened . . .?
GHOST My hour is almost come. People who lived uselessly like me can't even go to hell. But after this, maybe I will be truly able to die . . . I couldn't die . . . I wanted to . . . at least, tell you . . .
AKIHABARA Father, you're not useless . . .
GHOST I'm sorry . . . I'm sorry for troubling you. It's time to tell you everything . . . Please forgive me for the way I look.
AKIHABARA What is it, father. Say it, I'll listen to anything you say . . .
GHOST Listen to me. You have to take revenge.

Scene Six

AKIHABARA   Revenge?

GHOST   Yes. When you've done it, I'll finally be able to die.

AKIHABARA   Tell me, father. Everything.

GHOST   Ah ... the truth is, your mother isn't your real mother ...

AKIHABARA   My mother ...?

GHOST   Your real mother is dead. She died in a traffic accident just after you were born. Your mother now – you probably can't really call her your mother ... She was my lover back then. My life became a wreck after she died ... I drowned in drink ... I came to Elsinore and got drunk on the pleasures of S&M. I didn't have a good job ... I was just scraping by, and so ... I borrowed money, got in deep, corrupted my soul ... at first I thought it would only be an escape. The alcohol, this rope ... But then I couldn't draw out the poison dart. The lump collected at the bottom of my heart crushed sincerity, my hope, and dragged on the sickness of depression.

AKIHABARA   Father ...

GHOST   I stopped talking to your mother ... She knew all about me. She knew all about my shameful habits ... The woman who was my lover ... Pieces of shit like me soon use up people's civility ... and then ... She became violent, to me and to you too. I warned her to stop ... Even I said that ... But she always said she was thinking of you, that she didn't want you to become like me, that she wanted you to succeed in society ... she didn't listen ... she shouted at you to make you strong, so that you wouldn't become useless, spineless. Like me. I hate this world. Breathing in the fumes of this city, rank with the poisonous ruins of desire that burn the lungs, struggling to breathe, I thought it would be better if I died quickly; to shake off that thought I would climb this slope again, to the top of Dogenzaka, to Hotel Elsinore ... I came to be bound by Ophelia. It was my only peace ... Ah, why did things fall so far, why does your mother raise her hand to you ... Ah, why have you been unloved by everyone.

I can't bear it anymore, I beg you, please, save me from my heavy, corrupt, filthy heart. Revenge.

AKIHABARA   Revenge?

GHOST   Revenge. Is there somewhere for trash like me, earning one million yen a year, labour for hire, with a family that's caving in, who lost his lover, who has no stamina – is there a place for someone like that to die? ... Ah, revenge, revenge, revenge on this *world*, please let me die, let me die, I'm not dead yet, take revenge on this *world*, I beg you ...

AKIHABARA   I'll do anything for you, father. I'm begging you, father, father, come back, father ... I'll start with my mother!

GHOST   Wait! Do not touch your mother. No matter how she torments you, don't touch your mother ... leave her to heaven. But do not taint yourself. Taint not thy mind. It's enough that I had that kind of life. Do not taint yourself. And then with your uncorrupted heart, take revenge on the *world*, kill me ... take revenge on the *world* ... take revenge, and then kill me ... I cannot look at the *light* when it comes in with the morning. I must go, adieu, adieu! Remember me.

The GHOST *vanishes.* AKIHABARA *turns to the camera.*

AKIHABARA   Ah, father, can it be! What! Hold, hold, my heart; and you my sinews grow not instant old but bear me stiffly up. Remember thee! Ay, thou poor ghost. I was born to follow after my father, to reform this rotten *world*. Abused by my mother, burned by cigarette ash to become stronger. I'll wipe away all the morals I've been taught, the inane things I learnt at school, the idiotic social niceties spewed out by the television, and carve only my father's words into my head and heart! 'With an uncorrupted heart, take revenge on this *world*' ... uncorrupted heart? It's the *world* that's corrupted ... Ah, father. I'll do it, I'll finish this revenge. So, please, father, rest in peace.

Scene Six

The SEX WORKER *rushes in.*

SEX WORKER   Wait, wait, you!
AKIHABARA   . . . I finally understood.
SEX WORKER   Understood what?
AKIHABARA   I . . . from now on . . . have to take revenge.
SEX WORKER   What?
AKIHABARA   The crazy bastards that . . . drove my father to his limit . . . I'll . . . kill them all.
SEX WORKER   What?
AKIHABARA   You won't tell anyone . . . what happened here today?
SEX WORKER   I'll say nothing, so don't send me away.
AKIHABARA   Nay, but swear't.
SEX WORKER   Swear on what?
AKIHABARA   Upon my knife.
SEX WORKER   What?
AKIHABARA   Please.

The world *echoes with the voice of the* GHOST *saying 'swear'.* AKIHABARA *starts to become agitated.*

SEX WORKER   I got it. I swear.
AKIHABARA   More seriously! Swear 'I won't tell anyone'!
SEX WORKER   I won't tell anyone.
AKIHABARA   More truthfully!
SEX WORKER   I swear I won't tell anyone what I saw here today.
AKIHABARA   With your heart, swear that you won't tell anyone.
SEX WORKER (*Loudly.*)   I swear that I won't tell anyone what I saw here today.

The GHOST*'s voice goes quiet.* AKIHABARA, *relieved, cries.*

AKIHABARA   Rest, rest, perturbed spirit . . . That is finally, finally enough.
SEX WORKER   What on earth . . .

AKIHABARA   That's enough. I'm going to kill them . . . there at the crossing, one after another . . . I'll kill them.
SEX WORKER   What are you saying? Are you an idiot? I'm leaving, alright?
AKIHABARA   (*Taking money from his pocket.*)   Alright. Here's some money . . . you can go . . .
SEX WORKER   Thank you. I don't totally get it, but don't do anything bad. Your mum will be worried. Go home, sleep. I feel sorry for you because your dad killed himself, but it'll be terrible for your mum if you go crazy.

AKIHABARA wails.

AKIHABARA   Thank you for today . . .

The SEX WORKER goes to leave. AKIHABARA suddenly calls to her.

AKIHABARA   Wait . . .
SEX WORKER   What?
AKIHABARA   It's . . .
SEX WORKER   I said, what?
AKIHABARA   Can you let me touch your boobs . . .?
SEX WORKER   Seriously?
AKIHABARA   Please . . . is it no good? . . . It's no good, right?
SEX WORKER   Your father was a pervert, and you are too. All men love it. But I can't relax in this job unless a guy asks me that. So tell me who is the bigger pervert here? (*Moving towards* AKIHABARA.)

Moving close to the SEX WORKER, he touches her chest. Agitated. And then he starts to cry.

SEX WORKER   I'm telling you, killing others won't change anything. Many people have done it to get revenge on the *world*. But nothing changes. It only dirties the town with blood. So that's why, boy, it's better to touch mama's chest and cry . . . That's all you need to do . . .

*The sound of a lullaby and the noise of the city.
Gradual black out.*

Scene Seven

The lullaby world. SHIBUYA*'s memories tremble. Is it a dream,
a vision or reality?*

CHORUS   The night gradually spreads out. If you concentrate you can hear singing.

CHORUS   A song – that cheerfully sings to the *world* the end of despair and love.

CHORUS   A lullaby but not a lullaby.

CHORUS   Your heart lurches. You don't know how to recover from her death.

CHORUS   And then, you start to dream. Guided by the lullaby, the dream begins.

CHORUS   While falling into sleep, awaken.

The young SHIBUYA *appears. Watching over him is
the older* SHIBUYA. *This is perhaps a fantasy of a
large crossing in Tokyo. The chatter of
contemporary youths' voices can be heard.*

YOUNG SHIBUYA   Where's Ophelia?
CHORUS (*Points.*)
YOUNG SHIBUYA   Ophelia!
CHORUS or GHOST OF OPHELIA   Ophelia?
YOUNG SHIBUYA   No. (*To a different youth.*) Where's Ophelia? My Ophelia, where is she?
CHORUS (*Points.*)
YOUNG SHIBUYA   Ophelia, Ophelia?
CHORUS or GHOST OF OPHELIA   How about it, me and you tonight? 20,000 yen.
YOUNG SHIBUYA   Ah, where the hell is my Ophelia? (*To a different youth.*) Excuse me, where is Ophelia, my, the real Ophelia?

CHORUS (*Points.*)
YOUNG SHIBUYA   Ophelia? Hey, you're Ophelia, right?
CHORUS or GHOST OF OPHELIA   Shibuya. That voice is Shibuya.
YOUNG SHIBUYA   That voice . . .?
CHORUS or GHOST OF OPHELIA   You're saying weird things again.

The shadow regains form and it is the MOTHER.
The lullaby vanishes.

The MOTHER *is cutting carrots in the kitchen. At the side of the stage,* the FATHER *is reading a newspaper.*

YOUNG SHIBUYA   Mother!
MOTHER   You're still not good enough, you know.
YOUNG SHIBUYA   My love is not enough.
MOTHER   Your head. You have to try harder.
YOUNG SHIBUYA   If I try harder, will you notice me?
MOTHER   Of course I will.
YOUNG SHIBUYA   Will you love me more than your new husband?
MOTHER   I love my new husband more than my old one.
YOUNG SHIBUYA   You're lying!
MOTHER   And then, above that, I love you.
YOUNG SHIBUYA   How much?
MOTHER   How much? As much as the university you get into.
YOUNG SHIBUYA   Is your love determined by my university?
MOTHER   Your father did very well.
YOUNG SHIBUYA   I hate my new dad.
MOTHER   What are you saying? So suddenly.
YOUNG SHIBUYA   It's not sudden, I've always hated him.
MOTHER   Please forget about the past.
YOUNG SHIBUYA   The past makes me 'me' now.
MOTHER   That man is my love now.
YOUNG SHIBUYA   If he wasn't here –
MOTHER   Not here?

Scene Seven

YOUNG SHIBUYA and SHIBUYA   Then I wouldn't have done it!
MOTHER   It's not good to blame others.
YOUNG SHIBUYA   But!
MOTHER   I won't tolerate 'buts'.
YOUNG SHIBUYA   But!
MOTHER (*Slaps* SHIBUYA.)   Shibuya, your father has been very angry with you recently.
SHIBUYA   Mother, father has been very angry with you recently.
MOTHER   Come, come, you answer with an idle tongue.
SHIBUYA   Go, go, you question with a wicked tongue.
MOTHER   Whatever is the matter, Shibuya?
SHIBUYA   What is it now?
MOTHER   Have you forgot me, Shibuya?
SHIBUYA   No, by the rood, not so. You are the new wife of my new father, and – would it were not so – you are my mother.
MOTHER   Nay then, I'll set those to you that can speak.
SHIBUYA   Come, come, and sit you down, you shall not budge. You go not till I set you up a glass where you may see the inmost part of you.

  YOUNG SHIBUYA *seizes the* MOTHER. SHIBUYA
  takes a knife out of his pocket.

MOTHER   What are you doing?
SHIBUYA   I wonder.
MOTHER   You will not murder me?
SHIBUYA   I won't murder you, but let you live.
MOTHER   Help, help, ho!
FATHER   What, ho! Help, help!
SHIBUYA   How now? A rat? Dead for a ducat, dead!
FATHER   Oh, I am slain.
MOTHER   O me, what hast thou done?
SHIBUYA   Nay, I know not . . . Could it really be . . . my . . . father . . . ?
MOTHER (*Falling on the body.*)   What have you done!

Peeling off the face on the body, it also looks like
OPHELIA . . . *News alert.*

Interrogation room. SHIBUYA*'s lines below are overlaid with another self's voice.*

POLICE OFFICER   Is the act of killing just?
SHIBUYA   The act of killing is wrong.
POLICE OFFICER   Why did you do something bad?
SHIBUYA   I didn't do it.
POLICE OFFICER   Then who did it?
SHIBUYA   Hamlet or another me.
POLICE OFFICER   How do you know that?
SHIBUYA   There's a spot of light in the pitch dark, and inside there Hamlet or another me is in the act of killing.
POLICE OFFICER   You saw that?
SHIBUYA   I didn't want to see it. I was forced to see it, I was scared.
POLICE OFFICER   You seem scared now, too.
SHIBUYA   I am.
POLICE OFFICER   Do you know what you are?
SHIBUYA   What I am?
POLICE OFFICER   Yes – in short, who are you?
SHIBUYA   Who?
POLICE OFFICER   And whose blood was shed . . .

And, the POLICE OFFICER *takes a photograph out of his breast pocket and passes it to* SHIBUYA.

SHIBUYA (*Looking at the picture, comparing himself with the corpse and the photo.*)   Who the hell am I?

SHIBUYA *tumbles down . . .*

The sound of breaking glass and the sound of the news vanishes.

The vision of the MOTHER, *the* POLICE OFFICER *and* YOUNG SHIBUYA *vanish.*

Scene Seven

OPHELIA *appears.*

OPHELIA'S GHOST   Is it fun to lock yourself away and revisit the past?

SHIBUYA   Ophelia?

OPHELIA'S GHOST   You're checking to see if I really existed in this world.

SHIBUYA   Ophelia . . . You've come! Thank you. What should we talk about? How were things lately? Recently I've been a bit depressed, so I can't really express things well, you were . . . Ah, sorry. Here's a cushion. Sit here. So you've really come. I thought we wouldn't meet anymore. Here, sit. Come on.

OPHELIA'S GHOST   (*Shakes her head.*)

Pause.

OPHELIA'S GHOST   Did you remember my name? I've come to say goodbye. I have remembrances of yours that I have longed long to re-deliver. (*Scattering numerous flowers.*)

SHIBUYA   No, what is this . . . I never gave you aught.

OPHELIA'S GHOST   Then what's this photograph? Are the you and me pictured here just our shadows? Will that night by the seashore when you kissed me with sweet words not have happened? If I disappear, will none of that have happened?

SHIBUYA   Ophelia, were you really my lover?

OPHELIA'S GHOST   It was so before. But now things are different. Since I've become a shadow, I can only wander beside you. Love is now in the past. It's just memories. Something you have to return to the living when you die. So that's how you'll look at photographs of me, isn't it?

SHIBUYA   I want to recover your beauty and honesty that's shown in this picture.

OPHELIA'S GHOST   Beauty and honesty are the privilege of the living. My body shelters maggots, I'm already complicit in the dirt of this world. The blood that burst from me calls for more blood. This was sometime a paradox, but now the time gives it proof.

SHIBUYA   Don't corrupt my memories! I loved you!

OPHELIA'S GHOST   Indeed, Shibuya, you made me believe so.

SHIBUYA   You shouldn't have believed me! If loving someone means all your memories will disappear when they die, I won't sell my heart to such a filthy love. You're the same as my mother. Go and become a whore and fuck other men!

SHIBUYA breaks down crying like a child.

Around this time, the MOTHER *and* POLICE OFFICER *secretly peep out from the shadows.*

OPHELIA'S GHOST   Hey, Shibuya, don't hoard all the memories to yourself. Don't live in the *world* of stories. When I died, who turned the edge of that knife my way? There was dirty blood on that knife, and who was the accomplice to that corruption? You can remember. Remember my name. And then, one day it will be time to rip up that photo. It was so with me. On the eighth afternoon I ran to the beach looking for shadows, I was careful not to step on them but with the setting sun I trampled on everything. The same day will come for you too. From now on, do what you've decided to do. That's your only answer.

AKIHABARA or SHIBUYA   And in this harsh *world* draw thy breath in pain, to tell my story . . .

Sound of sirens in the distance. The ring bites into OPHELIA*'s finger, blood wells up.*

OPHELIA'S GHOST   I tried to take that droplet that shone amber in my hands but I couldn't hold it, as I desperately searched for the shadow I lost that day. While lying to myself, like a little girl collecting shards of broken shells, thinking all will be well, as long as I at least have a shadow, I searched desperately. But it was no use. The shadow wasn't anywhere . . . Since then, I became good at lying. Hey, can you remember my name?

SHIBUYA Not yet . . .
OPHELIA I see . . .

> OPHELIA *slowly breaks away from him.*

SHIBUYA or AKIHABARA For murder, though it have no tongue, will speak with most miraculous organ.
OPHELIA (*Begins to vanish.*)
SHIBUYA I'll have these players play something like the incident at the crossing before him . . .
OPHELIA (*Vanishes.*)

> *The* MOTHER *and* POLICE OFFICER *watching from the shadows make a noise.*

SHIBUYA Who's there!

> *They fall completely silent, and holding their breaths vanish.* SHIBUYA *looks around* . . .

SHIBUYA Who's over there . . .

> SHIBUYA *is left alone. Staring at the photograph and flowers, he steps firmly on the shadow of loneliness.*

SHIBUYA . . . Ophelia . . . Ophelia . . . Ophelia . . . Ophelia . . . Ophelia . . . (*Soundlessly expresses isolation.*)

> SHIBUYA*'s voice is overlaid with* AKIHABARA*'s voice.*

AKIHABARA . . . Father . . . father . . . father . . . father . . . father . . . father . . . father . . .

> SHIBUYA*'s room slowly changes into* AKIHABARA*'s room.*
>
> *The sound of* AKIHABARA*'s typing fills in the theatre.*

Scene Eight

> AKIHABARA*'s room.*

AKIHABARA Will I pollute my heart, or grasp the truth – or both? Which is more human? To see through my own lies or rather believe in them, betray my morals and push on towards true love? Or do I become a cog in human activity, play the fool and continue to lie to myself? To live is to become corrupted, and that's all. In this dirt even the things that should be loved will be lost. That's who I am, now. If I could at least kill myself. The suicide of someone I loved has cast on me the dread of something after death. Treachery! Who? Who calls me villain? Breaks my pate across? Blames me for it all? Who does me this? Blows smoke in my face, and makes me drink piss? Who? Who forced my father's hand? Made him commit suicide in a whorehouse? O, vengeance! Is there no one here . . .! Real love doesn't seek payment. Real love doesn't thrash about looking for compensation. It's up to me whether or not I believe the ghost. Do I love it, that spirit? The answer is no. Because I have no right to love anyone. So, do I not love it then? The answer is still no. Because I was saved by that flesh that was once my father. But, all I can say is this. I won't think anything of it, even if the price of my actions from now on is my death. Even if I lose my life. This is true love. Love isn't a choice ... We are corrupted by love. I'm going to go beyond morality. To the other side, where once you've stepped in you can no longer go back. Am I alone? I'm tired of drinking the poison of loneliness. Dishonest acts become more evil out of fear of evil. Then it follows that being conscious of the right of my actions, my revenge will not be stained: because my heart knows nothing of filth but only love for my father. Love will always warm you. By drawing in my father's lifeblood I can continue on this path in the name of love. When I've finished my revenge with a pure heart, my body can melt away in that sun. Then for the first time me and my father will become one, and the two of us will overcome this lonely *world*. That is an unpolluted revenge.

Scene Nine

A phone vibrates.

Father? Is that you? Come out. One more time. Father? Father? You're my father, aren't you?

He grabs the phone and answers it.

CALLER Is this Akihabara?
AKIHABARA Yes...
CALLER It's about the truck you reserved the other day.
AKIHABARA Yes...
CALLER It'll be ready in five days as you requested.
AKIHABARA Yes...
CALLER There's the matter of payment: if you could pay in cash on delivery, please.
AKIHABARA Yes...
CALLER Well then, thank you for your time.

The line goes dead. Staring straight ahead,
AKIHABARA *stands motionless.*

AKIHABARA I... can't do it... I... can't do... I...

Scene Nine

In the darkness, SHIBUYA *is cheerfully acting out a scene from Hamlet, alone. As though he is rehearsing with some actors. But there is no one else around.*

SHIBUYA The rugged Pyrrhus, he whose sable arms, black as his purpose, did the night resemble when he lay couched in the ominous horse, hath now this dread and black complexion smeared with heraldry more dismal, head to foot. Now is he total gules, horribly tricked with blood of fathers, mothers, daughters, sons, baked and impasted with the parching streets that lend a tyrannous and a damned light to their lord's murder; roasted in wrath and fire, and thus o'ersized with coagulate gore, with eyes like carbuncles, the hellish Pyrrhus old grandsire Priam seeks. ... 'Fore God, my lord, well spoken – with good accent and good discretion. ... Anon he finds him striking too short at Greeks. His antique sword, rebellious to his arm, lies where it falls.

Around this point, in a different space the interrogation of the woman who seems like the boy's MOTHER *is being held. The contents of that are below. At the same time,* SHIBUYA *continues with his one-man show.*

POLICE OFFICER   So he was always alone?
MOTHER   That boy was extremely introverted. He always took the streets with the fewest people when he came home from work.
POLICE OFFICER   There's a rumour that he was muttering strange things to himself during the incident ...
MOTHER   Yes. He would drift into his fantasy *world*, all alone, and make odd gestures like he was acting something out.
POLICE OFFICER   Was he ... alone?
MOTHER   Although it seemed as though there were others in that dream *world* with him, he was alone.
POLICE OFFICER   Hm ...
MOTHER   He always had this book with him (*Holds it out.*) ... It was probably something from this part he was muttering to himself.
POLICE OFFICER   This is ... Hamlet.
MOTHER   (*Nods.*)

The actors appear around the young man and continue the lines.

SHIBUYA   ... anon, the dreadful thunder doth rend the region, so after Pyrrhus' pause, a roused vengeance sets him new a-work.

Scene Nine

CHORUS   And never did the Cyclops' hammers fall on Mars's armour, forged for proof eterne, with less remorse than Pyrrhus' bleeding sword now falls on Priam.

CHORUS   Out, out, thou strumpet Fortune!

CHORUS   All you gods in general synod take away her power.

CHORUS   Break all the spokes and fellies from her wheel and bowl the round nave down the hill of heaven as low as to the fiends.

CHORUS or POLICE OFFICER (*Staring fixedly at the book.*)   This is too long.

MOTHER   Yes.

SHIBUYA (*To* ACTOR 5 *or to the* POLICE OFFICER.)   It shall to the barber's with your beard. Prithee say on – he's for a jig, or a tale of bawdry, or he sleeps. Say on, come to Hecuba.

CHORUS   But who – ah woe – had seen the mobled queen –

HAMLET   The mobled queen?

CHORUS or POLICE OFFICER (*Coming across a page.*)   That's good, mobled queen is good.

MOTHER   Excuse me?

POLICE OFFICER   No, nothing . . .

HAMLET   Go on.

CHORUS   Run barefoot up and down, threatening the flames with bisson rheum, a clout upon that head where late the diadem stood.

CHORUS   And, for a robe . . .

The CHORUS *continue. The young man listens and directs them. At the same time, the following occurs:*

POLICE OFFICER   On the day of the incident he seemed to be muttering something terrible, according to witnesses. While he carried out this tragedy. It's probably from this book. (*Staring hard at the book.*)

MOTHER   . . . He was a good boy. He wasn't the kind of boy who would do something like this. I brought him up so he'd live an honest life, I didn't want him to be like his dead father. I wanted to raise a strong and resilient child . . . (*She crumbles.*)

POLICE OFFICER (*Staring at one page in the book, a little afraid, thinking deeply.*) That day, pedestrian paradise, your child got in a truck and drove it straight into them. Just like . . .

MOTHER   No!

The POLICE OFFICER *and the* MOTHER *vanish.*
The CHORUS *finish the speech.*

SHIBUYA (*Applauding and praising the actors.*) Brilliant! Brilliant! This is the scene in Hamlet of Priam's slaughter. No, brilliant! In order to take revenge on Priam's son who killed his father, Pyrrhus hides in the belly of the wooden horse to get into Troy. By destroying Troy, he fulfils his duty of revenge. This is that scene. No, great! The revenge scene where Pyrrhus, hidden in the horse, suddenly appears in the middle of a crowd got me the most worked up! Really, brilliant!

CHORUS   Thank you.

SHIBUYA   The abstract and brief chronicles of the time! But be careful. Now this overdone, or come tardy off, though it makes the unskilful laugh, cannot but make the judicious grieve. The purpose of playing whose end, both at the first and now, was and is to hold as 'twere the mirror up to Nature to show Virtue her own feature, Scorn her own image, and the very age and body of the time his form and pressure. It should also reflect the truth. To spin out stories that were never seen or never happened in reality. A woman may have a beautiful face but be rotten to the core. And villains thought by the world to be ugly may have unpolluted hearts. So, see things as they are. That's what is important.

CHORUS   I hope we have reformed that indifferently with us.

SHIBUYA   O, reform it altogether.

CHORUS   Yes.

Scene Nine

SHIBUYA   By the way, the real show will be the final scene of Hamlet, at that crossing. Hamlet and Laertes duel in public and the King is killed. I want to do that scene. The climax of Hamlet. At the very least, it should be enjoyable even for people in the audience who don't know the story.

CHORUS   Um, but I have a question.

SHIBUYA   What is it?

CHORUS   How will we do Fortinbras's army?

SHIBUYA   Right, that. Since Fortinbras arrives suddenly at the end of Hamlet, I'm thinking about styling it after that 'revenge of Pyrrhus' you just did. Fortinbras comes into Denmark to defeat his father's enemies. So, I want to use the image of the wooden horse. Pyrrhus's revenge is the Trojan War. And the Trojan War is the wooden horse. Fortinbras probably hid in some big vehicle, too, to break into Denmark – and bursting out of it, took his revenge. I want to change it to that.

CHORUS   I see, I see.

SHIBUYA   So . . . I decided we could use a truck as the wooden horse and have the army appear from there.

CHORUS   Oh, that's a great idea! We can do that!

SHIBUYA   Don't forget to learn your lines. The show is soon! Get to work.

The CHORUS *get dressed and start getting ready for the performance.*

POLICE OFFICER   Is it better to rush towards oblivion? It may be a mistake to assume that this city is the same as the cracked universe in this book. Oblivion gives birth to oblivion, and divides the *world* into a *world* of happiness and a *world* of sadness. Asked which of the two you would rather go to, it's likely the former. Revenge . . . I want to go far away from this city . . . (*And, reading aloud from a page.*) ''Tis now the very witching time of night when churchyards yawn and hell itself breathes out contagion to this world. Now could I drink hot blood and do such business as the bitter day would quake to look on'.

Holding up the book. An image is reflected on it.

Projection.

Hamlet is the record of events brought about by a young man's insanity.

HAMLET X SHIBUYA is not Hamlet.

This is the record of two young men, SHIBUYA *and* AKIHABARA.

Scene Ten

'8th June, the day of the incident – the performance begins!' is projected.

We can see the CHORUS*'s performance of Hamlet.*

Mournful music. However, there's a rich element to it. A video of the incident is shown faintly in the background.

Seven ghosts . . .

CHORUS (*female*)   I think it was probably just after twelve. The blue sky appeared between the gaps of the buildings, and the warm sunlight shone on us all. I came to the city to look for gifts before I went to my hometown in Hokkaido with my second son. Because the Yamanote line was a little crowded, we talked about going to a café for some tea before we went looking for the presents. My son seemed surprised by how many people there were, and he was more excited than usual. He took my hand and tugged me towards a backstreet. It was then. I heard some kind of loud noise from behind.

Scene Ten

The noise of a truck, and light.

CHORUS (*male*)   That day the three of us had come into town to hang out. We were looking for something we couldn't get our hands on anywhere else. This place is really special, after all, and because it has that 'something' we tend to just end up here. What were we after? Like I can say it out loud! Right? (*Laughs.*) My friend really likes that 'thing' but he was saying he didn't have the guts to go in alone so we were kind of on edge. We were getting close to the shop, messing around and telling jokes, when those two started running. My bag was heavy so I readjusted it before going after them. I shouted at them to wait for me. When they turned around, a huge object came from the shadows and crashed into me.

The noise of a truck, and light.

CHORUS (*male*)   I was walking straight ahead. I'd just been discharged from hospital, so I was pretty proud of being able to walk. When I looked around, there was a huge noise and the screaming started. I started hurrying in that direction. My legs still hurt but I didn't notice. There was something huge pushing at my back. It was that kind of feeling. Thinking about it now, I probably shouldn't have gone there.

The noise of a truck, and light.

CHORUS (*female*)   There was a loud noise, and something huge stopped about fifteen metres in front of me. I was disoriented. I could guess what was happening, but I didn't want to believe it. And then a lone man appeared from out of that thing. I couldn't see his face well, but it was like he was possessed and being controlled by something.

The noise of a truck, and light.

CHORUS (*female*)   I heard screaming and started running. I had no idea it was anything like that, so I just had a strange sinking feeling about the atmosphere. It couldn't be expressed in words. I thought there might be something I could do to help, so I should head towards the screaming. I broke into a run. There was something around the corner. It was then. Suddenly, a lone man appeared in front of me. I don't remember clearly what he had in his hands, but it was about this size. I don't remember anything else after that. Even if I try, I can't remember it.

The noise of a truck, and light.

AKIHABARA   I remember the scene from that time. I remember the wrinkles in the corners of the eyes of someone who was bleeding in front of me. I remember the sensation of plunging the knife into flesh. I remember the terrible darkness in the back of the eyes that pleaded with me: no, not me. I couldn't move my legs and I couldn't stop shaking. But everything had already been put in motion. I had already reached a point I could no longer come back from. My untarnished revenge was in progress. This place was now not like any space in the *world*. Emptier than outer space, yet it was more real than anywhere else on Earth. Each time I cut someone down, I was lost. I was no longer myself. There must have been butchered people behind me. But I couldn't look back. I told myself: this is theatre. Theatre. Like the play Hamlet carved into the nobles. I'm Hamlet. I'm performing Hamlet in the middle of this crossing!

SHIBUYA   It was then I realized I had to stop this play; were Akihabara's deeds actually my own? Yes, I asked myself that, I might have been Akihabara . . . While performing on the crossing, I had no choice but to run through the unresponsive audience and cry out, 'give o'er the play! Give o'er the play! Give o'er the play!'.

OPHELIA (*girl*)   That day, I'd gone to buy a bag for my boyfriend in return for a ring he'd given me. He always had

Scene Ten

lots crammed into his bag, so I wanted to buy him a big, strong new one as a present – but one that looked cool. I found something that fit, and thinking it wasn't quite enough I thought I'd hide some music from my favourite band inside it. I was sure he'd be surprised. I wandered about the busy streets daydreaming about it.

AKIHABARA Another person appeared in front of me. I raised my arm.

SHIBUYA Give o'er the play! Give o'er the play! I tried to put a brake on it. I tried to put a brake on his madness that was spilling out.

AKIHABARA I could no longer stop myself. I was no longer myself. The spirit of my father was the devil. I'd been tricked by the devil.

SHIBUYA I'm begging you, stop the show!

AKIHABARA My heart was controlling my body. I have to stop right now. I have to stop the play. I wasn't Hamlet. I was Fortinbras. Fortinbras who came into another country in his dirty boots and ruined everything.

SHIBUYA Stop the play!

AKIHABARA and OPHELIA meet. AKIHABARA goes to stab her. SHIBUYA tries to stop it. Their eyes meet. But AKIHABARA knocks SHIBUYA over and stabs OPHELIA.

AKIHABARA I am you, and you are me. Since Akihabara and Shibuya are both part of Tokyo. Forgive me, forgive me, I can't forgive myself. But since you are my other self, please at least forgive me in your voice. Forgive me.

SHIBUYA Ah . . . I . . . can't . . . forgive you!

AKIHABARA Of course . . . I can't be forgiven.

The sound of sirens comes close. An announcement that the criminal is on the run.

The police enter and blow whistles. They say things like 'Stop the play!' 'Did you get permission to put on a performance here?' The CHORUS. *They gather up the small props and run.*

SHIBUYA *is left on his own.*

SHIBUYA   While watching my own play, what the hell did I see . . .?

SHIBUYA *opens his hands, and there is warm blood on them. He is handcuffed by the police.*

Scene Eleven

News report.

NHK PRESENTER   At one o'clock today, a young man named himself as the perpetrator of yesterday's indiscriminate attack at the crossing in Shibuya. Police are currently investigating. It seems as though there's little chance this is the same perpetrator. The young man put on a performance at the Shibuya crossing without permission from the police and while apparently becoming distressed part way through interrupted his own performance and ran wild, with no understanding of what he himself was saying. To repeat . . .

ASAHI PRESENTER   We've just received new information. New information is coming in about the young man who named himself as the perpetrator of yesterday's attack. We've just learnt that the young man was carrying a knife in a paper bag that closely resembled the knife used in yesterday's incident. The police have taken this suspicious individual into custody, while the investigation continues. To repeat . . .

YOMIURI PRESENTER   This is the newest information about the suspicious male just arrested. We understand that the results of his psychological evaluation are in, and that he has lost nearly all of his memory and is unable to answer coherently. It seems as though even he cannot determine whether he is possessed, feigning madness or in the grip of insanity. The young man is repeating his story that he is the criminal and according to the police he has told them his name is Shibuya. He states he planned and carried out yesterday's attack. Because he wanted to reclaim the shadow of Ophelia; because he wanted to reclaim the shadow of Akihabara. He is only repeating these strange claims. It seems as though the paper bag he was carrying contained a knife and large amounts of clippings from a script.

The clippings are scattered everywhere. The CHORUS *read them aloud.*

Scene Twelve

> AKIHABARA *on the run. He is covered in blood. The unbloodied* SHIBUYA. *He is in handcuffs.*

AKIHABARA   I've heard some strange news.

SHIBUYA   Ever since that day my memories are gradually fading.

AKIHABARA   A performance of Hamlet at the crossing. The one who committed that attack was me.

SHIBUYA   I can't even remember the name of the person I loved.

AKIHABARA   I did it?

SHIBUYA   Ophelia?

AKIHABARA   The one who did it was me, right here. So, who is this kid?

SHIBUYA   ... Your name only carries with it the smell of blood now.

AKIHABARA   I had lost my shadow before I realized it.

SHIBUYA   I feel like my life is no longer my own.

AKIHABARA   Maybe that other shadow is making a mess somewhere else.

SHIBUYA   Maybe I've become someone's alter ego, and I'm doing things without being aware of it.

AKIHABARA   Who is this boy they've got instead of me? Who is this boy, burdening his heart with my sin instead of me, while I shamelessly live on in the deep forest of this city? Did I play Hamlet but get lost in Claudius's sins?

CHORUS   O, my offence is rank: it smells to heaven; it hath the primal eldest curse upon't – a brother's murder. What if this cursed hand were thicker than itself with brother's blood? Is there not rain enough in the sweet heavens to wash it white as snow?

SHIBUYA   I played Hamlet in Shibuya. Blood was stuck to my hands then. Warm, warm red blood that had only just been in someone's beating heart. Blood so warm it burns bright red. I could imagine this smell of blood was her warmth. Oh, my memories are drifting. Why did I do such a cruel thing . . . ?

CHORUS   Forgive me. I have sinned. But . . .

AKIHABARA   To be or not to be, that is the question. Do I let him take up all my sins and live as I am? Or do I confess to all of it? How all occasions do inform against me, making the dull lump of my heart heavier and full of barbs. What are humans, if they spend their lives just eating, sleeping? Beasts, no more.

CHORUS   How all occasions do inform against me.

SHIBUYA   Everything is growing faint. I'm no longer myself. Just like the people who died at the crossing, I'm vanishing from this world. My memories are fading . . .

AKIHABARA   I'll trace my memories. I lost my father.

SHIBUYA   My name is Shibuya.

AKIHABARA   And I went to the hotel where my father killed himself. Elsinore.

SHIBUYA   And I staged Hamlet.

AKIHABARA   And I met my father's ghost there.

SHIBUYA   And there was a terrible murder.

AKIHABARA   And I decided to take revenge.

SHIBUYA   And real, not stage, blood was spilled.

Scene Twelve

AKIHABARA   I swore to take revenge on this dirty *world*.
SHIBUYA   Her blood was mixed in with it . . .
AKIHABARA   I promised my father. That I wouldn't taint my heart . . .
SHIBUYA   Her name was . . . Ah, I can't remember it.
AKIHABARA   But my heart was already tainted. It's dirtied with warm blood, and I'm entrusting the settlement of my sins onto this boy, my other self. I do nothing, even after hearing of this. Now, whether it be bestial oblivion, or some craven scruple of thinking too precisely on the event, a thought which, quartered, hath but one part wisdom and ever three parts coward, I do not know why yet I live to say 'This thing's to do'. It is not nor it cannot come to good.
CHORUS   O that this too too sullied flesh would melt . . .
SHIBUYA   I can't remember her name. The smell of her blood has driven awareness out of my mind.
CHORUS   They bore him barefaced on the bier . . .
SHIBUYA   I can hear something. A sound that always follows her. The sound of waves. Ophelia lived in Elsinore. In Hamlet, Elsinore is next to the sea.
CHORUS   They bore him barefaced on the bier . . .
SHIBUYA   I close my eyes to meet her. Abandon yourself to the secret rhythm of waves, heard on the other side, when you soak in the smell of blood. I am falling. While my memories are fading, I'm falling down into the police interrogation room. Falling down to Elsinore, by the sea, where Ophelia is and my girlfriend whose name I've forgotten lingers . . .
AKIHABARA   My legs were taking me in a different direction. There's no use in shamelessly surviving here. I couldn't stop my feet anymore. Once more. Let's go and meet him. Let's go once more to Elsinore and meet my father's spirit. I'll question it whether my heart has been tainted, or whether I was right. I love my father. That loving father must know everything. I headed to Hotel Elsinore . . .

Scene Thirteen

The seashore in SHIBUYA*'s mind.* OPHELIA *is standing there.*

SHIBUYA   I knew you'd be here. I don't know who I am.
OPHELIA   Why?
SHIBUYA   My memories have slowly started to fade since you died . . . I should have realized sooner that I killed you.
OPHELIA   Is that so?
SHIBUYA   Of course.
OPHELIA   Do you know where this is?
SHIBUYA   The sea next to Elsinore. The sea of memory in the farthest depths of my mind.
OPHELIA   Yes. How did you know I'd be here?
SHIBUYA   I know everything about you.
OPHELIA   So what's my name? Not yet, hm?
SHIBUYA   Not yet . . .
OPHELIA   Do you know why I'm always here?
SHIBUYA   Here by the ocean, you mean?
OPHELIA   Yes. At Elsinore bordering the sea.
SHIBUYA   Something happened by the sea. Like Ophelia, Ophelia who lived in Elsinore . . . Something was lost.
OPHELIA   Just like a virus that develops without you knowing, people can be dragged into something painful without realizing.
SHIBUYA   I understand. Since I killed you without knowing it.
OPHELIA   Did you really kill me?
SHIBUYA   I performed Hamlet at the crossing. That was what killed you.
OPHELIA   You're making a big mistake. You should throw away all those memories. And I want you to think more carefully about who you should hate. I want you to look at my blood and think about who you should hate.
SHIBUYA   I'm slowly losing my memories . . . I've even started to forget things like the names of my parents, things that happened with my friends, what I liked and what I didn't.

Scene Thirteen

Blood, for example. Is that really such a frightening thing? The sea, for example. Is that really so beautiful? Humans, for example. Are they really so precious? I'm frightened because I'm beginning to forget. But at the same time, the more I forget absolutely everything . . .

OPHELIA   What happens if you do?

SHIBUYA   I feel like I'm getting closer to you. Your name is on the edge of my tongue. I should be able to remember it soon.

OPHELIA   Revenge . . .

SHIBUYA   What?

OPHELIA   You lost me. You are carrying that as your sin on your back. But, you're wrong. There is someone you should take revenge on. There is someone you have to hate. Unlike me, there is someone you can hate. To do so, you have to leave the fantasy *world*. And then you have to throw away all your memories and take revenge.

SHIBUYA   Please, stop! That argument won't work on me. Leave the medication for people who are sick. I'm fine. I can't be loved by anyone, and I can't hate anyone. Because I killed someone I loved. That fact is everything.

OPHELIA or the POLICE OFFICER   That fact is wrong. Why are you sticking to that? You really did carry out that attack, then?

SHIBUYA   . . . Yeah.

OPHELIA or the POLICE OFFICER   You really did carry out that attack, then?

SHIBUYA   . . . Yes.

OPHELIA or the POLICE OFFICER   You really did carry out that attack, then?

SHIBUYA   . . . Yes, I did.

OPHELIA *gradually changes into the* POLICE OFFICER. *The sound of waves also vanishes.*

POLICE OFFICER   You really did it?

SHIBUYA   Yes. I drove into the crossing and killed people.

POLICE OFFICER   According to people who witnessed the attack, the criminal was taller than you.
SHIBUYA   I was taller then.
POLICE OFFICER   Is that possible?
SHIBUYA   The unthought of happens in this *world*.
POLICE OFFICER   Alright. So why do you want to be the perpetrator so badly?
SHIBUYA   Because I'm a killer.

Pause.

POLICE OFFICER   Didn't you lose someone in the incident? We looked into it. You lost your girlfriend of two years that day.
SHIBUYA   Stop . . .
POLICE OFFICER   You'd made an eternal vow with her.
SHIBUYA   Please stop . . .
POLICE OFFICER   You'd given her a beautiful ring as a present.
SHIBUYA   Please stop it . . .
POLICE OFFICER   But, your girlfriend . . .
SHIBUYA   Ahh . . .
POLICE OFFICER   She was stabbed that day by the criminal and died. But you weren't there.
SHIBUYA   Stop!
POLICE OFFICER   You're alive. And your beloved girlfriend is dead.
SHIBUYA   Stop it!
POLICE OFFICER   You can't forgive yourself for living.
SHIBUYA   Stop!
POLICE OFFICER   So that's why you decided to let go of your memories. Just like Hamlet who feigned madness, you decided to pretend to know nothing.
SHIBUYA   No, stop!
POLICE OFFICER   And didn't you come here, to the police station, to fool both yourself and everyone else?
SHIBUYA   Stop!

POLICE OFFICER   Well then. Please leave, Shibuya. We don't have time for you. We have to concentrate our energy on catching the real criminal. (*Pushing* SHIBUYA *aside.*)
SHIBUYA   Please stop it. I really killed them! Please believe me!
POLICE OFFICER   Please leave! So we can help you. It'll take time to catch the person who killed your girlfriend.
SHIBUYA   Please stop. I killed them all. I'm not Hamlet. I'm Fortinbras. Fortinbras who came into another country in his muddy boots and ruined everything.
POLICE OFFICER   Go to the hospital! I can empathize with you because you lost your girlfriend, but we have work we need to do. The hospital, not the police station, deals with injuries. Farewell.
SHIBUYA   Ahh . . .
POLICE OFFICER   The remedies you need are available. To a hospital go, and quickly too.
SHIBUYA   I did it. Believe me! I did it all.
POLICE OFFICER   Be quiet! You can't live in a fantasy *world*. I've arranged for you to be introduced to a good psychiatrist, you'll get good treatment there. Amnesia! Ridiculous. You should know which reality you need to live in. To a hospital, go.

The POLICE OFFICER *pushes* SHIBUYA *away and leaves.*
SHIBUYA *wails. His memory fades further.*

Scene Fourteen

Hotel Elsinore. Rain.

SEX WORKER   It really was you.
AKIHABARA   Yes.
SEX WORKER   I thought it might be when I heard the news.
AKIHABARA   Did you talk to anyone . . . ?
SEX WORKER   I said nothing. Didn't I promise? Swear? That I wouldn't tell anyone?

AKIHABARA   My father's ghost appeared in front of me and I couldn't bear it.
SEX WORKER   There aren't any ghosts.
AKIHABARA   There are! Even if you can't see them, I can.
SEX WORKER   You're saying you saw a ghost?
AKIHABARA   Yes.
SEX WORKER   You believe that?
AKIHABARA   It's the truth.
SEX WORKER   What are you talking about? That's why you did it?
AKIHABARA   'It'? Are you objecting to what I did?
SEX WORKER   Of course I am! I'm afraid to be alone with someone who's spilt as much blood as you.
AKIHABARA   Everyone bleeds. When cut, anyone's blood will spill out! It's nothing particularly special.
SEX WORKER   What? Are you crazy?
AKIHABARA   Crazy? My pulse as yours doth temperately keep time and makes as healthful music. It is not madness that I have uttered.
SEX WORKER   Why did you come here?
AKIHABARA   I wanted to meet my father again.
SEX WORKER   That ghost?
AKIHABARA   Yes . . . But it won't appear, even though I've waited.
SEX WORKER   So why did you call me? Are you going to bring me here and then send me away again? Don't go silent . . . Don't send me away, and don't drag me into it.
AKIHABARA   But . . .
SEX WORKER   But?
AKIHABARA   You're my mother.
SEX WORKER   What?
AKIHABARA   You are my mother.
SEX WORKER   Don't be an idiot! Why would I be your mum?

Scene Fourteen

AKIHABARA That was the first time I touched a woman's chest. And it made me feel a bit more normal.

SEX WORKER Then isn't it strange for me to be your mum? That kind of transformation doesn't happen in this *world*.

AKIHABARA Sorry. But, I . . .

SEX WORKER And if you're really the one behind what happened, I don't want to be around you.

AKIHABARA Why?

SEX WORKER Why! You're a murderer, you've dirtied this town with the blood of seven people. News of that event has tied up the hearts of the people in this city with fear. Now we can't even look each other in the face. It was already a faceless *world* . . . And you pushed it further. But those of us who sell our bodies do it to re-tie that open seam in the heart. That's why I call myself Ophelia. Ophelia who was driven mad by this bloodstained *world* and who fell into the water. I think even as she was losing herself, she was praying for the *world*'s recovery.

AKIHABARA Stop distorting things. This bloodstained *world*? In such a *world* as this, blood is there just to be shed! Look at this city. The blood that should be flowing in each person's veins is clogged and decaying in this rotten *world*. All of my father's blood was swallowed by the *world*. We'll soon be killed if we don't shed blood.

SEX WORKER Don't be so stupid! I don't want to talk to you anymore.

AKIHABARA Wait, mother. You shall not budge. You go not till I set you up a glass where you may see the inmost part of you. Look, here's a mirror. Look well. Why do you fornicate with so many men? Let beer-bellied salarymen tempt you to bed, take their money, pinch wanton on your cheek, call you their mouse and let them for a pair of reechy kisses, or paddling in your neck with their damned fingers, make you to ravel this matter out. That I am on the run for that incident. Why would you betray me like that, mother?

The scene in GERTRUDE*'s bedroom and* AKIHABARA*'s past and present overlap.*

SEX WORKER and MOTHER   What is this? I already told you I'm not her, didn't I?
AKIHABARA   Mother?
SEX WORKER and MOTHER   I'm your mother but I'm not her.
AKIHABARA   I knew it!
SEX WORKER   I'm not her.
AKIHABARA   I knew it!
MOTHER   I'm not her.
AKIHABARA   I knew it!
SEX WORKER   But if that's what you want, I'll do it.
AKIHABARA   Become my mother?
SEX WORKER   Yes. I'll trade places with your dead mother, and from today on I'll be her.
AKIHABARA   Mother!

As though he is being drawn in, AKIHABARA *rapes her. The* MOTHER *looks on, with tears in her eyes.*

CHORUS   I'll be consumed.
CHORUS   I'll be consumed.
CHORUS   You'll be consumed.
CHORUS   Her sea.
CHORUS   You'll wade into her sea.

AKIHABARA *undresses. He rapes her.*

CHORUS   You hasten your feet.
CHORUS   You're running into the sea as fast as you can.
AKIHABARA   Mother . . .
CHORUS   The one you call so as you violate her
CHORUS   is of course not your mother,

Scene Fourteen

CHORUS and neither is she Hamlet's mother Gertrude.
AKIHABARA Mother . . .
CHORUS She is Ophelia.
CHORUS You violate her. You violate the person you should love.
AKIHABARA Mother . . .
CHORUS You pollute the person you should love.
SEX WORKER I'm on my period right now. We don't do that kind of thing here.
AKIHABARA I can smell the sea . . .
SEX WORKER Really?
AKIHABARA Yeah, this is the ocean. It smells like the ocean.
SEX WORKER You can smell the sea?
AKIHABARA Yes.
SEX WORKER That's bullshit. I'm on my period. I'm on my period, so it's not the ocean . . .
AKIHABARA Not the ocean?
SEX WORKER It should smell like blood.
CHORUS Blood hangs in the air.

AKIHABARA screams. Sudden black out. Pitch black.

SEX WORKER Is the news true?
AKIHABARA What news?
SEX WORKER That someone impersonating you turned himself in at Shibuya police station . . .
AKIHABARA I heard it too. I think it's probably true.
SEX WORKER So, are you intending to pollute even that person? Kill seven people, pollute their memories, pollute the city, pollute me, and then even that boy who has no connection to any of it – pollute him too?

Pitch black. She cries.

SEX WORKER Hasn't there been enough bloodshed? I'm Ophelia. There's already enough blood.

Half-light.

SEX WORKER (*Singing.*) Tomorrow is Saint Valentine's Day, all in the morning betime, and I a maid at your window to be your valentine. Then up he rose and donned his clothes and dupped the chamber door – let in the maid that out a maid never departed more.

AKIHABARA Ophelia–.

SEX WORKER Now, get out of here! (*Hitting* AKIHABARA.) (*Sings.*) By Gis and by Saint Charity, alack and fie for shame, young men will do't if they come to't: by Cock they are to blame. Quoth she, 'Before you tumbled me you promised me to wed.' He answers: 'So would I ha' done by yonder sun an thou hadst not come to my bed.'

AKIHABARA Ophelia–.

SEX WORKER Get out! (*Hitting* AKIHABARA.)

AKIHABARA Can I meet you again?

SEX WORKER I hope all will be well. We must be patient. Get out of here and unravel young Narcissus' mistake. I'm Ophelia, I can't leave Elsinore. I can't get out of this hotel.

AKIHABARA I'm sorry.

SEX WORKER Get out! (*Shoving* AKIHABARA *away.*)

AKIHABARA I'm sorry. I'm sorry. I'm sorry. I'm sorry … (*Continuing to say it.*)

SEX WORKER Get out!

She shuts the door. Alone, he continues to apologize. Music.

Scene Fifteen

AKIHABARA *goes to turn himself in.* SHIBUYA *is thrown out of the police station. The* CHORUS. *Music.*

CHORUS And so, that man walked.
CHORUS Judged, accused, he walked to obliterate himself.
CHORUS The thoughts that piled up in his mind

Scene Fifteen

CHORUS   were already defiled.
AKIHABARA   I'm filthy, I'm filthy.
CHORUS   He walked desperately.
CHORUS   Each step was an ordeal.
CHORUS   It truly was a fight.
CHORUS   He wanted to negate every part of himself.
CHORUS   He wanted to erase every possible past.
CHORUS   But he
CHORUS   could never have
CHORUS   imagined another past
CHORUS   even if God gave him
CHORUS   the chance.
AKIHABARA   Filthy, filthy.
CHORUS   Since
CHORUS   he
CHORUS   could only be himself.
CHORUS   He walked.
CHORUS   He walked down the Dogenzaka slope in Shibuya.
CHORUS   He went down that slope that he would never climb again.
CHORUS   He gazed around
CHORUS   to brand into his eyes
CHORUS   this *world*
CHORUS   he was seeing for the last time.
CHORUS   And then he thought,
AKIHABARA   Let's give a new name . . .
CHORUS   to this dirty *world*.
CHORUS   In his mind, perhaps by naming it
CHORUS   he tried to
CHORUS   re-do his life.
AKIHABARA   This is the last chance. The last chance to shake off this dirt.

SHIBUYA *enters.*

CHORUS   At the same time, a young man

CHORUS   was kicked out of the Shibuya police station.
CHORUS   He imagined that
CHORUS   his name was
CHORUS   Shibuya.
CHORUS   Stupid.
CHORUS   Stupid.
CHORUS   Stupid.
CHORUS   But, he chose the stupid route
CHORUS   in his mind
CHORUS   to search for his lost girlfriend's name.
SHIBUYA   Ophelia, Ophelia . . .
CHORUS   He concentrates his mind.
CHORUS   Focusing on that one goal
CHORUS   of remembering her name.
CHORUS   And while doing so, he
SHIBUYA   I've lost my memories. I've lost my memories.
CHORUS   While saying that he was Shibuya, he
CHORUS   lost the entire city.
SHIBUYA   What was that?
CHORUS   He has no memories.
CHORUS   All the names have been lost from the *world*.
CHORUS   You're losing everything but her name.
CHORUS   And the more you lose them.
SHIBUYA   I'm closing in on her. I'll forget everything and then be close to her.
CHORUS   He continues to walk. He names things anew.
AKIHABARA   I'll think of new names and burn them into my memory.
CHORUS   He continued to forget.
SHIBUYA   I can't remember . . . her name . . . What's that?
CHORUS   A guardrail.
AKIHABARA   Annabelle Lee's collarbone.
SHIBUYA   What's that?
AKIHABARA   A plastic bag.
CHORUS   A soft white bird.

Scene Sixteen

SHIBUYA   I can't remember her name!
AKIHABARA and CHORUS   Traffic lights.
CHORUS   A tomato on your Twitter timeline.
CHORUS   Sunset.
CHORUS   Gertrude's thick make-up.

It continues. Continues. AKIHABARA's *voice is absorbed by the* CHORUS.

Like this, the CHORUS *start to give* SHIBUYA *a new name.*

Scene Sixteen

SHIBUYA *and* AKIHABARA's *lives meet in the middle of that crossing in* SHIBUYA. *A possible dialogue between two people who might have been.*

There is no sound but their voices.

AKIHABARA   Hey . . .
SHIBUYA   H, e, y . . .
AKIHABARA   Shibuya. You're my shadow, aren't you?
SHIBUYA   A, ki, ha, ba, ra, I, wa, s, wa, i, ti, ng, fo, r, yo, u.
AKIHABARA   Sorry . . .
SHIBUYA   . . . Yo, u, ki, ll, e, d, O, ph, e, li, a.
AKIHABARA   Sorry . . . Not just that. I murdered other people too.
SHIBUYA   Gi, ve, he, r, ba, ck.
AKIHABARA   Sorry. Sorry. Sorry. I'll give myself up.
SHIBUYA   Gi, ve, he, r, ba, ck, gi, ve, O, ph, e, li, a, ba, ck.
AKIHABARA   Sorry. I'll give myself in to the police. I'll throw everything away. I don't think I can be forgiven, but I'll throw everything away.
SHIBUYA   Gi, ve, he, r, ba, ck.
AKIHABARA   Sorry. I'll give myself up and then kill myself.
SHIBUYA   A, t, lea, st, gi, ve, m, e, he, r, na, me, ba, ck.
AKIHABARA   What?
SHIBUYA   Revenge.

Lines from Hamlet violently intervene.

SHIBUYA   Hamlet. Gi, ve, m, e, ba, ck, O, ph, e, li, a's, na, me.

And then, what is seen beyond this . . . SHIBUYA*'s revenge tragedy.* SHIBUYA *stabs* AKIHABARA. *Blood flows.*

Police sirens. The world is bright red. Breaking news.

'The criminal behind the terror attack has killed himself in the middle of the SHIBUYA *crossing . . .'*

The POLICE OFFICER *appears, carrying a book.*

POLICE OFFICER   That amnesiac boy from before came to the station again. He still said his name is Shibuya. And in his hands he was holding this script stained red with blood. He said: I've regained my shadow. I've regained all the shadows. And with the shadows I remembered her name. There are things that can't be seen without a shadow. According to the expert's opinion, he really had lost his memories – and he was cutting himself with the knife in his pocket. Just like Hamlet kills to grasp the truth . . . Everything is resolved. The real culprit killed himself, and the city has once more recovered a healthy rhythm. The city moves as it always does. The crossing, the Yamanote line, 109, Dogenzaka, Hachiko, salarymen, prostitutes, students, tissue hawkers, right-wing agitators . . .

And he continues to list motifs of Shibuya. And then at some point he vanishes . . .

Epilogue

The seashore. Dusk. OPHELIA *is watching the sea.* SHIBUYA *arrives on a bicycle. He's in handcuffs. He's covered in blood.*

SHIBUYA   I've finally understood that this is a slope.
VOICE   Really?
SHIBUYA   Yeah. It's gentle, but it's definitely a slope.

Epilogue

VOICE   You don't need to worry when you're riding a bike then, do you.

SHIBUYA   Yeah. And look, if I dig into the sand and bury it deeply, then the bike won't topple over anymore.

VOICE   And then if we stand side by side, we can look out at the view together.

SHIBUYA   That's it. (*Pause.*) And I remembered your name. It's taken me a long time to remember. I didn't think I could say your name again . . . You're not Ophelia. Your name is . . . Light. Your father gave you that name when you were born, when he was showered with hope. Your father who died here gave you that name.

The sea is dyed red by the dusk-light.

SHIBUYA   When it seemed like you were going to be swallowed, what you saw was not the spray of deep blue waves, nor eddies that rolled across a violent sea. It was the crimson sun that shone far away. When it sets it meets the sea and the *world* glows bright red and then pale, but the light never vanishes completely, it fills the *world*. The red-dyed sea. Gazing out at that, your body that had been an open vein ached to melt into the world. That gaze was fixed straight on the bright red, burning *world* as your heart beat and exhaled blood, that warm blood joined the sea and was then drawn up into the heavens beyond the glittering sunset. It wasn't the sea that captivated you. Let's look at the light from beyond all that, something no one has seen, suffocated by hate. Let's look at the light from beyond all that, stained by blood. That's right . . . Your name is Light. I didn't understand until I found my shadow. Now that shadows dominate this *world*, I could remember your name. . . . Light . . . I want to hold you once more . . . I want to feel your body once more, I want to kiss you . . . it doesn't matter that you bled . . . I want to feel your warmth again . . .

The beach seems to burn in the dusk. The sea is the colour of warm blood.

OPHELIA *begins to fade away as though she is melting into the dusk.* SHIBUYA *tries to hold her, but his hands only grasp air. He continues to reach out for her. His body stretches and his blood bursts out. The hands seeking for* LIGHT *are also dyed red.*

You really are going to vanish . . . I can't see you anymore . . . You really are going to vanish . . . I know. . . But I had to call you . . . Light . . . Light . . . Don't go . . .

The world begins to swallow LIGHT. SHIBUYA *runs towards the sea to try to prevent it. All the while, he is being dyed red.*

The curtain of night descends. SHIBUYA*'s body is by now in the sea. Darkness dominates the world.*

Only SHIBUYA *knows whether this darkness is the kind of clammy dark that invites panic and nightmares, or whether it's a peaceful night that might cover a mother and her sleeping baby.*

He could have told us, but he can no longer be seen . . .

The sound of the waves quietly commands the darkness, and the rest is silence.

Fin.

INTRODUCTION TO *THE NEW ROMEO AND JULIET*

Fumiaki Konno

The New Romeo and Juliet is part of a trilogy whose main purpose was to bolster through entertainment the spirits of people in the areas devastated by the Great East Japan Earthquake. Therefore, the three adaptations share three features: they are comedies, depict no death and are located in a hot spring setting. In *The New Romeo and Juliet*, the two households – alike in their dignity – are changed into a couple of rival inns in the Itari hot spring district: the International Tourist Hotel Verona and the Berona Hot Spring Inn.[1] The two

4 Ishii Rina (Juri) and Takahashi Toshiki (Romio) from the 2012 production of *The New Romeo and Juliet*.

---

[1] In the original text, 'Verona' is written in katakana script and 'Berona' in kanji script: this may indicate the fierce rivalry and hostility between the two hotels. The name 'Verona' also sounds a bit affected in Japanese, compared to 'Berona', which is also the name of the town.

feuding families each have one child: Monta Romio (Romeo) and Kafu Juri (Juliet) respectively. Romio is a senior in high school (between the ages of seventeen and eighteen) and Juri a senior in junior high school (between the ages of fourteen and fifteen), and both wear their school uniforms on stage. The two are young literary enthusiasts who love the works of such authors as Hermann Hesse and Kita Morio, a Japanese novelist and psychiatrist of the twentieth century. Romio and Juri meet at an inaugural party for the International Tourist Hotel Verona annex, and since they share such similar interests, it does not take long for them to understand each other and fall in love.

However, the Montas (the Montagues) and the Kafus (the Capulets) bear such a grudge against each other that members of both families, including Romio, start a brawl at the public bath of Berona Hot Springs, which results in both Maki Kyūshirō (Mercutio) and Chibō Ruto (Tybalt) being injured and taken to hospital for treatment. Fortunately, no one dies and their injuries are not serious, but Romio blames himself for Ruto's injury and despairs. Romio and Juri go to the hut of Rensu (Friar Laurence), a *matagi* hunter (traditional bear hunters in Tohoku) to ask for his help, and at his suggestion they take a mysterious drug contained in an empty bullet casing, which makes them appear dead for a while. To the surprise of both families, Romio and Juri come back to life during their funeral and there is a happy ending.

The play is full of nostalgia for the good old days when Japan was a flourishing economic power and people were extremely high-spirited, in stark contrast to the languishing economy in the Lost Decades after the bubble economy burst. Shimodate Kazumi and the creative team of his Shakespeare Company Japan (SCJ) adopted the period of the Shōwa[2] 30s (1955–64) and part of the 40s (1965–74) for the play, because

---

[2] The reign of Emperor Hirohito (Emperor Shōwa) was from 1926 to 1989, which is known as the Shōwa era.

that was a time when people had great 'vitality and a strong hope for the future' (Inamasu 2006: 47). There are references in the play to famous singers, teen idols, actors, superheroes, a journalist of a popular television programme, and an author and his literary work, all from the Shōwa 30s and 40s. They included: singers Saigo Teruhiko, Sono Mari, Tashiro Miyoko and the Mahina Stars, Funaki Kazuo and Hana Hajime & Crazy Cats; film stars Sada Keiji (1926–64) and Ōkawa Hashizō (1929–84); television superheroes *The Moonlight Mask* (1958–59) and *The Rainbow Mask* (1959–60); and *Myōjō* (1952–), a gossip magazine for teens. By evoking happy memories of 'the good old days' of their teens and twenties, the SCJ intended to raise the spirits of the elderly in the disaster-hit area.

Alongside such aims, their choice of the historical backdrop also reflected a growing interest in the Showa 30s and 40s, the 'Shōwa Retro Boom', which 'steadily gathered strength' in the first decade of the twenty-first century (Inamasu 2006: 46). The trend continued into the next decade, and films and television dramas which depicted the daily life of people in the Showa period were immensely popular. For example, the 2005 film, *Always: Sunset on Third Street*, was a smash hit and won the Japan Academy Prize for Best Film, Best Screenplay and ten other awards in 2006. Two sequels were released, respectively in 2007 and 2012.[3] Furthermore, the NHK television drama series of 2012, *Ume-chan Sensei*, also set in post-war Japan, was a great success.

The Shōwa 30s and 40s were the era of the 'Economic Miracle', a time of exponential economic growth following the recovery of the devastated Japanese economy during the post-war period of 1945 to 1954. An Economic White Paper in 1956 announced that Japan's post-war recovery had been a huge

---

[3] Kōno Kōhei argues that according to the director Yamazaki Takashi, the purpose of producing the film *Always: Sunset on Third Street* was not to reproduce a vision of the real past, but to create beautiful memories of the Shōwa 30s, which engendered the criticism that the film ignores the negative aspects of the period (2018: 296–99).

success, and real GDP grew at an average annual rate of about ten per cent during the following two decades. The 'three sacred treasures', the most wanted electrical appliances in the 1950s, were black and white television sets, washing machines and refrigerators, while there were also the 'three Cs', items which people in the 1960s wanted to purchase: cars, colour televisions and 'coolers' (air-conditioners). The lifestyle of the general public changed markedly and the average standard of living during this period in Japan rose sharply.

Another crucial factor is that the Showa 20s, particularly the years between 1947 and 1949, was the time of the '*dankai sedai*' (baby boomers), when the number of new-borns increased sharply to over 2.5 million, nearly three times that of 2018: 2,678,792 (1947), 2,681,624 (1948), 2,696,638 (1949) and 918,400 (2018) (Ministry of Health, Labour and Welfare 2019). This means that in the Showa 30s and 40s these baby boomers were in their teens and twenties and were enjoying their youth, just as Romio, Juri and their young friends in the play do. By setting the period in these two decades, *The New Romeo and Juliet* aimed to reproduce and represent the vibrancy of the Shōwa culture, and to evoke happy memories among the baby boomer generation in the audience.

In addition to triggering a sense of nostalgia, the play also brought home to the audience the message that we should remember the earthquake and tsunami and live on even in the depths of despair. When Kafu Kanako (Lady Capulet) and Juri discuss her current age, Onasu (Nurse) reminisces about a huge earthquake which occurred just before Juri was born, significantly expanding on the Nurse's reference to the earthquake that occurred when Shakespeare's Juliet was weaned:

> How cud I forget. It wis just as Juri wis about tae be born, when that earthquake hit. The previous mistress wis verra afeart o earthquakes, and once the rice bowls on the altar started tae clatter and shake, she shouted, Onasu, it's an earthquake, and rushed oot into the

street, at which point I thought the shaking would stop, but a vertical movement that made a thudding noise knocked over the chest of drawers and brought the picture frames clattering down, and just as I thought my life wis coming tae an end, whae gave out a thunderous cry as she wis born but Juri. My, I wis right flabbergasted. Then the shaking completely hauded. This is a very special child, said we as we all rejoiced. Ain't that right, mistress?

Here, Onasu's vivid memories describe the intense earth tremor and her sheer terror, though the story ends blissfully with the birth of Juri.

Similarly, the matagi hunter, egged on by his friend Sankichi (Chorus), recounts the story of his childhood, and elaborates on the landslide and tsunami caused by the huge earthquake which he experienced at the age of three. The victims of the tsunami included his mother and all of Sankichi's primary school friends, and while Sankichi has become senile and feeble, his memory of the disaster has not faded away.

MATAGI   With that catastrophic earthquake, ye ken, the mountain before me een collapsed like it had turned tae water, like the mountain became the sea. Me dad wis in Sendai and survived, but me mam hung her three-year-old bairn from that big beech tree and wis washed away.

SANKICHI   Ah, so it did, so it did. The sea in our parts rose like a mountain and the water wis like it's earth and sand. I wis at me elementary school, but all me freens were washed away by the tsunami.

MATAGI   That's right. Sanki, ye are from Shizugawa, ain't ye. Have ye remembered?

SANKICHI   Vaguely.

MATAGI	It's nae a bad thing, tae have yer lugs shut off and yer mind go foggy. Cannae gan on living without forgetting.
SANKICHI	Forgetting's nae guid. We cud be washed away by the tsunami again.

The important lesson learned from the past catastrophe is underscored here by Sankichi's vociferous acting when delivering the last line, as if to warn the audience not to forget the calamity of the great tsunami of 2011, just as hundreds of 'tsunami stones' (Fackler 2011) along the coast of Japan have been doing: 'Forgetting's nae guid. We cud be washed away by the tsunami again.'

Juri's lines in the balcony scene are also focused on the context of life and death. Romio is so happy to know Juri's love for him that he over-exaggerates his feelings a little: 'Noo I ken that I'm in yer heart, I'm so happy, I'd gladly die. Nay, I'm so happy I cud faint and die. That's whit I mean.' Juri, on the other hand, is very sensitive to the word 'die': 'Then dinnae die, but live and live on.' The reference to death, as well as to an earthquake and tsunami, would be a reminder for the audience of the tragedy they themselves had just experienced, and it would serve to transform their traumatic memories into something shared.

In addition to the use of dialects and the reference to the cataclysm of the earthquake and tsunami, another important aspect of Shimodate's works is the fieldwork and learning through experience involved in the process of preparing for productions. This has been something that Shimodate has continued since the forming of the SCJ. For example, in his version of *King Lear*, which attracted '100 spectators into a theatre in downtown Sendai' on a Sunday in 2014, the king was changed into the character of 'a sushi magnate' (Westhead 2014). Shimodate was inspired to add this twist when he enjoyed the traditional dish at a sushi restaurant with his three daughters. Together with some members of the Company, he began taking lessons from a sushi master and they actually made sushi after the performance of *The*

Introduction

New King Lear at SanSanKan. In the case of *The New Romeo and Juliet*, in order to familiarize himself with the ways of matagi hunters, Shimodate met a real matagi and learned a great deal about their culture and lifestyle while walking together in the mountains in winter. He hit on the idea of using an empty bullet casing as Friar Laurence's vial after he was given a cartridge by the matagi. Matagis hunt bears in groups and they use the casings as whistles or a syrinx to signal to members of the group without drawing the attention of the bears.[4] As a matagi Rensu speaks of this use of bullet casings in the play: 'Empty bullet casings used tae signal fellow hunters when we're in the mountain. Bears cannae hear this. So, we'll have tae gan with this.'

Shakespeare's *Romeo and Juliet* has always been amenable to various kinds of adaptations; *The New Romeo and Juliet* falls

5 Izumori Isamu (Rensu), Ishii Rina (Juri) and Takahashi Toshiki (Romio) from the 2012 production of *The New Romeo and Juliet*.

[4] For details of matagis' methods of hunting and their use of the whistle, see Chiba Katsusuke (2019: 86–98) and Nebuka Makoto (2018: 85–147 and 192–93).

into the category of the comic burlesque.[5] Shakespearean burlesque has often been set in the hospitality industry – the SCJ's Montagues and Capulets, owners of rival seafood-obsessed spas, is part of a long tradition of taming the Shakespearean tragedy by reimagining it in restaurant kitchens. Some other notable examples include the 2001 film *Scotland, PA*, which is set in a hamburger restaurant, and the 2005 *Macbeth* in the BBC *ShakespeaRe-Told* series. However, as I have discussed so far, *The New Romeo and Juliet* is burlesque with a difference. The play evokes memories of happier days and a time of economic prosperity. By combining the burlesque elements with Shōwa nostalgia, an examination of life and death, and a sense of the locality of the play created through the use of the Tohoku dialect, it not only aimed to mock the conventions of Shakespearean plays, but also contributed to lifting the spirits of audience members who had experienced a tragic disaster and whose ties to their community needed reconfirming.[6]

Finally, a few words must be said about the translation. One of the great charms of *The New Romeo and Juliet* and of the SCJ's works in general is the sense of warmth and vibrancy that comes from the use of the Tohoku dialect. In an attempt to convey this, the translator has opted to mix Scottish English from different

---

[5] According to Stanley Wells, in the long history of Shakespearean burlesque, 'the first substantial burlesques' were *The Empress of Morocco* and *The Mock-Tempest* in 1674, by Thomas Duffet (Wells 1965: 49). The popularity of *Romeo and Juliet* in the genre is illustrated by the following works: *Romeo and Juliet Travesty, in Three Acts* (1812), by Richard Gurney; *Romeo and Juliet: 'As the Law Directs' An Operatic Burlesque Burletta, in One Act* (1837), by Maurice Dowling; *Rummio and Judy; or, Oh, This Love! This Love! This Love! A Serio-Comic-Parodi-Tragedi-Farcical Burlesque, in Two Acts* (1841), by Horace Amelius Lloyd; *Romeo and Juliet Burlesque; or, The Cup of Cold Poison, A Burlesque, in One Act* (1859), by Andrew Halliday; *Capuletta; or, Romeo and Juliet restored. An Operatic burlesque* (1868), by George Melville Baker. For these works and Victorian Shakespeare burlesques, see Stanley Wells (1977–78) and Richard W. Schoch (2002).

[6] For a detailed discussion of how the SCJ's productions have helped rebuild a sense of community in the Tohoku region, see Motoyama and Konno (forthcoming in 2021).

regions with standardized British English, while retaining some Japanese expressions as well. The decision to adopt Scottish English comes partly from its sonorousness, a quality it shares with the Tohoku dialect. But it is also because the region's history of political struggles with England brings to mind the clashes Tohoku has historically had with the Japanese central government; when Shimodate premiered his *Macbeth* at the Edinburgh Fringe Festival in 2000, he introduced the SCJ and himself as having come 'from the Scotland of Japan'. The contrast between standardized English and Scottish English also helps highlight the formality of standardized Japanese in Harisu's lines and in scenes such as the first meeting between Romio and Juri.[7] The use of Japanese expressions such as *chan*, a term of endearment, and *matagi*, hunters of the Tohoku region, is intended to infuse the translation with a sense of the locale, which is another important aspect of the work. While this may seem like an odd mishmash, it is true to what Shimodate has been attempting to achieve through his work: the transformation of the local dialect, by combining it with variations from different regions and with standardized Japanese, into a theatrical language.

---

[7] The idea to translate the play using Scottish English came partly from the 1994 Japanese production of *Rosencrantz and Guildenstern Are Dead* (translated by Matsuoka Kazuko), which used standardized Japanese for Shakespeare's lines and the Kansai dialect for the private exchanges between the two protagonists.

INTERVIEW: SHIMODATE KAZUMI

What was your motivation for starting your theatre company, and how do you see your company in relation to the many other companies in Japan that stage Shakespeare?

It has been a desire to build a Globe Theatre in Tohoku. I would like to present a Tohoku version of Shakespeare produced by the people of Tohoku to those who come to the theatre to see Shakespeare.

What was the inspiration for the work translated in this volume, and how much of the work was created during the writing process and how much of it was created or changed through the rehearsals?

There were two inspirations. The first was what an elderly lady, who approached me in Sendai after 3.11, said, 'Please don't give up Shakespeare. It's something I always look forward to. Please stage something not sad and not long.'

The second was my experience at British Hills. By chance on business I visited British Hills, which had been the venue for our first stage production. A non-Japanese staff member proudly mentioned that he had seen our *Romeo and Juliet* sixteen years ago. That evening, I stood across from Shakespeare's statue in front of the manor house. The statue seemed to me to saying, 'Come again', and that was when I decided to restart the company and to give back to the people of Tohoku.

What are your thoughts on the reception of Shakespeare in Japan today, and where would you place your theatre company and its works in relation to that?

Translations of Western works have primarily been staged in Tokyo; while that has helped shape standardized Japanese, dialects have not been challenged and allowed to grow in the same way. I wanted to know if dialects could serve as languages for the arts. I followed the example of playwright and translator Kinoshita Junji to combine the 'right amount' of dialect and standardized Japanese to create a language for the theatre.

What do you envisage for the future of your theatre company?

I would like to build a theatre in Tohoku and hold an Olympics for the theatrical arts where stage directors and theatre companies might gather from countries such as South Korea, Singapore and India. I would like to give children the chance to learn about the *lingua franca* that is Shakespeare and about dialects. Theatres in Tokyo have an urban character; I would like this theatre in Tohoku to be down-to-earth and filled with human warmth. I would like it to be a place where people gather from around the world and converse without formalities, like the Dirty Duck pub in Stratford-upon-Avon. And where it is possible to engage with the audience during the intervals. I hope to build such a theatre where we can hold such events.[1]

---

[1] Shimodate is now in talks with Tagajo City in Miyagi Prefecture, which was once the political centre of Tohoku, for permission to build his Globe Theatre there.

THE NEW ROMEO AND JULIET

(2012)

THE SHAKESPEARE COMPANY JAPAN

LIST OF CHARACTERS

KAFU REIJIRō	Director of the International Tourist Hotel Verona
KAFU KANAKO	Director's wife
KAFU JURI	Daughter; a senior at Miyagino Gakuin Junior High School
CHIBō RUTO	KANAKO's nephew; Heir to the Kintoki Construction Company
ONASU	Maid to the KAFUs; Nurse to JURI
HARISU BONBON	Heir to Itari Hospital; a medical student
MONTA GYūEMON	Innkeeper of the Berona Hot Spring Inn
MONTA SATOKO	*Okami* hostess of the inn
MONTA ROMIO	Son; a senior at Itari Senior High School
MAKI KYūSHIRō	Friend of ROMIO
EN HORIO	Friend of ROMIO
RENSU NOBUO	A *matagi* hunter
SHIRATO SANKICHI	Bath attendant of the Berona Hot Spring Public Bath
CHūZAI MAMORU	Constable of Itari Police
EKINO TSUTOMU	Stationmaster of Berona Hot Spring Railway Station
SONO MARI	Singer
NOMIYA ASAKO	Landlady of the Itari Pub
SAMI ERI	Maid at the Berona Hot Spring Inn
KUREKO RI	Maid at the Berona Hot Spring Inn
ABURA Yō	Maid at the International Tourist Hotel
HARU SAZAKO	Maid at the International Tourist Hotel
MITO MASAYUKI	Also known as MāBO, the butcher
CHūKA KENJI	Also known as KENCHAN of Rairaiken, the Chinese diner
SARASHINA SABURō	Also known as SABUCHAN of the soba noodle shop
MAGURO SASHIMI	Also known as SACCHAN, the fishmonger

Bath attendants, a romantic couple, a student, a parent and a child, a peddler

THE NEW ROMEO AND JULIET

The Attendant's Booth at the Berona Hot Spring Public Bath

SANKICHI   Berona, in the Itari hot spring district is the best hot spa in the Tohoku region: there's nae denying it's the champion, the *yokozuna* when it comes to the Eastern Japan hot spring ranking. Twae right braw inns stand there: the International Tourist Hotel Verona and the Berona Hot Spring Hotel. But they be bearing each other such a grudge that the town of Berona's split right in half. The fishmongers, the greengrocers, the butchers, the *sake* merchants, the drycleaners, the rice dealers, the temples, the doctors, the timber merchants, the schoolteachers, why even the stray dogs and cats: none can stay in the toon less they be taking sides. But lo, what trick of the stars is this that the lass and lad of these twae feuding families are sweet on each other. And I dinnae mean they had a wee bit of a crush; they were right smitten with each other. Ready-to-die-if-kept-apart smitten. This wis a much bigger deal than the elections. The whole town, a right fankle. It wis a fankle and everyone realized it wis all daft. Ay right, even if ye be thinking how inept, how confusing, how all's a muddle and ye ain't sure whit's being said, rage ye nae. I beg ye, please forgive all faults for the sake of this here Sankichi.

Berona Hot Spring Station

EKINO   The ticket barriers are this way!

A weekend afternoon. The bath attendants serving as touts are divided into two groups and waiting for potential customers. A student, a parent and a child, a romantic couple and a peddler enter and the touts vie for their attention. Animosity spreads through the tranquil surroundings of the hot spring town.

The Hoke Street in the Berona Shopping District

SAMI ERI   I say, it gets me goat.
KUREKO RI   Sure, the building's right grand, but nae even a cur would eat that kind of scran.
ERI   Apparently, they're nae cooking it there.
RI   Awa ye go!
ERI   According to Mābo, the butcher... seems they're ordering from the diner serving Western-style scran in Furukawa.
RI   Awa ye go!
ERI   Seems at fower every evening, there's a truck parked aback the kitchie.
RI   And with their flyers mentioning bona fide French cuisine as the *spécialité* of the International Tourist Hotel.
ERI   Right ye are. Seems they started out creating their dishes right proper. But, my word, that cook wis quite the looker, wisnae he?
RI   The one with the deeply chiselled features of the matinee idol, Saigō Teruhiko?
ERI   Right ye are. And remember he took off with the bath attendant's wife.
RI   Well, that cook wis a looker. Whae wouldn't elope with him? And with that bath attendant looking like a goby fish.
ERI   Whit can you do when there's a tuna and a goby fish?
RI   Go for the tuna, no doubt. But why dinnae I git asked?
ERI   So wanton ye are, ain't you? Covering the walls of yer room with photos of that teen idol, Funaki Kazuo.
RI   Lo, here come the fowk from the Tempura Hotel.
ABURA YŌ   We heard that. Whit ye be meaning, calling us the Tempura Hotel?
RI   Crispy and tidy.

The Hoke Street in the Berona Shopping District

HARU SAZAKO   Much obliged.

ERI   The shrimp may be a wee little thing but the batter is oh so muckle.

RI   Like cotton candy?

ERI   (*Laughs.*)

YŌ   The gall of these bumpkin lassies from that run-down hotel to think they can laugh at us.

SAZAKO   Pshaw, ye best be giving up such dowie kimonos.

ERI   Ye are one to talk, looking like ye do, like a mosquito larva.

YŌ   Mos – mosquito larva? Ye, ye are . . .

SAZAKO   A mud snail.

ERI   A mud snail?!

RI   Mud snails we can eat, mosquito larvae we cannae.

ERI   Ay. Lo, here comes Horio.

EN HORIO   Whit's ganing on, Kureko, Sami? Ye are red in the face.

RI   Hear us. These fowk be insulting us, saying our kimonos are sad.

ERI   And calling our place run-down.

HORIO   That's rank, but the guests will be arriving and they wonnae want to see maids threaping so in the middle of the road.

With the entrance of CHIBŌ RUTO, *people begin to gather.*

CHIBŌ RUTO   Whit is this? Are they ganging up, with men an a', to abuse ye?

YŌ   Ruto, hear us, will ye? They taunt us, calling our place the Tempura Hotel.

RUTO   Tempura?

SAZAKO   So rank they are, saying Yō's like a mosquito larva.

RUTO   Mosquito larva?

YŌ   (*Cries.*)

RUTO   Horio, call yerself a man, picking on women? Whit a low life.

HORIO   Ye've got it all wrong. I wis just passing by when . . .

The New Romeo and Juliet

RUTO　Making excuses, even more cowardly.
HORIO　I wis just saying it would be a shame if the guests saw them so.
RUTO　Charming, you say? Being all goody-two-shoes, are ye? Get off yer high horse.
MITO　Ye tell him, Ruto!
SARASHINA　Horio, stand yer ground!
CHŪKA　The International Hotel, naething but lies. Shut 'em down!
MITO　The Hot Spring Inn deserves tae gan down in a pile of shite.
CHŪZAI　Whit ho, haud! Haud! (*Warning shot.*)
ALL　(*Scream.*)
CHŪZAI　How many warning shots will bring ye tae yer senses? Nae more than three shots are allowed each day, and so that wis the last one for today. It would be different if it were the fake guns used in sports events. But this here is a real gun; do ye have a death wish? Ruto and Horio, I'm asking ye, too. And all of ye – egging em on insteid of hauding the fight. Really, I've had enough of this, I tell ye. If only some superhero like Moonlight Mask or Rainbow Mask would come tae the rescue! I cannae deal with all this on me own. Noo, on yer way. Ye should be getting lots of business on Fridays; no time tae be loitering so.

Each leaves as does the CONSTABLE. ROMIO *enters.*

HORIO　Romio, where have ye been?
ROMIO　Naewhere.
HORIO　Yer dad and yer mam hae been fashed.
ROMIO　They complained they cannae figure oot whit's going through me head, didnae they?
HORIO　Ye have it figured out.
ROMIO　They complained that water in a goldfish bowl is better clear, didnae they?
HORIO　It is, int it nae?

The Hoke Street in the Berona Shopping District

ROMIO   Whit's wrong with it being muddy?
HORIO   There's nothing wrong, but it's difficult tae see.
ROMIO   For who?
HORIO   For who? For the owner of the goldfish.
ROMIO   This has nowt tae do with the goldfish. The water's better muddy.
HORIO   Whit's troubling you? Entrance exams?
ROMIO   That's nae completely off track – it's connected a wee bit.
HORIO   Only a wee bit?
ROMIO   If it weren't for the exams, I cud hail focus on me cares. Alone in the distance, in the space between boulders, to think on my troubles while thinking not of others' eyes.
HORIO   Is that Saigyō?
ROMIO   Ay.
HORIO   It's a smashing poem.
ROMIO   Ye think so, too?
HORIO   Ay. Cannae imagine how many tens of thousands of people have recited this poem. A thousand years since the Heian Period. Squeezed between rocks far away, all alone, untroubled by others' gazes, just thinking about that special person; if that were possible. Oh, do ye like someone?
ROMIO   Are ye seeing the smoke?
HORIO   Is there a fire?
ROMIO   Ay.
HORIO   Wh-where?
ROMIO   Here, that's where it burns.
HORIO   And the smoke?
ROMIO   Fumes of sighs. Day after day, just sighs.
HORIO   For who?
ROMIO   Someone just oot of reach.
HORIO   Tell me. Ain't we friends?
ROMIO   If I do, will I be feeling a wee bit better?
HORIO   That's how it works.
ROMIO   Tell nae one.

HORIO Ay. So would I reply, but that I might tell Kyūshirō.
ROMIO Do ye mean Maki Kyūshirō? I'm nae fashed about him.
HORIO So?
ROMIO It's Rozako.
HORIO Winner of the 'Miss Itari' pageant?
ROMIO Ay.
HORIO Forget her.
ROMIO How?
HORIO Whit do you mean, how?
ROMIO It's because she's niece tae the president of the International Tourist Hotel, ain't it?
HORIO That, too, but rumour has it that she's a flirt.
ROMIO Ye've seen her cheat?
HORIO I havnae witnessed anything, but she's luridly made up.
ROMIO Her face paint may be so, but she's bonnie.
HORIO Whit about her disposition?
ROMIO A fair visage is a sign of a fair disposition.
HORIO Is it truly so? I'm nae sure. One doesnae necessarily guarantee the other.
ROMIO You sound peculiarly certain.
HORIO I cannae help but think there's someone better for ye oot there.

The Living Room of the KAFU Residence

KAFU KANAKO (JURI'S MOTHER) Onasu, Onasu?
ONASU Ye called, madam?
KANAKO Where's Juri?
ONASU Lo, she's nae come, even though I called her a while back? Ho, Juri-chan, Juri-ppe, Juri-rin, Juri-pon!
JURI How noo, Onasu!
ONASU The mistress be calling.
KANAKO Juri, there's a wee matter I wish tae discuss with ye. Ah, Onasu, cud ye run an errand? Go call on my elder sister. I bought some *yatsuhashi* sweeties in Kyoto.
ONASU Noo?

The Living Room of the Kafu Residence

KANAKO Ay. Are ye busy?
ONASU Can it be later?
KANAKO Well, fine, stay with us, then.
ONASU As ye wish.
KANAKO Juri, what age are ye noo?
ONASU Thirteen. Fourteen next month?
JURI That's right.
ONASU How cud I forget. It wis just as Juri-chan wis about tae be born, when that earthquake hit. The previous mistress wis verra afeart o earthquakes, and once the rice bowls on the altar started tae clatter and shake, she shouted, Onasu, it's an earthquake, and rushed oot into the street, at which point I thought the shaking would stop, but a vertical movement that made a thudding noise knocked over the chest of drawers and brought the picture frames clattering down, and just as I thought my life wis coming tae an end, whae gave out a thunderous cry as she wis born but Juri. My, I wis right flabbergasted. Then the shaking completely hauded. This is a very special child, said we as we all rejoiced. Ain't that right, mistress?
KANAKO Ay, so it wis. But this must be close tae the hundredth time we hear this story. Enough of this.
JURI Nae matter how many times we hear it told, it's a kittling tale.
ONASU Amen.
KANAKO I'll be brief, being busy as I am. Ye've had a marriage offer.
ONASU Whit's this noo?
KANAKO Ye can stay here, but dinnae interrupt us.
ONASU Fine!
KANAKO Granted ye are young, but ye're our only daughter.
ONASU Heir tae the family name.
KANAKO Onasu.
ONASU Of course.
KANAKO In the future, ye may, at some point, in many years' time fall in love . . .

The New Romeo and Juliet

ONASU   Cannae say when, cud be the morn.
KANAKO   (*Mouthing 'Onasu' silently.*)
ONASU   (*Ignoring her.*)
KANAKO   Even if ye fall in love, keep in mind, things dinnae ayeweys gan as ye wish.
JURI   Mother, so whae made the offer?
KANAKO   Ay, ay, the son of Itari Hospital.
JURI   A doctor?
ONASU   A looker, he is.
KANAKO   Ay, he reminds me of someone . . .
ONASU   Haruki from the film *What's Your Name*, ye ken, played by Sada Keiji.
KANAKO   I'm sure she dinnae ken whae that is.
ONASU   The samurai film actor Ōkawa Hashizō; the sex appeal just drips off of him, ye ken.
KANAKO   I'm sure she dinnae ken whae that is.
ONASU   Juri, havnae ye seen him?
JURI   He plays the hero Zenigata Heiji, nae? (*Does his signature move of throwing coins as if they are ninja blades.*) I ken him.
ONASU   Blimey, ye think ye're auld enough noo to play dumb. How adorable. That's Harisu.
JURI   How should I ken him? After all, there's a mighty muckle age difference.
KANAKO   Oh. There might be a photo of him in the office. I'll show it tae ye so come with us.

The Director's Office at the International Tourist Hotel Verona

KAFU REIJIRŌ   Well, ye've certainly become a fine young man. And when did ye return?
HARISU   Yesterday evening. I arrived in Rabe'na station and took the bus from there to Berona.

The Director's Office at the International Tourist Hotel Verona

REIJIRŌ Tokyo's so much closer noo, ain't it. In my time, 'twas a two-day journey.

HARISU My father said the same. By the way this is a small souvenir, something for all of you.

REIJIRŌ Lo, we're ayeweys grateful for yer thoughtfulness. How noo, fried sweeties from Nakamura-ya, me gran's favourite. Well, ain't ye become a full-fledged Tokyoite. Nae a trace of the Berona dialect in ye.

HARISU Not really. Once you have me munching on the likes of rice cakes with a chestnut filling and enjoying a dish of sea squirts with a drink in hand, I'll be back to speaking the Berona dialect.

REIJIRŌ Great prospects, blighted future ... (*Laughs.*) bright future ahead. Right radiant that I ain't able tae look straight at ye. Nae wonder yer dad's so happy and cannae contain himself.

HARISU My father's always had a weak heart and so it seems he'd like me to take over as soon as possible. But I have two more years as an intern and the National Examination for Medical Practitioners awaits after that.

REIJIRŌ Indeed. His complexion's improved recently. With bloody age, time accelerates. When young, it's languorous like the flow of the River Eai, but when ye reach the age of yer dad or me, it races by like a river just as it plummets down the Niagara Falls.

HARISU Mr Kafu, you've been to Niagara?

REIJIRŌ Nay, just seen it on the telly. The show with the bonnie lass who prates on in fluent English.

HARISU Oh, yes, the journalist Kanetaka Kaoru.

REIJIRŌ Ay, Kanetaka Kaoru.

HARISU Uh, my father must have spoken with you ...

REIJIRŌ Ah, about Juri. Bon-chan, have ye met with Juri?

HARISU I first saw her as a senior at Itari Junior High, during the *bon* festival dance.

REIJIRŌ And Juri must have been in the third grade or so. Oh, those baby teeth with cavities.

HARISU And last year at the *kokeshi* doll festival during the summer break, we ran into each other for the first time in ages. My bride, I thought. I desired her for my bride.

REIJIRŌ I've been chums with yer dad since we were yea high and yer dad noo and ye yerself are fine fowk, so I cudnae be wishing for aught better.

HARISU Thank you.

REIJIRŌ But Juri's still a child.

HARISU I'll wait until Juri graduates high school.

The Reception Desk at the Berona Hot Spring Inn

MONTA SATOKO (ROMIO'S MOTHER) Dearie, how be ye looking like a dried radish?

MONTA GYŪEMON This here.

SATOKO Monta Gyūemon, Esquire, Director of the Berona Hot Spring Inn. Inaugural celebration for the International Tourist Hotel Verona Annex.

GYŪEMON I dinnae want tae gan.

SATOKO Ay. But one of us will have tae make an appearance.

GYŪEMON That's why I be looking so.

SATOKO I've been given a general idea of what it'll be like from Ochiyo. Seems like all the luminaries of Berona, ye ken, like the politician Sasaki Gōzō, are invited.

GYŪEMON Even that Sasa-go?

SATOKO After all, old man Kafu is head of Sasa-go's campaign. I heard they've even invited the singer Sono Mari.

GYŪEMON She'll really be coming?

SATOKO Ye are a fan, ain't ye?

GYŪEMON Of that trio, she's the sexiest.

SATOKO Ha, whit's so sexy about her?

GYŪEMON Her voice.

SATOKO Uh-huh, if ye say so. We can complain all we like but ye and I still be needing to gan.

GYŪEMON I ken that. But I feel nae weel when I be seeing the mug of that Kafu.

The Reception Desk at the Berona Hot Spring Inn

SATOKO Noo, don't ye be ganing on like a wee bairn.

GYŪEMON I've got me feelings under control. But our manager and bath attendants and maids and the fowk we have business with like the sarashina soba noodle shop and the Chinese diner and the fishmonger and the butcher, they all say they cannae stand him. Why for send an invitation when he kens this? I wudnae be surprised if he's sent one tae everyone. Whit's going through that head of his?

SATOKO Must be he's being mature about all this.

GYŪEMON Nay, he's a show-off. I am the pillar that makes Berona hot spring a community, that's what he be wanting tae show the luminaries. It's all just for show.

SATOKO Ho, Horio.

HORIO Ma'am, have ye seen this?

SATOKO We have one here.

HORIO Dad told me tae ask ye.

SATOKO Whuther or nae we're attending?

HORIO Ay. Dad says he dinnae want tae gan and since he's trying tae get mam tae gan insteid, they're in the mids o' a catterbatter.

GYŪEMON What did I tell ye? Lo, another one's coming.

KYŪSHIRŌ Uncle, have ye seen this?

HORIO Got one here.

KYŪSHIRŌ Ye're here, too.

HORIO I'm just after arriving.

KYŪSHIRŌ Gran said they ain't ganing. Then granddad said they'd have tae, and so gran and granddad are quarrelling.

SATOKO (*Laughs.*)

GYŪEMON This ain't nae laughing matter.

SATOKO Sorry.

KYŪSHIRŌ Their daughter's right nice, but the old geezer and that cousin of theirs . . .

HORIO The son of Kintoki Construction, ain't he?

KYŪSHIRŌ Chibō Ruto. A right tosser. Flashy clothes, picking up birds in that car of his.

SATOKO As they say, once ye hate a man, ye hate everything about him.
GYŪEMON Ye sound like you're indifferent to all this.
SATOKO I'm nae. I ain't fond of the way the Kafus do things. But I ain't happy about how we're feuding in this here wee town, either. Ain't there anything tae be done?
KYŪSHIRŌ It all comes down tae Uncle Monta taking charge, I suppose.
GYŪEMON Ah, tae be or nae tae be, ain't it?
HORIO As in *Hamlet*.
GYŪEMON There wis that performance in Berona Hot Spring some time ago.
SATOKO Dearie, ye be coming?
GYŪEMON Ay. After we get a drink.
KYŪSHIRŌ That's a fine idea. We best be keeping a close eye on them tae see what they're doing, whit they're saying.
HORIO By the way, auntie, has Romio been invited, too?
SATOKO Ay, it's the three of us.
GYŪEMON That lad just reads novels, has his head in the clouds. Cannae tell what he's thinking. Nae need tae take him.
KYŪSHIRŌ It'll get his mind off of things. Right, Horio?
HORIO Indeed.
KYŪSHIRŌ Nae worries, we'll be taking him along.
GYŪEMON Then tell your dad and mam, your granddad and gran, that's what we'll do. And give them our best.

The Itari Pub

ERI Phew, I'm pure done in. Good mistress, a pint, a proper cauld one!
RI Whit'll we be harking tae today?
ERI Me brother, when he goes tae a sushi place, ayeweys orders the same things. First squid, then next octopus and tuna. After that he debates whit tae get, but it has tae be squid! Them three are the only things he'll have.

The Itari Pub

RI Whit's your point?
ERI Ye're going tae play that teen idol Funaki Kazuo again, ain't you?
RI Of course. There ain't naething wrong with that.
ERI Put yerself in our shoes.
RI But it's me own money I be spending tae listen tae him. I barely make meself up, and I work and work, and I be sending money tae me mam back home. The only thing I got tae look forward tae is buying the gossip magazine *Myōjō* every week at the bookshop and harking tae songs here every noo and then. (*Begins to cry.*)
ERI Ain't nae need tae cry.
LANDLADY My, whit's the matter? A fellow break up with ye?
ERI Kure-chan, let's drink.
RI Ay.
ERI Cheers.
RI My, that hits the spot.
ERI Sure does.
LANDLADY Come tae think of it, there's that inaugural party at the International Tourist Hotel the morn.
ERI It's supposed tae be a big deal.
LANDLADY That's fine, but it fashes me.
ERI Whit does?
LANDLADY Seems like that annex will have everything from a muckle souvenir shop and a pub tae a ramen shop. Ho, stationmaster. Come on in. Finished for the day? Ye must be beat. My, so ye've come with Sashimi the fishmonger.
EKINO The usual, please. I ran into Sashimi just around the corner.
SASHIMI I felt I cud use a drink. And that made me think of ye.
LANDLADY Ye sure ken how tae mak a woman happy.
EKINO Lo, Sami-chan, ye're early today.
ERI That's cause I had the late shift the streen.
LANDLADY Sashimi, are ye thinking of your mam in Ōma?

The New Romeo and Juliet

SASHIMI   When I be cleaning tuna, I sometimes hear me mam calling, 'Sashimi!'

LANDLADY   It wis just after ye finished junior high, so it must have been about five years ago. That being said, how did she come tae name ye Sashimi?

SASHIMI   Me family name's Maguro, me given name's Sashimi. I got me a ridiculous name, ain't I? Must be 'cause she wis so skint she cud never eat sashimi.

ALL   Mm-hmm . . .

ERI   So, ma'am, whit ye were saying.

EKINO   Anything the matter?

NOMIYA   Well, ye ken the International Tourist Hotel built that annex? Everyone's fashed that it'll keep people from coming into the town of Berona Hot Spring.

EKINO   That's understandable. The head of the local business association wis fashed for the same reason.

RI   Uh, would it be alright if I turned on the jukebox?

EKINO   I dinnae mind. Kure-chan, are ye playing 'High School Senior' again?

RI   Sorry.

NOMIYA   The International Tourist Hotel dinnae care aboot naething but whit lies outwith. Seems they're tight with politicians, too. They're nae so much part of Berona Hot Springs as – whit's it called? – a franchise. They probably want to build the same kind of place here and there. Rumour has it they've bought an inn in Akiu Hot Springs.

EKINO   Kafu is a developer, after all.

ERI   I dinnae like that maun.

SASHIMI   I do. He's a fine fellae.

RI   (*Sings along to 'High School Senior',*)

LANDLADY   The constable's pistol went off three times today. Everyone must be ganing radge today.

ERI   Well, one of those three shots wis mine. Sashimi wis there too.

SASHIMI   Ah, that shot.

LANDLADY   What's tae come of all this flyting in such a wee town as this?

EKINO   Dinnae I ken it, but I cannae haud it, (*sings*) '*hore sui sui sui dararatta sura sura sui sui sui*' (*So sings everyone as they exit.*)

Inaugural Party for the International Tourist Hotel Verona Annex

REIJIRŌ   Well, well, welcome.

KANAKO   It's ayeweys good tae see ye.

The guests of the KAFU*s arrive one after another and the couple are busy greeting them.*

Music plays and people crowd the room.

KYŪSHIRŌ   Those fireworks, were they for this party?

HORIO   Seems so.

KYŪSHIRŌ   Whit a waste.

HORIO   They say there'll be a hundred consecutive fireworks tonight.

KYŪSHIRŌ   Blimey. Where's Romio?

HORIO   Whit, he wis with us till a moment ago. I'll gan search for him.

KYŪSHIRŌ   I ain't surprised since that lad ain't fond of crowds. There's nae clear reason for him tae come here.

ROMIO   Uh, where's Horio?

KYŪSHIRŌ   Looking for ye. How noo, it's Chibō. Romio, dinnae ye look at him.

RUTO   Whit book's that?

KYŪSHIRŌ   Whit do ye care?

RUTO   Herman Hesse, is it? 'Schön ist die Jungend, sie kommt nicht mehr'. How sentimental. Ain't there other things ye should be reading?

KYŪSHIRŌ   I'm warning ye, back off.

ROMIO   Kyūshirō, it's fine.

KYŪSHIRŌ   What an eejit!
RUTO   I dare ye tae call me that agane.
KYŪSHIRŌ   We ain't here out of our own choice. We were asked, by yer uncle.
RUTO   Invited, are ye? I didnae realize that. I thought ye were a door-to-door salesman.
KYŪSHIRŌ   Ye scunner!
ROMIO   Kyūshirō!
HORIO   Romio, I went looking for ye. Whit happened?
KYŪSHIRŌ   That poser there's picking a fight with us.
HORIO   Sono Mari's just arrived. There's a huge crowd in front of the station.
KYŪSHIRŌ   Nae kidding? We shouldnae let our invitation gan to waste. Let's eat.

ROMIO, EN HORIO *and* MAKI KYŪSHIRŌ *wander around the venue for a while.* SONO MARI *appears amid applause. She sings* 'So So Desperate to See You'.

SONO MARI (*Sings.*)
   The only one I loved is you and only you, this I know but even so
   Can't tie together these heartstrings of ours, we two are such lovers
   I am so in love, I am so in love
   A kiss, that's what I wanted, even so
   I am so sad, how can I not cry.
ROMIO   Horio, whae's that?
HORIO   Huh? That lass? Dinnae ken. Whae is she, Kyūshirō?
KYŪSHIRŌ   I dinnae ken is what I'd like tae say, but I'll tell ye. A wean in junior high.
HORIO   She's bonnie. Ain't she, Romio?
ROMIO   Ah.
HORIO   Gan on.
KYŪSHIRŌ   A senior at the Miyagino Gakuin Junior High. A member of the art society.

HORIO   Gan on. Lo, Romio's gone.
KYŪSHIRŌ   That lad's surprisingly ballsy. There he gans.
HORIO   Where?
KYŪSHIRŌ   Close tae her. There.
HORIO   Uh-oh.
ROMIO   This dumpling is delectable. Have you tried it?
JURI   No, not yet.
ROMIO   With so many people here, it's impossible to savour the food properly, isn't it?
JURI   No. And I am not hungry.
ROMIO   I'm famished. This is my tenth dumpling.
JURI   (*Laughs.*)
ROMIO   I've not seen you in these parts. Do you go to school in Berona?
JURI   No, I have been at a school run by the university in Sendai since I was seven. I've always been schooled outside my school district.
ROMIO   Indeed? No wonder.
JURI   What is that in your pocket?
ROMIO   Eh, this paperback? Don't mind this.
JURI   I love books.
ROMIO   Do you? For example?
JURI   Do you know Kita Morio?
ROMIO   *The Voyages of Doktor Mambo*!
JURI   Such a wonderful novel, isn't it.
ROMIO   For sure. Undoubtedly delightful.
JURI   Did you know that Kita Morio studied at the medical school of Seihoku University in Sendai? Being in Sendai makes me feel close to him, which is why I love being there.
ROMIO   I know what you mean.
JURI   And this?
ROMIO   Hesse.
JURI   Oh, 'Schön ist die Jungend, sie kommt nicht mehr'.
ROMIO   Have you read it?

The New Romeo and Juliet

JURI   I love it!
ONASU   Juri-chan, yer mam be wanting a word with ye.
JURI   Of course. Well, I'll be seeing you.
ROMIO   Of course. I'll definitely be seeing you.
KYŪSHIRŌ   Romio, ye cad!
ROMIO   What are ye talking about?
KYŪSHIRŌ   A lady's man. Swifter than the strides of the number one sprinter of Itari Senior High's track and field team, Maki Kyūshirō.
ROMIO   Ye have it all wrong.
KYŪSHIRŌ   Riddy, are ye?
HORIO   Romio, ye are aware, ain't ye?
ROMIO   About what?
HORIO   That lass, she's Kafu's only child.
ROMIO   Aye right . . .
KYŪSHIRŌ   So ye didnae ken. Jumped the gun, did ye?
HORIO   Time tae head home.
KYŪSHIRŌ   Ho, let's go, Romio.
JURI   Onasu, can ye tell me something?
ONASU   Anything ye'd like tae ken.
JURI   Do ye ken that lad?
ONASU   Kyūshirō, heir to the Maki Timber business.
JURI   Nae, next tae him.
ONASU   This side of Horio the milkman?
JURI   Yes, yes.
ONASU   He's a Monta.
JURI   A Monta? Of the Berona Inn?
ONASU   Ay. He's the heir, Romio. For why?
JURI   Nae reason.
ONASU   Best be avoiding the crack with him. Since the master will scold ye.

The party continues for a while, then it ends.

The Balcony of the KAFU Residence

ROMIO   How can I gan hame when my heart still bides here?
HORIO   Romio! Romio! Where are ye?
KYūSHIRŌ   He's snuck hame.
HORIO   The Berona Inn's that way. Romio went this way. I cud swear he climbed this here wall . . . Kyūshirō, ye call him, too.
KYūSHIRŌ   So I will. Romio! It's I, Rozako. Where are ye? Ho, Romio!
HORIO   Romio will be vexed at ye.
KYūSHIRŌ   Let him be vexed. I vex him so he'll appear.
HORIO   Shh! What noise wis that?
KYūSHIRŌ   Must be nerves. The sound of the heart beating.
HORIO   I dinnae think so.
KYūSHIRŌ   Of my heart.
HORIO   How now?
KYūSHIRŌ   Come with us. We won't find him if he disnae want tae be found.

EN HORIO and MAKI KYūSHIRŌ exit.

ROMIO   Phew! Whit's that light? The east? The sun, then? That's Kafu Juri. Does she speak? Nay, she does nae speak. Does she? She does nae. It does nae matter. Her een speak. They be twinkling. I ain't sure if they be stars in the night sky or Juri's een. Lo, she moves. She leans her cheek on her haun. Ah, that haun. I be wanting tae be that haun.
JURI   Ay me.
ROMIO   She be speaking. This time, I'm sure. For her mouth opened so.
JURI   Monta, Monta, Monta Romio . . . why for are ye a Monta? If ye leave behind the Montas, I'll put the Kafus behind me . . .
ROMIO   Whit to do . . . Shall I haud me weesht and hear more? Ho.

The New Romeo and Juliet

JURI   Even if ye be nae a Monta, ye are yerself. What's Monta? It ain't yer face nor haun nor foot. A cherry blossom, by any other name, would bloom as sweet. So yer name, yer surname disnae matter.

ROMIO   Ay, as a matter of course, then, I'll nae more be Monta!

JURI   How noo! Whae's it?

ROMIO   I donae want tae tell ye by name. Nay, I have nae name nae more. I'm just after writing 'Monta' on paper and tearing the word.

JURI   Ho, the voice . . . that me lugs have heard before. Whit a familiar sound. Are ye nae Romio, and a Monta?

ROMIO   Neither. They lie right here rejected.

JURI   How did ye sneak into this yard, I wonder. These walls are right tall.

ROMIO   With these, these wings.

JURI   Whit, wings?

ROMIO   Love's wings. This is whit is known as a metaphor, a figure of speech.

JURI   A form of rhetoric, ain't it?

ROMIO   I'm impressed.

JURI   We learned this in language arts.

ROMIO   So, ye are a canny lass.

JURI   Nay, but I kinda like language arts.

ROMIO   I do, too. I dinnae like maths, though.

JURI   Same here.

ROMIO and JURI (*Laugh.*)

ROMIO   Whit were we speaking about?

JURI   Wings.

ROMIO   Of love.

JURI   Ay, but if anyone sees ye, ye'd be in peril.

ROMIO   Dinnae fash yerself, for I don the cloak of night.

JURI   In any case, they might murder ye.

ROMIO   How?

JURI   With a gun, like this.

The Balcony of the Kafu Residence

ROMIO   Like they'd shoot a bear? But I'm nae even a wee bit scared of that. There lies more peril in yer een.

JURI   Peril? How?

ROMIO   How do I explain this . . . As they twinkle, they stab us here. There lies the peril. But I dinnae care. Stab away. I would happily die.

JURI   How? Do ye hate me, tae die happily?

ROMIO   How cud I hate ye? I would die happily since I ken whit's in yer heart, whit's in your thoughts. Noo I ken that I'm in yer heart, I'm so happy, I'd gladly die. Nay, I'm so happy I cud faint and die. That's whit I mean.

JURI   Then dinnae die, but live and live on.

ROMIO   I'll live, I'll live on. But if I'm nae at all in yer thoughts, life has nae purpose, so I might as well be killed by a stray bullet from a matagi hunter's gun.

JURI   Dinnae I tell ye? And dinnae ye hear?

ROMIO   Ay, it wis like I wis dreaming. I asked meself, is this really happening?

JURI   It wis actually a right mortifying thing. Like having a diary read, nay even more mortifying. After all, I wis speaking those words. We'd only just met. And such thoughts that had only just formed in my heart, unshapen thoughts too early tae ken if they be true or nae; I voiced such thoughts even before I wis certain of them; and I had those thoughts overheard.

ROMIO   Are ye sorry for it?

JURI   A wee bit.

ROMIO   Indeed.

JURI   But dinnae mind. When I realized ye were listening, there wis another side of me that cud have taken over and said, 'Scram ye eejit. Of course, it's all a lie' or 'It ain't about ye. Whit a self-involved lad, ye are' but it didnae . . .

ROMIO   For why did ye decide ye liked me?

JURI   I hae never met anyone like ye. Honest and passionate and kind and a wee bit uncouth and . . .

ROMIO   And?

JURI   With a twinkle in yer een.

ROMIO   It's too dark, ye cannae see me een.

JURI   At the party, when I first met ye.

ROMIO   Ah. That must be because ye were reflected in them.

JURI   And ye can make me heart skip a beat with such words.

ROMIO   Ah, me friends and me mam keep saying that I read so muckle and so everything I say sounds pretentious.

JURI   I dinnae think so. I like it. That's whit I like about ye. I like books and I like novels and stories and plays.

ROMIO   I'm gled we share these loves. I've never met anyone like ye aither. Where have ye been hiding yerself in such a wee town as Berona.

JURI   I've ayeweys been here.

ROMIO   Have ye?

JURI   Perhaps you cudnae see me since I'm such a toatie thing.

ROMIO   (*Laughing.*)   Dinnae think so.

JURI   And nae bonnie.

ROMIO   Ye are bonnie. Right bonnie. More than that moon.

JURI   The moon, it grows thin and grows fat.

ROMIO   More than the stars. More than the sun.

JURI   Dinnae compare me tae anything.

ROMIO   Right ye are, naething compares tae ye.

JURI   (*Laughs.*)

ROMIO   Do ye find it funny?

JURI   Tae hear ye say that with such a serious look on yer face . . .

ROMIO   Is that daft?

JURI   Ye are bonnie, though it's nae something that's said tae an older man.

ROMIO   The night is full of stars.

JURI   So it is.

ROMIO   Tae look at them thus, I see yer een among them. Pure bonnie.

JURI   Oh, such joy ... But ain't it too rash, too sudden? Why, like lightning that lights up and fades even before it's mentioned.
ONASU   Juri-chan, whit ye be doing?
JURI   Oh, I maun be awa'.
ROMIO   Will ye gan already? Bide a while longer.
JURI   Well, another three minutes.
ONASU   For why are ye talking tae yerself in such a loud voice?
JURI   I'll be there anon.
ROMIO   I wanted tae tell ye ...
JURI   Whit?
ONASU   Why's yer bum oot the windae? It'll be thought ye've gane radge.
ROMIO   I've forgot.
JURI   (*Laughs.*)
ROMIO   Will I see ye the morn?
JURI   Ay.
ROMIO   So then.
JURI   So then, guid night.
ROMIO   See ye.
JURI   See ye.

The Matagi Hunter's Hut

SANKICHI   That wis close. Ye were almost done for, chief.
MATAGI (RENSU NOBUO)   Really. It cud hae been me funeral about noo. But, well, it's been like I've been living on borrowed time since I wis three, so I'll have lived much longer than expected nae matter when I die.
SANKICHI   Whit happened?
MATAGI   Dinnae ken how many times I've told ye; ye ayeweys ask, whit happened, dinnae ye?
SANKICHI   But whit happened?
MATAGI   With that catastrophic earthquake, ye ken, the mountain before me een collapsed like it had turned tae

water, like the mountain became the sea. Me dad wis in Sendai and survived, but me mam hung her three-year-old bairn from that big beech tree and wis washed away.

SANKICHI   Ah, so it did, so it did. The sea in our parts rose like a mountain and the water wis like earth and sand. I wis at me elementary school, but all me freens were washed away by the tsunami.

MATAGI   That's right. Sanki, ye are from Shizugawa, ain't ye. Have ye remembered?

SANKICHI   Vaguely.

MATAGI   It's nae a bad thing, tae have yer lugs shut off and yer mind go foggy. Cannae gan on living without forgetting.

SANKICHI   Forgetting's nae guid. We cud be washed away by the tsunami again.

MATAGI   So ye are able tae speak words of wisdom noo and again.

SANKICHI   And that three-year-old bairn, did he die?

MATAGI   Still lives. I'm that bairn.

SANKICHI   Thank heaven, that's a relief, such a relief. Guid tae have ye living.

ROMIO   Old man, are ye in?

SANKICHI   Whae is it?

MATAGI   We're here. It's Romio.

SANKICHI   From the Berona Inn?

MATAGI   Ay.

ROMIO   Good morning.

MATAGI   Ye are up right early, ain't ye.

SANKICHI   Well, I'll be leaving noo.

MATAGI   Take some bear meat stew with ye. It's tidy with all the gamey gust taen oot.

SANKICHI   Thank ye for ayeweys being so generous. Well, I'll be around again. See ye.

MATAGI   Take care.

ROMIO   This here's a souvenir from the school trip.

MATAGI   Thank ye. So where did ye gan?

The Matagi Hunter's Hut

ROMIO   Hokkaidō.
MATAGI   Ah, and how wis it?
ROMIO   Muckle. The roads were twice as wide as the ones here, and the sky wis muckle, and the air so fresh.
MATAGI   Ay.
ROMIO   We had miso ramen noodles in the Susukino part of Sapporo. It wis right tidy.
MATAGI   Wis it, noo. And are ye visiting this early tae talk about ramen noodles?
ROMIO   Nay.
MATAGI   Ye didnae sleep last night, did ye?
ROMIO   How can ye tell?
MATAGI   Look in a mirror, ye've got rings under yer een.
ROMIO   So I do.
MATAGI   Ye've been with a lass.
ROMIO   Ay. How do ye ken?
MATAGI   Out of breath and a glare deep in yer een.
ROMIO   Ye can tell?
MATAGI   How many years do ye think I've observed bears in heat?
ROMIO   I'm nae a bear.
MATAGI   (*Laughing.*) Is it Rozako?
ROMIO   Nay, it's nae longer her.
MATAGI   Whit? Nae even bears are so fickle.
ROMIO   I'm nae fickle. This time, it's the real thing.
MATAGI   Such a heartbreaker, ye are.
ROMIO   Old man, let me explain.
MATAGI   Ye've brought me a souvenir, so I'll listen.
ROMIO   Do ye ken Kafu Juri of the International Tourist Hotel Verona?
MATAGI   Course I do. She's their only child and in junior high.
ROMIO   Seems she's gane to another school district, to a private junior high in Sendai.
MATAGI   A school for rich lasses. What about her?
ROMIO   . . .

MATAGI Ye ain't saying . . .
ROMIO I've fallen in love with her.
MATAGI Whit do ye mean, ye've fallen in love with her. Ye, whae, till just noo wis curled up in that corner there, sighing and weeping as ye cried out the name Rozako, Rozako. Unbelievable.
ROMIO Hear me, it's different this time. I'm really. . .
MATAGI Gan there and splash some water on yer face.
ROMIO In love.
MATAGI Unbelievable.
ROMIO I'm really, really, from the bottom of my heart, in love.
MATAGI But ye realize that here in Berona Hot Springs, from the Taishō and the Meiji periods and even as far back as the Edo period, yer Monta clan and the Kafus of which she's the only child have gotten along nae better than cats and dogs.
ROMIO But whit happened?
MATAGI Ye widna understand. Grown-ups have their reasons.
ROMIO That makes nae sense.
MATAGI Romio.
ROMIO Then I dinnae want to grow up
MATAGI (*Poses with his rifle to polish it.*)
ROMIO Old man, shoot me.
MATAGI Stop yer havering, ye dafty.
ROMIO I'm daft. But, old man, for the longest time, I didnae ken for why I wis living. I dinnea like school and I'm nae that fond of studying, so for why do I need tae gan to university? Dad dinnae say naething but just give it a try and me mam only keeps reminding me that I'm heir to the Berona Hot Spring Inn with its three-hundred-year history. Whit am I?
MATAGI Ye are the grandson of the previous Monta Gyūemon and the son of the present Gyūemon.
ROMIO I am. But I'm Romio. Simply Romio.
MATAGI Simply, say ye?
ROMIO Ay. I thought if I did some reading, I would ken whae I am, whit I want tae do and where I ought tae go, but I

dinnae. The words build up within me, but I still dinnae ken.

MATAGI (*Plays a syrinx made from empty bullet casings.*)

ROMIO But the moment I saw her, I saw Kafu Juri and I kent, I felt I kent.

MATAGI Ye felt ... feelings are whit rules life. But that's whit's important in life. Truth manifests itself through chance.

ROMIO Truth manifests itself through chance? Whit do ye mean?

MATAGI Exactly whit I said. Ye've been waiting all this time.

ROMIO Waiting?

MATAGI For Juri.

ROMIO And Juri?

MATAGI Probably the same for her.

ROMIO How do ye ken?

MATAGI It's like a mirror. People reflect people. Ye've touched Juri with the intensity of yer feelings, that's why ye are here. I've kent ye since ye were yea high, but have never seen ye look so serious, so impressive. In the expression of yer face, I see Juri's face.

ROMIO Whit should I do?

MATAGI The strife that's continued here in the town of Berona of the Itari hot spring district for yonks, even yont our imagination; whit will bring about its end cud be the twae of ye.

JURI'S Room in the KAFU Residence

KANAKO So they've suggested we all get together once for a meal.

JURI Ye and dad should gan without me.

KANAKO Dinnae ye be difficult.

JURI I've told ye, I dinnae want tae gan.

KANAKO Haud pouting like a petulant bairn.

JURI It ain't naething more than a simple meal, is it?

KANAKO Nae exactly, but it's nae a proper engagement dinner, either.
JURI I'm nae ganing. And me finals are coming up.
KANAKO Dearie, ye've come at the right moment.
REIJIRŌ Whit has Juri said?
JURI Why do I have tae gan all the way tae Hamada?
REIJIRŌ Well, Dr. Harisu's family's from Hamada and it seems there's a place that serves mighty tidy fish there. So, ye see, they thought it would be the perfect opportunity and invited us.
JURI I winnae.
REIJIRŌ I've told ye, we're deeply indebted tae Dr. Harisu. He wis even yer reference when ye entered Miyagino Gakuin Elementary School.
JURI It's just an excuse tae matchmake, ain't it?
REIJIRŌ Blimey, ye are an impossible bairn.
KANAKO Dearie, there be nae need tae shout so.
REIJIRŌ How dare ye question yer parents when ye're naething more than a wee bairn in junior high. In yer position, ye need to hold yer tongue and agree with everything we say. I have nae need for a daughter like ye. I dinnae even want to see yer mug.
KANAKO Dearie, there be nae need tae gan that far. And Juri, dinnae ye be so hard-headed. Apologize tae yer dad.
REIJIRŌ It's a chore commuting all that way tae school, anyway, so we'll have ye stay with Bonbon's mam in Hamada. Till ye finish high school.
JURI I willnae gan.
REIJIRŌ Nay, ye will.
JURI I willnae gan.
REIJIRŌ Ye will.
JURI . . . fine. I'll gan. Does that make ye happy? Ye want me tae dine in Hamada? I'll gan. I'm sorry.
REIJIRŌ Ye should have answered obediently, as noo ye've done, from the start.

KANAKO   All's well, all's well. I'll give Dr Harisu a call.
REIJIRŌ   Ye ken the quid o this, dannae ye, Juri?
JURI   Ay.

The Public Bath of Berona Hot Springs

In the women's bath downstage are KUREKO RI, SAMI ERI *and the landlady.* SANKICHI *sits where the attendant's booth is.*

RI   My, that's nice, Sankichi, the bath's the perfect temperature today.
SANKICHI   Whit did ye say?
ERI   Just telling ye, the bath's perfect.
SANKICHI   Guid tae hear, guid tae hear. Kure-chan, sing something for us.
RI   Sure thing. Whit shall I sing?
ERI   There ain't that many tunes ye can sing.
RI   I've learnt a few more recently. Sankichi, is there anyone in the gents' bath?
SANKICHI   Nae one at the moment, so don't ye fash.
RI   Ye ken Tashiro Miyoko and the Manly Sisters?
LANDLADY   It's the Mahina Stars.
RI   The Manly Sisters, the Mahina Stars ... it's the same thing.
LANDLADY   Nae at all.
RI   All this time, I thought they were the Manly Sisters.
ALL THREE (*Laugh.*)
RI (*Sings.*)   I ended up loving you,
ALL THREE (*Sing.*)   La la lan lan.

The singing continues. SANKICHI *begins to dance, and the butcher and the proprietor of Rairaiken, entering the men's bath, follow suit. It is then that* MAKI KYŪSHIRŌ *and* EN HORIO *enter, and shortly after they are followed by* CHIBŌ RUTO. *Into the women's bath enter* HARU SAZAKO *and* ABURA YŌ.

RI I ended up loving you,
ALL La la lan lan
RI No one else but you, I could die for you
ALL La la lan lan
RI When I'm awake, when I'm asleep, there is no one else but you
KYŪSHIRŌ It sounds like ye are having fun. What are ye doing?
THE BUTCHER It's Kure-chan's solo part.
HORIO Ho, I think I might join ye. I am in love with you, but . . .
RUTO This here's a public bath. What are ye doing? Don't ye agree, Sankichi?
SANKICHI Ah, well.
RUTO Having *tae* listen tae such terrible singing when it's already this baltic only makes me skin crawl even more. Brrr, it's chankin'. Ye are even making the hot water freeze over, don't ye agree, Yō-chan, Saza-chan.
YŌ It be, brrr, right chankin'.
SAZAKO So I see, this is the difference between having central heating throughout the building and using a wood burning stove.
ERI Just where do ye see this difference?
SAZAKO The hot water's turning cauld in just that one spot where ye are, there.
YŌ and SAZAKO (*Laugh.*)
KYŪSHIRŌ All ye do is find faults here and there. Whit's wrong with everyone in the town of Berona singing together? It should be acceptable precisely because this is a public bath. So shut yer gob.
RUTO We're complaining because it's a public bath. Maki Kyūshirō, ye are even more of a bampot than I thought. If ye are so desperate tae sing, ye should go tae the Itari Pub.
YŌ and SAZAKO Ye tell them.

KYŪSHIRŌ Whit's that, ye tosser? It's because of eejits like ye that Berona is gane tae the dogs.

RUTO I dare ye tae say that again.

ROMIO Whit are ye doing?

KYŪSHIRŌ Romio, ye've come just in time.

RUTO Ye run-down hottle! Ye reek! Won't y quickly wash yerselves.

ROMIO Do ye think we smell?

RUTO Ye reek, ye reek, the smell of a jessie (*laughs.*)

KYŪSHIRŌ Enough.

ROMIO Haud yer catterbattering!

KYŪSHIRŌ Romio, how can ye let him talk tae ye like that?

ROMIO We're all like kinfolk here.

RUTO Kinfolk? Ye ain't got some hackit scheme up yer sleeve, have ye?

ROMIO Like whit?

RUTO Like making our Juri yer bride.

ROMIO Whit if that's me plan.

RUTO I'll kill ye.

MAKI KYŪSHIRŌ *and* CHIBŌ RUTO *in the men's bath start grappling with each other and a brawl begins in the women's bath, as well.* MAKI KYŪSHIRŌ, *attempting to stop* CHIBŌ RUTO *from attacking* ROMIO, *slips and sustains a concussion. Seeing that,* ROMIO *becomes enraged and clobbers* CHIBŌ RUTO, *who loses consciousness. Both* MAKI KYŪSHIRŌ *and* CHIBŌ RUTO *are rushed to the Itari Hospital.*

The Matagi Hunter's Hut

MATAGI Whit do ye think ye're doing? The beasts in the mountains have more sense than ye. The beasts trust one another; whit they are feart of the most are humans. Matagis as well, we are nae feart of bears. Whit we are feart of are stray bullets from fellow hunters and jealousy. That's why

The New Romeo and Juliet

we never gan into the mountains alone and shoot muckle bears. We gan in together and share our triumphs. Noo, haud those unmanly tears!
ROMIO Whit am I tae do?
MATAGI It's fortunate that naither injury wis serious. Juri-chan, how is Ruto?
JURI Seems he had tae have about seven stiches.
MATAGI And I suppose he bled plenty.
JURI That he did. Me aunt fainted after seeing the bluid.
MATAGI Ye are much tougher than ye look. (*To* ROMIO, *who begins crying.*) Haud yer greeting! It'll do ye nae guid sulking and pouting. Come noo, collect yerself.
JURI And it seems there wis nae damage tae the brain.
MATAGI That's a relief . . .
JURI Dear old man, please help us.
MATAGI (*Plays the syrinx made from empty bullet casings.*)
JURI Whit is that?
MATAGAI Empty bullet casings used tae signal fellow hunters when we're in the mountain. Bears cannae hear this. So, we'll have tae gan with this.
JURI Wi' whit?
MATAGI Juri-chan. Ye are still a quine but right sensible, so I'll ask ye. Are ye ready for a life together with this lad?
JURI Ay.
MATAGI How so?
JURI (*Placing her hand on her chest.*) I am drawn tae this in Romio.
MATAGI Right then. Romio and Juri-chan, listen closely. This, before ye win asleep tonight, ye will each drink in yer own rooms. It ain't pleasant, but make sure ye drink it all.
JURI And then?
MATAGI The morn's morn, ye both will be cauld.
ROMIO And we'll be dead.
MATAGI Did ye lie when ye said ye cud die?
ROMIO It wis nae lie. But will I be seeing Juri again?

MATAGI   Ye will. If ye do exactly as I tell ye. This drug will place ye in a death-like state for twenty-four hours, but ye will awaken without fail, so dinnae fash yerself. Juri-chan are ye nae feart?
JURI   I am nae feart.
MATAGI   Romio, whit about ye?
ROMIO   I am nae feart.
MATAGI   Leave the rest tae me. I've been thinking, I'd like tae risk me life doing guid while I still have a life tae risk. Well, this is me chance. Noo, dinnae ye spill that.

The KAFUs and the MONTAs stumble back and forth in confusion. The screams of their families. The sound of an ambulance siren.

The Attendant's Booth of the Public Bath of Berona Hot Spring

SANKICHI   The whole of Berona Hot Spring, leaving the guests completely unattended, wis in a pure state of pandemonium. Up and down and right and left. A right fankle. When Dr Harisu of Itari Hospital, with a mighty sad face, said in a voice nae louder than the sound of a mosquito, 'I'm sorry', there wis naething but tears and tears and tears. But there wis also such a peaceful, gentle calm, that we'd never experienced before, and the Kafus and the Montas and all the young fowk bowed and took one another's hauns. We were miserable and troubled by the thought, 'Alack, did it have tae take something like this tae bring us together?' Can ye believe it? Ren-chan, the matagi hunter, kept mum even with me, like we wernae friends. Must have been fashed I'd blether. In the end, that's how things turned out.

The corpses of the two are laid out in the compound of Furaia Temple and as the head priest recites the Buddhist sutra, the funeral quietly takes place. The monotonous beat of the wooden mokugyo *drum continues. But then the sound of the drum changes into what seems to be strange, joyous music and* ROMIO *and* JURI, *who should be dead, suddenly rise and start dancing. Those attending the funeral are bewildered; but being drawn in by the deputy head priest, who begins to dance while matter-of-factly continuing the sutra, they start to dance. Everyone exits the stage dancing.*

Fifty years pass. SANKICHI, *whose age is indeterminate, appears.*

SANKICHI   Since then, Berona Hot Spring has improved all together and everyone has become neighbourly with one another. A tidy feat by Rensu, the matagi hunter. Worthy of a Nobel Prize, ye cud even say. And whit of Romio and Juri? See there, they stand together happily. The International Tourist Hotel Verona and the Berona Hot Spring Inn merged to become the Berona Hikari Hotel; and the twae of them have been its happy owners ever since.

APPENDIX 1

A list of stage productions by the three theatre companies

THE TOKYO SHAKESPEARE COMPANY

Shakespeare productions

1991 September	*The Two Gentlewomen of Verona*§ (Jean-Jean)
1992 February	*Giulietta**§ (Jean-Jean)
1993 April	*Cleopatra VII** (Jean-Jean)
1993 October	*Twelfth Night*§ (Umewaka Noh Gakuin Hall)
1994 September	*The Female Merchant of Venice* (Jean-Jean)
1995 August	*Macbeth* (Edinburgh Fringe Festival)
1996 July	*As You Like It* (Yorozu Studio)
1997 July	*Measure for Measure: Uogokoro areba mizugokoro* (*Tit for Tat*) (Jean-Jean)
1998 December	*Hamlet* (Jean-Jean)
1999 November	*Antony and Cleopatra* (Jean-Jean)
2005 September	*Pericles* (Theater X)
2006 June–July	*A Midsummer Night's Dream* (Ad-lib Theater)
2007 March	*Damashi damasare karasawagi* (*Deceiving and Deceived: Much Ado about Nothing*)* (Yorozu Studio)
2007 October	*Love's Labour's Lost**# (Yorozu Studio)
2008 July	*Queen Margaret* (based on *1*, *2* and *3 Henry VI*)* (Theatre Iwato)

Appendix 1

2009 February	*Falstaff**[1] (Yorozu Studio)
2010 February	*Twelfth Night* (Theatre Iwato)
2010 July	*Jajauma wa ikaga?* (*Fancy a Shrew?*, based on *The Taming of the Shrew*)* (Theatre Iwato)
2011 February	*Hamlet* (Theatre Iwato)
2011 July	*Cymbeline* (Aye Pit Mejiro)
2012 November–December	*Nagai nagai yume no ato ni* (*After a Long, Long Dream*, based on *1* and *2 Henry IV* and *Henry V*)* (Box in Box Theater)
2014 January	*The Merchant of Venice* (Shimokitazawa Geki Shōgekijō)
2015 January	*Falstaff* * (Nippori d-Sōko)
2016 November–December	*Meja meja*: *Measure for Measure* (SPACE Zatsuyū)
2017 June	*Love's Labour's Lost** (Shimokitazawa Geki Shōgekijō)

* Adaptations or reworkings of Shakespeare's plays
§ Translation by Tsubouchi Shōyō
# Adaptation by Okuizumi Hikaru

'Shakespeare through the Looking-Glass' series

1995 March–April	*Ria no sannin musume* (*The Three Daughters of Lear*)** (Jean-Jean)
1996 March	*The Three Daughters of Lear*** (Sendai)
1996 December	*Makubesu saiban* (*The Trial of Macbeth*)** (Yorozu Studio)
1997 September	*The Three Daughters of Lear**** (Kushibiki and Mikawa)

[1] Although this and the 2015 revival production are not part of the 'Shakespeare through the Looking-Glass' series, they are original works that make use of Shakespeare's characters. In 1990, Edo appeared in a different work with the same title that was adapted and directed by Inoue Masaru.

Appendix 1

2000 June	*The Three Daughters of Lear 2000* (Theatre Zamza)
2001 October	*Pōsha no niwa* (*Portia's Garden*) (Momo)
2003 December	*The Trial of Macbeth 2003: Chikyū saigo no hi* (*Earth's Last Day*) (Ad-lib Theater)
2004 July	*The Three Daughters of Lear* (Shimokitazawa Ekimae Theater)
2004 September–October	*Soshite Richādo wa shinda* (*And Thus Richard Died*) (Ad-lib Theater)
2009 September	*The Trial of Macbeth* (Sasazuka Factory)
2012 February	*Mugen enten* (*A Far and Distant Point*, inspired by *Romeo and Juliet*) (Theatre BONBON)
2013 February	*The Three Daughters of Lear* (Shōgekijō Rakuen)
2014 January	*Portia's Garden* (Shimokitazawa Geki Shōgekijō)
2017 November	*Kagami no naka no Henrī VIII* (*Henry VIII through the Looking-Glass*) (Shōgekijō Rakuen)
2019 February	*Kigeki: Romio to Julietto* (*A Comedy: Romeo and Juliet*)[2] (Shimokitazawa Geki Shōgekijō)

** Directed by Maekawa Shirō
***Directed by Yoshida Kōtarō
All other productions directed by Edo Kaoru

---

[2] This is a revised version of the 2012 *Mugen enten*.

Appendix 1

KAKUSHINHAN THEATRE COMPANY

2012 April	*HAMLET X SHIBUYA ~ Light, Was Our Revenge Tarnished?* (GALLERY LE DECO 4)
2012 September	*Romeo and Juliet on the Seashore* (GALLERY LE DECO 4)
2014 June	*King Lear* (SPACE Zatsuyū)
2014 June	*A Midsummer Night's Dream* (SPACE Zatsuyū)
2014 August	*No Justice Titus Andronicus* (SPACE Zatsuyū)
2014 November	*Hamlet* (SPACE Zatsuyū)
2015 April	*Othello – Black or White* (BIG TREE THEATER)
2015 October	Kakushinhan Pocket *The Taming of the Shrew* (GALLERYLE DECO 4)
2016 January	*Julius Caesar* (BIG TREE THEATER)
2016 May	Kakushinhan Pocket *Henry VI* (Theatre Fūshikaden)
2016 May	*Richard III* (Theatre Fūshikaden)
2016 July–August	Pocket *The Taming of the Shrew* (Shinjuku Golden Gai Theater)
2017 January	*Macbeth* (Tokyo Metropolitan Theatre)
2017 March	Pocket *A Midsummer Night's Dream* (Theatre Fūshikaden)
2017 August	*Titus Andronicus* (Kichijoji Theatre)
2018 April	*Hamlet* (BIG TREE THEATER)
2018 July	Pocket *The Winter's Tale* (WestEndStudio)
2018 November–December	Pocket *The Merchant of Venice* (Harajuku VACANT)
2019 February	Kakushinhan Studio *Romeo and Juliet* (Theatre Fūshikaden)

Appendix 1

2019 May	*HAMLET X SHIBUYA ~ Light, Was Our Revenge Tarnished?* (reading) (GALLERY LE DECO 4)
2019 July–August	*Wars of the Roses* (Theatre Fūshikaden)
2019 December	Pocket *Romeo and Juliet* (Atelier Fanfare)
2019 December	*Romeo and Juliet on the Seashore* (reading) (Atelier Fanfare)
2020 February–March	Kakushinhan Studio *Julius Caesar* (Theatre Fūshikaden)

THE SHAKESPEARE COMPANY JAPAN

1995 August–September	*Romeo and Juliet* (British Hills, El Park Sendai Studio Hall, Tome Festival Hall)
1996 March	*Umi e nori yuku mono tachi* (*Riders to the Sea*) (Translated and written by Kanomata Masayoshi, directed by Shimodate Kazumi) (Event Forum Yamaguchi)
1996 August–September	*A Midsummer Night's Dream in Matsushima Bay* (Urato Islands General Development Center in Nonojima, El Park Sendai Studio Hall)
1997 August–September	*Much Ado About Nothing in the Jōmon Period* (Fujisawacho Ceramic Art Center, El Park Sendai Studio Hall, Sannai-Maruyama Site)
1998 August–September	*Twelfth Night of the Sendai Clan* (Yūbikan Forest Park, Ezuko Hall, El Park Sendai Studio Hall)

1999 summer/winter and 2000 summer	*Macbeth of Mt. Osore* (Osore-zan Bodai-ji Temple, Korakukan Theatre, El Park Sendai Gallery Hall, Rikkōkai Hall, Tagajo City Cultural Center, C too of the Edinburgh Festival Fringe)
2001 September–December	*As You Like It in a Hot Spring Inn* (Naruko Waseda Sajikiyu, El Park Sendai Gallery Hall, Morioka Theatre, Korakukan Theatre)
2006 March, June, September, November, 2007 December and 2008 January, March	*Hamure* (*Hamlet*) *in Ōshū under the Late Tokugawa Shogunate* (El Park Sendai Studio Hall, Osaki-shi Matsuyama Seinen Kōryūkan, Rikkōkai Hall, Morioka Theatre, Izumity 21, Warabi-za Small Theatre, Yūgakukan, Hachinohe City Community Center Culture Hall)
2008 June–September	*The New As You Like It in a Hot Spring Inn* (Naruko Waseda Sajikiyu, El Park Sendai Studio Hall, Rikkōkai Hall)
2009 August–September	*A Midsummer Night's Dream* (Written and directed by Iwazumi Kōichi) (Fujisawacho Nikoniko Dome, Oroshimachi Hato no Ie)
2010 June	Special Performance for the 125th Anniversary of the Waseda University Alumni Association: *Hamure* (*Hamlet*) *in Ōshū under the Late Tokugawa Shogunate* (Okuma Auditorium, Waseda University)
2010 November–December and 2011 February	*Atuy Othello* (Osaki-shi Matsuyama Seinen Kōryūkan, El Park Sendai Gallery Hall, Hachinohe City Community Center Culture Hall)

2012 November–December and 2013 January–April	*The New Romeo and Juliet* (Sake Museum, Ishinomaki City General Welfare Center, Noh Box, Naruko Waseda Sajikiyu, Onagawa Dai-ni Elementary School, Yamamotochō Central Community Center, Yū Hall, Heisei-no Mori Arena, Ikegami Jissōji Temple, Osaki-shi Matsuyama Seinen Kōryūkan, Hisanohama Dai-ichi Elementary School)
2013 November–December and 2014 January–March	*The New King Lear* (Sake Museum, Naruko Waseda Sajikiyu, Hōkokuji Temple, Noh Box, Yamamotocho Central Community Center, Onagawa Dai-ni Elementary School, SanSanKan, former Urato Dai-ni Elementary School, Ikegami Jissōji Temple)
2015 May–November and 2016 February–March	*The New Merchant of Venice* (Naruko Waseda Sajikiyu, Noh Box, Urato Katsurashima Stay Station, SanSanKan, Yamamotocho Central Community Center, Natori City Takadate Elementary School, assembly room of Temporary Housing at Onagawa Multipurpose Sports Park, Ikegami Jissōji Temple)
2016 June	Special performance given by Shimodate Kazumi at the 27th International Japanese-English Translation Conference: *The New Merchant of Venice*, *Atuy Othello*, *Macbeth of Mt. Osore*, *The New King Lear*, and *Hamure in Ōshū under the Late Tokugawa Shogunate* (Sendai International Center)
2018 January–August and 2019 August	*Ainu Othello* (El Park Sendai Studio Hall, International Christian University, Kaderu Hall, Tara Theatre (London))

Appendix 1

2019 November	*Juliet of Tohoku* (A shortened version of *The New Romeo and Juliet*) (Michinoku Jōseki Hanaza)
2020 January	*Lear Sushi* (A shortened version of *The New King Lear*) (Michinoku Jōseki Hanaza)

APPENDIX 2

A list of Shakespeare productions in the Tokyo area in 2019

This list is created from the website, *Tokyo kinkō Shēkusupia geki sukejūru* (*Schedule of Shakespeare Plays in the Tokyo Area*),[1] which is extensive but may not be comprehensive. Lectures on Shakespeare that are not accompanied by a performance and screenings of recorded performances have been left out. When the performance is not a straightforward stage adaptation of Shakespeare or if the performance is in English, there is a short note at the end of the entry.

Date	Title	Theatre Company / Director / Translator / *etc.*	Venue
6, 9 Jan.	*Comedy of Errors*	Shakespeare Theatre	Kichijoji Theater
7–8 Jan.	*A Midsummer Night's Dream*	Shakespeare Theatre	Kichijoji Theater
12 Jan.	*5 nin de 55 fun no Ria Ō nyūmon / 5 nin de 55 fun no Oserō nyūmon* (*King Lear with 5 people in 55 min / Othello with 5 people in 55 min*) Performance of an abridged version of *King Lear* and *Othello*	Gekidanza Nabari Otome	Lilia Hall
18–27 Jan.	*Macbeth*	Gekidan Himawari	Theater Daikanyama

[1] http://iamnotthatiplay.sensyuuraku.com/plays2019.html

Appendix 2

Date	Title	Theatre Company / Director / Translator / *etc.*	Venue
25–26 Jan.	*TIC-TAC Hamlet* Contemporary dance	CHAiroiPLIN dir. and choreo. Suzuki Takurō	The Tokyo Globe
26–27 Jan. & 31 Jan.–3 Feb.	*Twelfth Night*	RoMT dir. Tano Kunihiko trans. Kawai Shōichirō	Wakabacho Warf
28 Jan.	*Sannin de Shēkusupia* Japanese production of *The Complete Works of William Shakespeare (Abridged)*	Chōjūgiga	Theater Green
30 Jan.–4 Feb.	*Hamlet* Stage reading	Koe no Sugureta Haiyū ni yoru Dorama Rīdingu dir. Fukasaku Kenta	Kinokuniya Southern Theater, Takashimaya
1–2 Feb.	*Romio to Jurietto kara umareta mono 2018 tsuā* (*Things Born out of Romeo and Juliet 2018 Tour*) Adaptation by and about people with disabilities	Bird Theatre Company dir. Nakajima Makoto and Saitō Yoriaki	Tokyo Metropolitan Theatre
1–10 Feb.	*Ame no yoru, sanjūnin no Jurietto ga kaette kita* (*On a Rainy Night 30 Juliets Returned*) Original play about performing R&J in Hokuriku	Ryūzanji Company dir. Ryūzanji Shō book Shimizu Kunio	Za Koenji
2 Feb.	*Chōyaku King Lear* One-woman adaptation set in contemporary Japan	Kusunoki Mitsuka Hitori Shakespeare	Asakusa Little Theatre

Appendix 2

Date	Title	Theatre Company / Director / Translator / etc.	Venue
2 Feb.	*Venisu no shōnin Shairokku kara no saishin seikyū* (*Request for a Retrial from the Merchant of Venice, Shylock*) Lecture, stage reading and concert	Machida Danjo Byōdō Festival	Machida Shimin Forum
2–3 Feb.	*Hitoribocchi Richādo* (*Richard All Alone*) One-man adaptation of *Richard III*	Bocchi Kikaku trans. Matsuoka Kazuko adapt. Komase Yui	Subterranean
6 Feb.	*Dezudemōna no shi: Shakespeare Osero yori* (*Desdemona's Death: From Shakespeare's Othello*)	Sōzō Shūdan g-Guraundo dir. and adapt. Kuraudo	Shinjuku Bunka Center
8–24 Feb.	*Henry V*	Sai no Kuni Shakespeare Series dir. Yoshida Kōtarō trans. Matsuoka Kazuko	Saitama Arts Theater
9–10 Feb.	*Macbeth*	Syake-speare trans. Tsubouchi Shōyō	Yamate Gaiety Theater
14–17 Feb.	*Macbeth*	TY Promotion dir. Yokouchi Tadashi trans. Odashima Yūshi	Mitsukoshi Theater
14 Feb.–17 March	*Saishū chinjitsu: soredemo chikyū wa mawaru* (*Final Statement: The Earth Will Continue to Revolve*) Musical about Galileo and Shakespeare meeting	dir. Watanabe Satsuki book Lee Hee-joon	Asakusa Kyūgeki

Appendix 2

Date	Title	Theatre Company / Director / Translator / etc.	Venue
16–24 Feb.	*Joyū tachi no tame no fuyu no yo no yume* (*A Winter Night's Dream for Actresses*) Musical about performing *Midsummer Night's Dream*	LIVEDOG GIRLS dir. and adapt. Yoshida Takehiro trans. Matsuoka Kazuko	Shinjuku Mura LIVE
20–24 Feb.	*Kigeki: Romio to Julietto* (*A Comedy: Romeo and Juliet*) Sequel to *Romeo and Juliet*	Tokyo Shakespeare Company dir. Edo Kaoru book Okuizumi Hikaru	Shimokitazawa Geki Shōgekijō
20–24 Feb.	*Tsuki no hitomi ni akogarete* (*Drawn to the Moon's Gaze*) Fable based on *Measure for Measure* and *Much Ado about Nothing*	Perrot dir. and book Iwamoto Yoshiyuki	Hanamaru Group Ōji Fringe Theatre
22–24 Feb.	*A Midsummer Night's Dream*	Bungakuza trans. Odashima Yūshi	Bungakuza Atelier
23–24 Feb.	*Romeo and Juliet*	Theatre Company Kakushinhan dir. Kimura Ryūnosuke trans. Matsuoka Kazuko	Theatre Fūshikaden
23 Feb.–10 March	*Musical Romeo and Juliet* Japanese production of Presgurvic's *Roméo & Juliette: de la haine à l'amour*	dir. Koike Shūichirō book Gérard Presgurvic	Tokyo International Forum
1–2 March	*Pericles*	Itabashi Engeki Center dir. Endō Ēzō trans. Odashima Yūshi	Itabashi Culture Hall

Appendix 2

Date	Title	Theatre Company / Director / Translator / etc.	Venue
2 March	*Chōyaku Two Gentlemen of Verona* One-woman adaptation set in contemporary Japan	Kusunoki Mitsuka Hitori Shakespeare	Asakusa Little Theatre
2–3 March	*Roméo et Juliette* Opera	Tokyo Opera Produce comp. Charles François Gounod	Nakano ZERO
2–4 March	*Macbeth* Student stage reading	Waseda University dir. Ikuta Miyuki trans. Odashima Yūshi	Waseda Drama-Kan Theatre
11 March	*San'nin de Shēkusupia* Japanese production of *The Complete Works of William Shakespeare (Abridged)*	Chōjūgiga	Theater Green
13, 16, 17 March	*Richard III* Stage reading	New National Theatre KOTSU-KOTSU Project dir. Uyama Hitoshi trans. Odashima Yūshi	New National Theatre
19–21 March	*Much Ado about Nothing*	Gekidan Haiyūza Kenkūjo dir. Mori Hajime trans. Odashima Yūshi	Akasaka Civic Center
21–24 March	*Hamlet*	Gekidan Oshare Daigaku dir. Aoyanagi Mizuki adapt. Itagaki Nanoka trans. Odashima Yūshi	Waltz Tokorozawa

Appendix 2

Date	Title	Theatre Company / Director / Translator / *etc.*	Venue
22–24 March	*Hamlet*	Gekidan Unit Statice dir. Yoshida Kazushi trans. Anzai Tetsuo	Sannō Hills Hall
22–24 March	*Poison* Contemporary dance based on Shakespeare's plays and quotations	dir. and choreo. Hirayama Motoko	Setagaya Public Theatre
23–24 March	*Measure for Measure*	Za Shakespeare DRAMA SHIP dir. and adapt. Jō Haruhiko	Echo Gekijō
24 March–7 April	*Macbeth*	Gekidan Tōen dir. and adapt. Valery Belyakovich trans. Satō Shirō	Theatre Tram
5–7 April	*Richard III* Production from China	National Theatre Company of China dir. Wang Xiaoying	Tokyo Metropolitan Theatre
9–21 April	*Sannin no prinshiparu* (*The Three Principals*) Female pop group entertainment that includes a performance of *Romeo and Juliet*	Nogizaka 46 dir. and adapt. Tani Ken'ichi	Sunshine Theatre
12–28 April	*The Macbeths*	Theatrical Company THE MODERN CLASSICISM dir. and adapt. Natsume Kiriri	THE MODERN CLASSICISM Atelier
13 April	*Chōyaku Taming of a Shrew* One-woman adaptation set in contemporary Japan	Kusunoki Mitsuka Hitori Shakespeare	Asakusa Little Theatre

Appendix 2

Date	Title	Theatre Company / Director / Translator / etc.	Venue
15 April	*San'nin de Shēkusupia* Japanese production of *The Complete Works of William Shakespeare (Abridged)*	Chōjūgiga	Theater Green
18–21 April	*Hamlet*	SKE 48 dir. and book Maruo Maruichirō	Shinagawa Prince Hotel
26–29 April	*Romeo and Juliet*	Willow's dir. and adapt. Yanaginuma Takuya	Meiji University Art Studio
26–29 April	*A Midsummer Night's Dream*	Machi no Seiza dir. and adapt. Toyokawa Ryōta	Hanamaru Group Ōji Fringe Theatre
9 May–2 June	*Hamlet*	dir. Simon Godwin trans. Kawai Shōichirō	Bunkamura Theatre Cocoon
11 May	*Sir Thomas More* One-woman adaptation set in contemporary Japan	Kusunoki Mitsuka Hitori Shakespeare	Asakusa Little Theatre
12 May	*King Lear* Stage reading in English and Japanese	SAYNK dir. Senuma Tatsuya	Kanagawa Kindai Bungakukan
12–19 May	*As You Like It*	Nuthmique dir. and adapt. Nukata Masashi trans. Matsuoka Kazuko	Komaba Agora Theatre
14, 16, 18, 29, 30, 31 May	*A Midsummer Night's Dream* Touring production from Britain	International Theatre Company London dir. Paul Stebbings	Seijo Gakuen University *et al.*
16–19 May	*Othello*	Gekidan AUN dir. Yoshida Kōtarō trans. Odashima Yūshi	Asakusa Kyūgeki

Appendix 2

Date	Title	Theatre Company / Director / Translator / etc.	Venue
22–26 May	HAMLET X SHIBUYA ~ Light, Was Our Revenge Tarnished? Original play inspired by Hamlet	Theatre Company Kakushinhan dir. and script Kimura Ryūnosuke	GALLERY LE DECO 4
22–26 May	Romeo and Juliet	THEATRE UBUNTU dir. Okada Kyōhei	Nippori d-Sōko
22–29 May	K. Tempest 2019	dir. Kushida Kazumi trans. Matsuoka Kazuko	Tokyo Metropolitan Theatre
23–26 May	A Midsummer Night's Dream Shakespeare combined with an audience participation game	pika kika x Jinrō dir. pika	Area 543
23–26 May	King Lear	Performing Arts Theater Company GEKI-Kisyuryuri dir. and adapt. Yanai Bunshō	Kisyuryuri Theater
24–26 May	A Midsummer Night's Dream	Types dir. Park Bangil trans. Odashima Yūshi	Za Koenji
24–29 May	Romio to Jurietto tachi (The Romeos and Juliets) Original play inspired by Romeo and Juliet	Gekidan Ōtake Sangyō dir. Ōtake Takumi book Yamazaki Yōhei	Shinjuku Ganka Gallery Space 0
25 May	Sakuradoki zeni no yo no naka (Life Is as Fragile as Cherry Blossom in a World of Money) Stage reading of a Meiji period kabuki adaptation of The Merchant of Venice	MSP Indies Shakespeare Caravan book Katsu Genzō	Waseda University Theatre Museum

Appendix 2

Date	Title	Theatre Company / Director / Translator / etc.	Venue
25–26 May	*The Little Mermaid / A Midsummer Night's Dream* Ballet performance	NBA Ballet Company choreo. Christopher Wheeldon (*A Midsummer Night's Dream*) comp. Michael Moritz	New National Theatre
27 May	*Sannin de Shēkusupia* Japanese production of *The Complete Works of William Shakespeare (Abridged)*	Chōjūgiga	Theater Green
29 May–1 June	*#Macbeth*	Theatre Moments dir. and adapt. Sagawa Daisuke	Sengawa Theater
7–9 June	*Owari nakereba subete nashi (All's Lost When the End's Lost)* Original comedy about performing *Hamlet*	Kawasaki Theatre Company dir. and script Kurashige Satoshi	Kawasaki H&B Theater
9, 22, 30 June	*Reiwa gannen no Shēkusupia: Macbeth vs. Hamletmachine (Shakespeare in the First Year of the Reiwa Era)* Stage reading	Kyoshoku Shūdan Kaiten Hyakume dir. and book Ishii Asuka	Nakano Gallery O2 Studio
13–14, 16–17 June	*A Midsummer Night's Dream*	Yume Fantasy	J.F. Oberlin University
14–15 June	*Sannin kurai de Shēkuspia: Tenpesuto (Shakespeare by Three or So: The Tempest)* Abridged stage reading of *The Tempest*	Kodomo no tame no Shakespeare dir. Kashiwagi Toshihiko trans. Matsuoka Kazuko	Kanack Hall

Appendix 2

Date	Title	Theatre Company / Director / Translator / *etc.*	Venue
14–23 June	*Rock Opera R&J* Musical version of *Romeo and Juliet*	dir. and book Suzuki Katsuhide comp. Ōshima Gorō	Nippon Seinen-kan Hall
18 June	*Sannin de Shēkusupia* Japanese production of *The Complete Works of William Shakespeare (Abridged)*	Chōjūgiga	Theater Green
18–23 June	*A Midsummer Night's Dream*	RASMY dir. Satō En	Rabinest
20–30 June	*Danjo gyakuten no Makubesu* (*Reverse Gender Macbeth*)	One Two-WORKS dir. and adapt. Kojō Toshinobu trans. Odashima Yūshi	Akasaka Red Theater
29 June	*Chōyaku Richard III* One-woman adaptation set in contemporary Japan	Kusunoki Mitsuka Hitori Shakespeare	Asakusa Little Theatre
29–30 June	*5 nin de 55 fun no Richard III nyūmon / 5 nin de 55 fun no natsu no yo no yume nyūmon* (*Richard III with 5 people in 55 min / A Midsummer Night's Dream with 5 people in 55 min*) Performance of an abridged version of *Richard III* and *A Midsummer Night's Dream*	Gekidanza Nabari Otome	Lilia Hall
30 June–2 July, 7–10 July	*Hamlet* Original music performance	Shiawase Gakkyū Hōkai	Sound Studio Noah / Bass on Top Nakano / nagomix

Appendix 2

Date	Title	Theatre Company / Director / Translator / *etc.*	Venue
5 July	*Shēkusupia asobi katari: Ima anata ni shitte hoshii Shēkusupia* (*Playful Talk about Shakespeare: The Shakespeare You Need to Know Now*) Book launch event with performances of selected scenes from Shakespeare	perf. Miwa Erika	Lutheran Ichigaya Center
6–7 July	*Othello* Student production of *Othello* in English	Sophia Shakespeare Company dir. Tōgō Takanori	Asagaya Arche
12–15 July	*A Midsummer Night's Dream*	Gekidan Sharekōbe dir. Kida Hiroki trans. Odashima Yūshi	Theatre Fūshikaden
13–14 July	*Coriolanus* Production in English	Yokohama Shakespeare Group dir. Ebizuka Yūya	Yamate Gaiety Theater
16 July	*Sannin de Shēkusupia* Japanese production of *The Complete Works of William Shakespeare (Abridged)*	Chōjūgiga	Theater Green
18–20 July	*Twelfth Night*	Musashino Kita High School Playing Club adapt. Musashino Kita High School Playing Club	Musashino Kita High School
19–21 July	*Taming of the Shrew*	Kodomo no tame no Shakespeare dir. and adapt. Yamasaki Seisuke trans. Odashima Yūshi	Kanack Hall

Appendix 2

Date	Title	Theatre Company / Director / Translator / etc.	Venue
24 July	*Henry VI Sanbu saku: Ie no danzetsu to wakai hen* (*Henry VI Trilogy: End of a Clan and Reconciliation*) Stage reading in English and Japanese	Shinchikyū-za curated by Arai Yoshio dir. Takahashi Masahiko adapt. Takagi Noboru trans. Tsubouchi Shōyō	Violon
25 July–12 Aug.	*Bara sensō* (*War of the Roses*) (*1, 2, 3 Henry VI* and *Richard III*)	Theatre Company Kakushinhan dir. Kimura Ryūnosuke trans. Matsuoka Kazuko	Theatre Fūshikaden
27–28 July	*Ongakugeki Hamlets!* (*Hamlets! A Play with Music*) Original musical play about an English sanatorium	DANCETERIA-ANNEX dir. and book Sawamura Miyuki comp. Goh Iris Watanabe	ST Spot Yokohama
28 July–4 Aug.	*Musical A Midsummer Night's Dream*	G Force Produce dir. Gotō Hiroyuki and Katō Hideo adapt. Nakai Yuriko	G Force Atelier
30 July–18 Aug.	*As You Like It*	dir. Kumabayashi Hirotaka trans. Hayafune Kaeko	Tokyo Metropolitan Theatre
1–12 Aug.	*Twelfth Night*	Willow's dir. and adapt. Yanaginuma Takuya trans. Matsuoka Kazuko	Meiji University

Appendix 2

Date	Title	Theatre Company / Director / Translator / *etc.*	Venue
3 Aug.	*Chōyaku Twelfth Night* One-woman adaptation set in contemporary Japan	Kusunoki Mitsuka Hitori Shakespeare	Asakusa Little Theatre
7–12 Aug.	*A Midsummer Night's Dream*	Gaikotsu Sutorippā dir. Kamisato Morihito	Hitsuji-za
16–19 Aug.	*Taming of the Shrew*	Kodomo no tame no Shakespeare dir. and adapt. Yamasaki Seisuke trans. Odashima Yūshi	Akasaka Civic Center
20–25 Aug.	*A Midsummer Night's Dream*	Gekidan Himawari dir. Kurita Yoshihiro trans. Matsuoka Kazuko	Theater Daikanyama
21 Aug.	*Richādo III + Richard III* Stage reading of *Richard III* in English and Tsubouchi's translation of the play	Zoshigaya Shēkusupia no Mori trans. Tsubouchi Shōyō	Zoshigaya Chīki Bunka Sōzō-kan
27 Aug.	*Sannin de Shēkusupia* Japanese production of *The Complete Works of William Shakespeare (Abridged)*	Chōjūgiga	Theater Green
31 Aug.	*As You Like It* Stage reading in English and Japanese and a lecture	SAYNK dir. Senuma Tatsuya	Yokohama Kindai Bungakukan
6–7 Sept.	*The Winter's Tale*	Itabashi Engeki Center dir. Endō Ēzō trans. Odashima Yūshi	Itabashi Culture Hall

Appendix 2

Date	Title	Theatre Company / Director / Translator / etc.	Venue
8 Sept.–6 Oct.	*Hamlet*	Tokyo Globe dir. Mori Shintarō trans. Matsuoka Kazuko	Tokyo Globe
10–16 Sept.	*The Merry Wives of Windsor*	Types dir. and adapt. Park Bangil trans. Odashima Yūshi	Studio Applause
11 Sept.	*Sannin de Shēkusupia* Japanese production of *The Complete Works of William Shakespeare (Abridged)*	Chōjūgiga	Theater Green
14–16 Sept.	*Supein no Higeki~Hieronimo no ikari~* (*The Spanish Tragedy ~Hieronimo Is Mad Again~*)	Theatrical Company THE MODERN CLASSICISM dir. and adapt. Natsume Kiriri	Cofrelio Theater
16 Sept.	*Roméo et Juliette*	Tokyo MET SaLaD Music Festival comp. Louis Hector Berlioz	Tokyo Metropolitan Theatre
25 Sept.	*Troilus and Cressida* Stage reading in English and Japanese	Shinchikyū-za curated by Arai Yoshio dir. Takahashi Masahiko adapt. Takagi Noboru trans. Tsubouchi Shōyō	Violon
25–28 Sept.	*Tarumae Kahei* Rakugo version of *King Lear*	Shimeko no Usagi dir. Imai Kōji	Art Space Plot
26 Sept.	*Musical Fantasy A Midsummer Night's Dream ~ Love ~*	Gunji Produce dir., adapt. and choreo. Gunji Yukio	Move Hall

Appendix 2

Date	Title	Theatre Company / Director / Translator / *etc.*	Venue
29–30 Sept.	*Hamlet* British touring production in Early Modern English pronunciation	The Shakespeare Ensemble curated by David Crystal	Meiji University / J.F. Oberlin University
1 Oct.	*Sannin de Shēkusupia* Japanese production of *The Complete Works of William Shakespeare (Abridged)*	Chōjūgiga	Theater Green
1–25 Oct.	*Musical Love's Labour's Lost* Japanese production of an American musical	dir. and trans. Ueda Ikkō adapt. Alex Timbers comp. Michael Friedman	Theatre Creation
3–13 Oct.	*The Merchant of Venice*	Engeki Syudan En dir. Ogawa Kōhei trans. Matsuoka Kazuko	Kichijoji Theater
5 Oct.	*Chōyaku Cymbeline* One-woman adaptation set in contemporary Japan	Kusunoki Mitsuka Hitori Shakespeare	Asakusa Little Theatre
8–15 Oct., 9 Nov.–11 Dec.	*Q* Sequel to *Romeo and Juliet* inspired by Queen's *Night at the Opera*	Noda Map dir. and script Noda Hideki	Tokyo Metropolitan Theatre
9–13 Oct.	*Romeo and Juliet in Tokyo*	Theatre Company Kakushinhan dir. Kimura Ryūnosuke trans. Matsuoka Kazuko	GALLERY LE DECO
11–14 Oct.	*Much Ado about Nothing*	Gekidan Pajama Party dir. Yoshitake Saori book Tanaka Yūnosuke	Komaba Shōkūkan

Appendix 2

Date	Title	Theatre Company / Director / Translator / etc.	Venue
14 Oct.	*Comedy of Errors*	Types dir. Park Bangil trans. Odashima Yūshi	Edo-Tokyo Museum
15–22 Oct.	*Musical Hamlet* Musical version of *Hamlet*	Artist Japan dir. Fujima Kanjūrō book Tobe Kazuhisa comp. Hashimoto Kengo	Tenkū Gekijō
24–26 Oct.	*The Merchant of Venice* Stage reading	dir. Ashiya Tōru adapt. Takagi Noboru trans. Tsubouchi Shōyō	Asagaya Work Shop
25 Oct.	*Saru gundan no Hamuretto* *Hamlet* by performing monkeys	Tarō Jirō perf. Murasaki Tarō	Jiji Press Hall
26–27 Oct.	*A Midsummer Night's Dream* Acting school graduation production	Human Academy Shinjuku dir. Kō Yoshinori *et al.*	Human Academy Shinjuku
29, 31 Oct.	*Timon of Athens* Stage reading	dir. Nomura Mansai trans. and adapt. Kawai Shōichirō	Setagaya Public Theatre
1–4 Nov.	*Richādo III~Sekai waru neko aruki ingurando hen ~* (*Richard III: Bad Cats around the World: England Version*) Play about an animal photographer and a black cat, inspired by *Richard III*	Shakespeare Play House dir. and adapt. Hōsubōn Yumi trans. Matsuoka Kazuko	Shakespeare Tea House

Appendix 2

Date	Title	Theatre Company / Director / Translator / etc.	Venue
2 Nov.	*A Midsummer Night's Dream*	Trompe l'œil dir. Nakamura Hiromi adapt. Koide Kazuhiko trans. Kawai Shōichirō	Kami Miharada Kabuki Stage
2 Nov.	*Chōyaku Pericles* One-woman adaptation set in contemporary Japan	Kusunoki Mitsuka Hitori Shakespeare	Asakusa Little Theatre
2–3 Nov.	*Romeo and Juliet* Student production of Presgurvic's *Roméo et Juliette: de la Haine à l'amour*	Kyoritsu Women's University Musical Society book Gérard Presgurvic	Kyoritsu Women's University
2–3 Nov.	*The Three Sisters of the King Lear* Original musical based on *King Lear*	Liebe dir. Wada Kei book Yokoyama Kazuma	Plaza East Hall
2–4 Nov.	*Romeo and Juliet*	Meguro Community Theatre dir. Ushio Hozumi trans. Odashima Yūshi	Woody Theatre Nakameguro
6–10 Nov.	*Macbeth*	Shakespeare Theatre dir. Deguchi Norio trans. Odashima Yūshi	Nakano the Pocket
7–8 Nov.	*The Merchant of Venice / Twelfth Night* Performance of the trial scene from *The Merchant of Venice* and the fake letter scene from *Twelfth Night*	Shakespeare Theatre Senior Production dir. Deguchi Norio trans. Odashima Yūshi	Shakespeare Theatre

Appendix 2

Date	Title	Theatre Company / Director / Translator / *etc.*	Venue
8–10 Nov.	*Julius Caesar* and *Antony and Cleopatra* Student production using their own translation	Meiji University Shakespeare Project dir. Taniguchi Yuka and Nishizawa Eiji	Meiji University
11 Nov.	*Sannin de Shēkusupia* Japanese production of *The Complete Works of William Shakespeare (Abridged)*	Chōjūgiga	Theater Green
13–17 Nov.	*The Merchant of Venice* No record of this production exists, other than in a notice about future productions on the theatre company's webpage	Types dir. and adapt. Ishikawa Yūdai	Theater Green
16–17 Nov.	*A Midsummer Night's Dream*	Toho Gakuen College of Drama and Music dir. Miura Gō trans. Tsubouchi Shōyō	Toho Gakuen College
18 Nov.	*Hamletmachine* Stage reading of Heiner Műller's *Hamletmachine* with jazz piano accompaniment	trans. Tawada Yoko perf. Takahashi Aki	Theater X
20–24 Nov.	*La Tempesta* Japanese production of an American musical	Tachi World dir. and trans. Katsuta Yasuhiko book Tom Jones comp. Andrew Gerle	Yorozu Theater

Appendix 2

Date	Title	Theatre Company / Director / Translator / *etc.*	Venue
21–22 Nov.	*Macbeth* Production combining Shakespeare's text and Verdi's opera	Wakai Ensōka no tame no Project dir. Takahashi Noritaka comp. Giuseppe Verdi	Denshō Hall
22–26 Nov.	*Taming of the Shrew*	Kotoba no Aria dir. Sasaki Yūtarō trans. Odashima Yūshi	Gazavie
27 Nov.	*Twelfth Night* Stage reading in English and Japanese	Shinchikyū-za curated by Arai Yoshio dir. Takahashi Masahiko adapt. Takagi Noboru trans. Tsubouchi Shōyō	Violon
6–7 Dec.	*Twelfth Night* Student production of *Twelfth Night* in English	Kanto Gakuin Daigaku Shēkusupia Eigogeki Kenkyūkai	Kenmin Kyōsai Mirai Hall
8 Dec.	*Heroines' Room* Original play about female literary protagonists including Juliet from *Romeo and Juliet*	Jōchi Eigo Gakka Gogeki Sākuru book and dir. Ogawa Kimiyo	Sophia University
9–10 Dec.	*Sannin de Shēkusupia* Japanese production of *The Complete Works of William Shakespeare (Abridged)*	Chōjūgiga	Theater Green
10–11 Dec.	*Pocket Romeo and Juliet*	Theatre Company Kakushinhan dir. Kimura Ryūnosuke trans. Matsuoka Kazuko	Atelier Fanfare

Appendix 2

Date	Title	Theatre Company / Director / Translator / *etc.*	Venue
11–15 Dec.	*Hamuretto no kimyō na bōken* (*The Strange Adventures of Hamlet*) All-female production of *Hamlet*	Shingekidan dir. and adapt. Kushida Goblin	Theater 711
12–22 Dec.	*Macbeth*	DULL-COLORED POP dir. and adapt. Tani Ken'ichi trans. Matsuoka Kazuko	Kanagawa Art Theatre
14 Dec.	*Chōyaku Othello* One-woman adaptation set in contemporary Japan	Kusunoki Mitsuka Hitori Shakespeare	Asakusa Little Theatre
14–15 Dec.	*Romeo and Juliet* Student production of *Romeo and Juliet* in English	Sophia Shakespeare Company dir. Tōgō Takanori	Asagaya Arche
14–15 Dec.	*Umibe no Romio to Jurietto* (*Romeo and Juliet by the Sea*) Stage reading of an original play inspired by *Romeo and Juliet*	Theatre Company Kakushinhan dir. and adapt. Kimura Ryūnosuke	Atelier Fanfare
15–21 Dec.	*Shēkusupia no umi o oyogu~Mumei Juku to Shēkusupia* (*Swimming in the Sea of Shakespeare: Mumei Juku and Shakespeare*) Stage reading of scenes from *Hamlet, Richard III, Merry Wives of Windsor, Macbeth* and *Romeo and Juliet*	Mumei Juku dir. and adapt. Yamasaki Seisuke trans. Odashima Yūshi	Nakadai Gekidō

Appendix 2

Date	Title	Theatre Company / Director / Translator / *etc.*	Venue
17–22 Dec.	*Twelfth Night*	Types dir. and adapt. Park Bangil trans. Odashima Yūshi	Studio Applause
17–22 Dec.	*Romeo and Juliet* Stage reading	dir. and adapt. Fukasaku Kenta trans. Hirata Ayako	Sunshine Theatre
21–23 Dec.	*Hamlet* Stage reading	Hyōgensha Kōbō dir. and adapt. Shichimi Mayumi	Hyōgensha Kōbō Noir
22 Dec.	*Geshi no yo no yume (A Summer Solstice Night's Dream)* Student production of *A Midsummer Night's Dream*	Ōtemon University STEP curated by Yokota Osamu trans. Kawai Shōichirō	Hachioji Art & Cultural Hall
26 Dec.	*Stella by Shakespeare ~ Shēkusupia hoshi meguri (Shakespeare Tour of the Stars)* One-woman stage reading of 2.2 from *Romeo and Juliet* and 1.2 from *King Lear*	Akatsuki Hitori Shibai trans. Odashima Yūshi	Café Muriwui
29–30 Dec.	*Gansaku Karasawagi (Mock Much Ado about Nothing)* *Much Ado about Nothing* set in contemporary Tokyo, followed by a drag show	Flying Stage dir. and book Sekine Shinichi	Shinjuku Theater Miracle

BIBLIOGRAPHY

GENERAL INTRODUCTION

Anzai, Tetsuo, ed., *Nihon no Shakespeare hyakunen* (A Hundred Years of Shakespeare in Japan) (Tokyo: Arachiku Shuppan, 1989).

Anzai, Tetsuo, 'A Century of Shakespeare in Japan: A Brief Historical Survey', in Tetsuo Anzai, Soji Iwasaki, Holger Klein, and Peter Milward, eds., *Shakespeare in Japan* (Lewiston, NY: Edwin Mellen, 1999), 3–12.

Brandon, James R., 'Some Considerations of Shakespeare in Kabuki', in Stanley Vincent Longman, ed., *Crosscurrents in the Drama: East and West* (Tuscaloosa: University of Alabama Press, 1998), 7–18.

Brown, Sarah Annes, Lublin, Robert I., and McCulloch, Lynsey, eds., *Reinventing the Renaissance: Shakespeare and his Contemporaries in Adaptation and Performance* (Basingstoke: Palgrave Macmillan, 2013).

Curran, Beverley, *Theatre Translation Theory and Performance in Contemporary Japan: Native Voices, Foreign Bodies* (London: Routledge, 2014).

Edmondson, Paul, and Holbrook, Peter, *Shakespeare's Creative Legacies: Artists, Writers, Performers, Readers* (London: Bloomsbury, 2016).

Edo, Kaoru, 'SPT09 Hondana no naka no gekijō' (The Theatre within the Bookshelves) (booklet by Setagaya Public Theatre, Tokyo, 2013).

Fischlin, Daniel, and Fortier, Mark, *Adaptations of Shakespeare: A Critical Anthology of Plays from the Seventeenth Century to the Present* (London: Routledge, 2000).

Fukuda, Tsuneari, '*Hamuretto* no hon'yaku' (The Translation of *Hamlet*), in Sadanori Bekku, ed., *Hon'yaku* (Translations) (Tokyo: Sakuhinsha, 1994), 132–39.

Gallimore, Daniel, 'Shoyo's Shakespeare: Theory and Practice', *Sophia International Review*, 28 (2006a), 1–14.

Gallimore, Daniel, '"Singing Like Birds i' th' Cage": The Voices of Shakespeare in Meiji Japan', *Studies in English and American Literature*, 41 (2006b), 169–79.

Gallimore, Daniel, 'Speaking Shakespeare in Japanese: Voicing the Foreign', in Dennis Kennedy and Yong Li Lan, eds., *Shakespeare in Asia: Contemporary Performance* (Cambridge: Cambridge University Press, 2010), 42–56.

Gallimore, Daniel, *Sounding Like Shakespeare: A Study of Prosody in Four Japanese Translations of* A Midsummer Night's Dream (Osaka: Kwansei Gakuin University Press, 2012).

Gallimore, Daniel, 'Shakespeare geki no nihongo butai hon'yaku "shi" to "geki" no deai' (The Japanese Translation of Shakespeare's Plays for the

Stage: The Meeting of 'Verse' and 'Play'), *Jimbunronken*, 63/1 (2013), 167–87.

Gallimore, Daniel, and Minami, Ryuta, 'Seven Stages of Shakespeare Reception', in Jonah Salz, ed., *A History of Japanese Theatre* (Cambridge: Cambridge University Press, 2016), 484–96.

Geilhorn, Barbara, and Iwata-Weickgenannt, Kristina, 'Negotiating Nuclear Disaster: An Introduction', in Barbara Geilhorn and Kristina Iwata-Weickgenannt, eds., *Fukushima and the Arts: Negotiating Nuclear Disaster* (London: Routledge, 2017), 1–20.

Hutcheon, Linda, *A Theory of Adaptation* (Abingdon: Routledge, 2006).

Kawatake, Toshio, *Nihon no Hamlet* (Hamlet in Japan) (Tokyo: Nansōsha, 1972).

Kawato, Michiaki, *Meiji no Shakespeare: Sōshūhen*, I (Shakespeare of the Meiji Period: A Compilation, I) (Tokyo: Ōzora-sha, 2004).

Kimura, Ryūnosuke, 'APAF: Participant Interview #01 – Ryunosuke Kimura / TC Team Assistant Director' (2013), http://butai.asia/wp-content/themes/apaf/pdf/2013_kimura_e.pdf.

Kinsui, Satoshi, *Virtual Japanese: Enigmas of Role Language* (Osaka: Osaka University Press, 2017).

Kishi, Tetsuo, and Bradshaw, Graham, *Shakespeare in Japan* (London: Continuum, 2005).

Laera, Margherita, *Theatre and Adaptation: Return, Rewrite, Repeat* (London: Bloomsbury, 2014).

Lamb, Charles, and Lamb, Mary, *Tales from Shakespeare* (London: Bickers & Son, 1878).

Loxton, Howard, 'Theatre Review: *Ainu Othello* at Tara Theatre', *British Theatre Guide* (August 2019), https://www.britishtheatreguide.info/reviews/ainu-othello-tara-theatre-17939, accessed 16 August 2019.

MacArthur, Michelle, Wilkinson, Lydia, and Zaiontz, Keren, eds., *Performing Adaptations: Essays and Conversations on the Theory and Practice of Adaptation* (Newcastle-upon-Tyne: Cambridge Scholars Publishing, 2009).

Matsuoka, Kazuko, 'Shakespeare Translation' (Lecture) (4 December 2016), Kyoto Sangyo University.

Matsuoka, Kazuko, 'What Does it Mean to Write? Vol. 6', *Life no Book* (2 February 2019), https://www.1101.com/store/techo/en/magazine/2019/kaku/2019-02-02.html, accessed 15 November 2019.

Minami, Ryuta, 'Shakespeare Reinvented on the Contemporary Japanese Stage', in Ryuta Minami, Ian Carruthers, and John Gillies, eds., *Performing Shakespeare in Japan* (Cambridge: Cambridge University Press, 2001), 146–58.

Minami, Ryuta, '"What, has this thing appear'd again tonight?": Re-playing Shakespeare on the Japanese Stage', in Poonam Trivedi and Ryuta

Minami, eds., *Re-Playing Shakespeare in Asia* (New York: Routledge, 2010), 76–96.

Minami, Ryuta, '"The very basics for all of us": Fragments of Shakespeare in Japanese *Anime* and *Manga*', in Bi-qi Beatrice Lei, Judy Celine Ick, and Poonam Trivedi, eds., *Shakespeare's Asian Journeys: Critical Encounters, Cultural Geographies, and the Politics of Travel* (New York: Routledge, 2016a), 239–54.

Minami, Ryuta, 'Finding a Style for Presenting Shakespeare on the Japanese Stage', *Multicultural Shakespeare: Translation, Appropriation and Performance*, 14/29 (2016b), 29–42.

Minami, Ryuta, Carruthers, Ian, and Gillies, John, 'Introduction', in Ryuta Minami, Ian Carruthers, and John Gillies, eds., *Performing Shakespeare in Japan* (Cambridge: Cambridge University Press, 2001), 1–14.

Ministry of Health, Labour and Welfare, 'Statistics of Suicide of Japan' (June 2020), https://www.mhlw.go.jp/content/202005-shinsai.pdf, accessed 20 June 2020.

Murakami, Takeshi, 'Shakespeare and *Hamlet* in Japan: A Chronological Overview', in Ueno Yoshiko, ed., *Hamlet and Japan* (New York: AMS Press, 1995), 239–304.

Natsume, Kinnosuke (Natsume Sōseki), *Teihon Sōseki zenshū*, VI (The Collected Works of Sōseki: The Standard Edition, VI) (Tokyo: Iwanami Shoten, 2019).

Noda, Hideki, 'Interview', in Ryuta Minami, Ian Carruthers, and John Gillies, eds., *Performing Shakespeare in Japan* (Cambridge: Cambridge University Press, 2001), 220–29.

Ohtani, Tomoko, 'Juliet's Girlfriends: The Takarazuka Revue Company and the *Shōjo* Culture', in Ryuta Minami, Ian Carruthers, and John Gillies, eds., *Performing Shakespeare in Japan* (Cambridge: Cambridge University Press, 2001), 159–171.

Okamoto, Shigeko, and Shibamoto-Smith, Janet S., *The Social Life of the Japanese Language: Cultural Discourse and Situated Practice* (Cambridge: Cambridge University Press, 2016).

Okuizumi, Hikaru, *Mephistopheles no teiri: Jigoku Shakespeare sambusaku* (Mephistopheles's Theorem: Shakespeare in Hell Trilogy) (Tokyo: Gengi Shobō, 2013).

Olive, Sarah, '*Othello*, Shakespeare Company of Japan and Pirikap, dir. Kazumi Shimodate and Debo Akibe, Tara Arts, London', *Reviewing Shakespeare* (7 August 2019), http://bloggingshakespeare.com/reviewing-shakespeare/othello-shakespeare-company-japan-pirikap-dir-kazumi-shimodate-debo-akibe-tara-arts-london-2019/, accessed 6 September 2019.

Otake, Tomoko, 'Blurring the Boundaries', *Japan Times* (10 May 2009), https://www.japantimes.co.jp/2009/05/10/general/blurring-the-boundaries/, accessed 10 June 2017.

Poulton, Cody, 'Antigone in Japan: Some Responses to 3.11 at Festival/Tokyo 2012', in Barbara Geilhorn and Kristina Iwata-Weickgenannt, eds., *Fukushima and the Arts: Negotiating Nuclear Disaster* (London: Routledge, 2017), 127–43.

Powell, Brian, 'One Man's *Hamlet* in 1911 Japan: The Bungei Kyokai Production in the Imperial Theatre', in Takashi Sasayama, J.R. Mulryne, and Margaret Shewring, eds., *Shakespeare and the Japanese Stage* (Cambridge: Cambridge University Press, 1998), 38–52.

Powell, Brian, 'Birth of Modern Theatre: *Shimpa* and *Shingeki*', in Jonah Salz, ed., *A History of Japanese Theatre* (Cambridge: Cambridge University Press, 2016), 200–33.

Sanders, Julie, *Adaptation and Appropriation* (Abingdon: Routledge, 2006).

Sano, Akiko, 'Shakespeare Translation in Japan: 1868–1998', *Ilha do Desterro*, 36 (1999), 337–69.

Sasaki, Takashi, ed., *Nihon no Shakespeare* (Shakespeare in Japan) (Tokyo: Elpis, 1988).

Senda, Akihiko, 'Artist Interview: Revealing the Inner World of Young Women, with Scenes Repeated as Refrains', *Performing Arts Network Japan* (Tokyo: Japan Foundation, 2011), http://www.performingarts.jp/E/art_interview/1111/1.html, accessed 1 July 2017.

Shimodate, Kazumi, *Shin Romio to Jurietto / Matsushimawan no natsu no yo no yume* (The New Romeo and Juliet / Midsummer Night's Dream of the Matsushima Bay) (Tokyo: Koko Shuppan, 2016).

Shimodate, Kazumi, *Hamuretto, Tohoku ni tatsu* (*Hamlet*, Standing in Tohoku) (Tokyo: Kokusho Kankōkai, 2017).

Smiles, Samuel, *Self-help: With Illustrations of Character and Conduct* (revised and enlarged) (Tokyo: Maruzen Kabushiki Kaisha, 1902; first published 1859).

Suzuki, Masae, 'The Rose and the Bamboo: Noda Hideki's *Sandaime Richādo*', in Ryuta Minami, Ian Carruthers, and John Gillies, eds., *Performing Shakespeare in Japan* (Cambridge: Cambridge University Press, 2001), 133–45.

Taira, Tatsuhiko, '*Venice no shōnin* to *Sakuradoki zeni no yo no naka*: Sono daihon to jōen o megutte (Concerning the Script and Staging of *The Merchant of Venice* and *Sakuradoki zeni no yo no naka*)', *Eibungakushi kenkyū*, 29 (1994), 165–78.

Takahashi, Yasunari, '*Hamlet* and the Anxiety of Modern Japan', *Shakespeare Survey*, 48 (1995), 99–111.

Takahashi, Yasunari, series ed., *Shakespeare kenkyū shiryō shūsei*, I (Anthology of Research Materials on Shakespeare, I) (Tokyo: Nihon Tosho Center, 1997).

Takahashi, Yutaka, 'Shakespeare geki mō hitotsu no monogatari' (Shakespeare Drama: The Other Story), *Mainichi shimbun* (morning edition, 13 September 2008), 14.

Tanaka, Nobuko, 'The Bard in Abundance in Edo Japan', *Japan Times* (22 September 2005), https://www.japantimes.co.jp/culture/2005/09/22/stage/the-bard-in-abundance-in-edo-japan/, accessed 12 January 2017.

Tanaka, Yukari, '"Ama-chan" ga hiraita atarashii tobira: "Hōgen kosupure dorama" ga dekiru made' (The New Door that "Ama-chan" Opened: Toward the "Dialect Cosplay Drama"), in Satoshi Kinsui, Yukari Tanaka, and Minako Okamuro, eds., *Dorama to hōgen no atarashii kankei: 'Kānēshon' kara 'Yae no Sakura', soshite 'Ama-chan' e* (The New Relationship of Dramas and Dialect: From 'Carnation' to 'Yae's Cherry Tree' and 'Ama-chan') (Tokyo: Kasama Shoin, 2014), 22–43.

Tara Arts, *Ainu Othello by The Shakespeare Company Japan* (theatre programme, London, August 2019).

Thornbury, Barbara E., *America's Japan and Japan's Performing Arts: Cultural Mobility and Exchange in New York 1952–2011* (Ann Arbor: University of Michigan Press, 2013).

Tierney, Robert, '*Othello* in Tokyo: Performing Race and Empire in 1903 Japan', *Shakespeare Quarterly*, 62/4 (2011), 514–50.

Tsubouchi, Shōyō, '*Hamuretto* no shinka' (The Evolution of *Hamlet*), in *Geki to bungaku* (Plays and Literature) (Tokyo: Fuzambō, 1911), 330–40.

Tsubouchi, Shōyō, *Shōyō senshū bessatsu*, 5 (Selected Works of Shōyō: Supplementary Volume 5), ed. Shōyō Kyōkai (Tokyo: Dai Ichi Shobō, 1978).

Watanabe, Emiko, 'Ninagawa's *Macbeth*: A Japanese Interpretation of a Shakespeare Play', *Bulletin of College of Foreign Studies, Yokohama*, 26 (2003), 81–97.

Yadorigi Henshūbu, 'Saihō no taidan' (Interview on Their Return), *Yadorigi* (13 July 2016), http://yadorigi.jp/%e5%86%8d%e8%a8%aa%e3%81%ae%e5%af%be%e8%ab%87%e3%80%82%e3%82%ab%e3%82%af%e3%82%b7%e3%83%b3%e3%83%8f%e3%83%b3%e6%9c%a8%e6%9d%91%e9%be%8d%e4%b9%8b%e4%bb%8b-x-%e6%bc%94%e5%8a%87%e5%88%b6%e4%bd%9c/, accessed 27 August 2020.

Yoshihara, Yukari, 'Is this Shakespeare? Inoue Hidenori's Adaptations of Shakespeare', in Poonam Trivedi and Minami Ryūta, eds., *Re-Playing Shakespeare in Asia* (New York: Routledge, 2010), 141–56.

THE TOKYO SHAKESPEARE COMPANY

Adelman, Janet, *Suffocating Mothers: Fantasies of Maternal Origin in Shakespeare's Plays, Hamlet to The Tempest* (New York: Routledge, 1992).

Bharucha, Rustom, 'Foreign Asia/Foreign Shakespeare: Dissenting Notes on New Asian Interculturality, Postcoloniality and Re-colonization', in Dennis Kennedy and Yong Li Lan, eds., *Shakespeare in Asia:*

Contemporary Performance (Cambridge: Cambridge University Press, 2010), 253–82.

Edo, Kaoru, 'Tokyo de Shakespeare wo jōen suru igi to wa?' (What is the Significance of Staging Shakespeare in Tokyo)?, in Masaru Inoue, ed., *Meiji Shakespeare Project: Nettō!* (Heated Battle!) *Midsummer Nightmare* (Tokyo: Meiji University Press, 2017), 154–57.

'*Engeki: Lear no sannin musume*' (Theatre: *The Three Daughters of Lear*), *Kōhō Kushibiki* (*Kushibiki* Newsletter), November 1997, 5.

Gearhart, Stephannie S., '*Lear's Daughters*, Adaptation, and the Calculation of Worth', *Borrowers and Lenders*, 7/2 (Fall 2012 / Winter 2013), http://www.borrowers.uga.edu/195/show, accessed 10 January 2019.

Joubin, Alexa Alice, 'Yukio Ninagawa', in Peter Holland, ed., *Brook, Hall, Ninagawa, Lepage: Great Shakespeareans*, XVIII (London: Bloomsbury, 2013), 79–112.

Kahn, Coppélia, 'The Absent Mother in *King Lear*', in Margaret W. Ferguson, Maureen Quilligan, and Nancy J. Vickers, eds., *Rewriting the Renaissance: The Discourses of Sexual Difference in Early Modern Europe* (Chicago: University of Chicago Press, 1986), 33–49.

Kidnie, Margaret Jane, *Shakespeare and the Problem of Adaptation* (Abingdon: Routledge, 2009).

Konno, Kaoru, 'Tokubetsu kikō' (Special Contribution), *The Three Daughters of Lear* theatre programme (Tokyo: The Tokyo Shakespeare Company, 1996).

'*Lear Ō o shin-kaishaku: higeki no nazo o toku*' (Re-interpreting *King Lear*: Solving the Mystery of the Tragedy), *Sankei shimbun* (evening edition, 31 March 1995), 8.

Massai, Sonia, 'Nahum Tate's Revisions of Shakespeare's *King Lears*', *Studies in English Literature, 1500–1900*, 40/3 (Summer 2000), 435–50.

Motoyama, Tetsuhito, 'Theatre Review: *Meja Meja*' (*Measure for Measure*), *Shakespeare Studies*, 55 (2017), 43–46.

Motoyama, Tetsuhito, and Edo, Kaoru, 'Strange Oeillades No More: *The Three Daughters of Lear* from the Tokyo Shakespeare Company's "Shakespeare through the Looking-Glass"', *Shakespeare*, 9/4 (2013), 462–80.

Sasaki, Yasuko, '*Lear no sannin musume o mite*' (On Watching *The Three Daughters of Lear*), *Geibun kaihō* (Newsletter on the Arts and Literature) (31 March 1997), 2.

Sisson, C.J., *Shakespeare's Tragic Justice* (London: Methuen, 1961).

Takadō, Kaname, '*Kigeki shitate no higeki*' (A Comedy-Coated Tragedy), *Christ Shimbun* (10 June 1995), 4.

Tate, Nahum, *The History of King Lear*, in Daniel Fischlin and Mark Fortier, eds., *Adaptations of Shakespeare: A Critical Anthology of Plays from the Seventeenth Century to the Present* (London: Routledge, 2000), 66–96.

Umehara, Hiroshi, '*Shiron: Shin Kokuritsu Gekijō o torimaita seiji jōkyō to engeki jōkyō – omoni kokka senryaku no kanten kara*' (Essay: The Political and Theatre-Related Circumstances Surrounding the Establishment of the New National Theatre – Mainly from the Point of View of National Strategy), *Theatre Arts*, 41 (Winter 2009), 16–26.

Welsford, Enid, *The Fool: His Social and Literary History* (London: Faber & Faber, 1935).

Yamamoto, Susumu, ed., *Rakugo Handbook* (3rd edition, Tokyo: Sanseidō, 2007).

Yūki, Masahide, '*Gekihyō: Tetteishita Macbeth no kaisaku*' (Theatre Review: Thoroughly Reworked *Macbeths*), *Teatreux* (February 1997), 71–73.

'*Zuisho ni yūmoa kirari, Lear no sannin musume*' (Humour Shines through in *The Three Daughters of Lear*), *Mainichi Shimbun* (evening edition, 27 March 1995), 9.

KAKUSHINHAN THEATRE COMPANY

Anan, Nobuko, *Contemporary Japanese Women's Theatre and Visual Arts: Performing Girls' Aesthetics* (Basingstoke: Palgrave Macmillan, 2016).

Biberman, Matthew, *Shakespeare, Adaptation, Psychoanalysis: Better than New* (London: Taylor & Francis, 2017).

Brienza, Casey, 'Did Manga Conquer America? Implications for the Cultural Policy of "Cool Japan"', *International Journal of Cultural Policy*, 20/4 (2014), 383–98.

Dodson, Steve, 'Kafka on Books', *Language Hat* (4 January 2004), http://languagehat.com/kafka-on-books, accessed 5 January 2019.

Eglinton, Mika, 'Young Dramatists Mark the Bard's Anniversary in Style', *Japan Times* (26 April 2016), https://www.japantimes.co.jp/culture/2016/04/26/stage/young-dramatists-mark-bards-anniversary-style, accessed 12 May 2016.

Grassmuck, Volker, '*I'm Alone, But Not Lonely*' (London: eeodo, 2016).

Hutcheon, Linda, *A Theory of Adaptation* (Abingdon: Routledge, 2006).

Joy, Alicia, 'A Short History of Tokyo's Shibuya Crossing', *Culture Trip* (4 July 2019), https://theculturetrip.com/asia/japan/articles/tokyos-most-iconic-attraction-shibuya-crossing, accessed 15 July 2019.

Kakushinhan Makubesu (Theatre Company Kakushinhan's '*Macbeth*') (29 January 2017), http://blog.livedoor.jp/ciao_waki/archives/52034393.html, accessed 30 June 2017.

Kimura, Ryūnosuke, 'APAF: Participant Interview #01 – Ryunosuke Kimura / TC Team Assistant Director' (2013), http://butai.asia/wp-content/themes/apaf/pdf/2013_kimura_e.pdf.

Laera, Margherita, *Theatre and Adaptation: Return, Rewrite, Repeat* (London: Bloomsbury, 2014).

Matsuoka, Kazuko, 'Metamorphosis of *Hamlet* in Tokyo', in Yoshiko Ueno, ed., *Hamlet and Japan* (New York: AMS Press, 1995), 227–38.

McCurry, Justin, 'Japan Stabbing: Two dead and 16 injured in attack on children in Kawasaki', *The Guardian* (28 May 2019), http://theguardian.com/world/2019/may/28/japan-mass-stabbing-children-among-injured-in-attack-kawasaki, 20 June 2019.

McGray, Douglas, 'Japan's Gross National Cool', *Foreign Policy* (11 November 2009), https://foreignpolicy.com/2009/11/11/japans-gross-national-cool/.

Tanaka, Nobuko, 'Kimura's Crazed *Macbeth* for Today', *Japan Times* (24 January 2017), http://www.japantimes.co.jp/culture/2017/01/24/stage/kimuras-crazed-macbeth-today, accessed 27 January 2017.

Theatre Company Kakushinhan, website, http://kakushinhan.org/artist.

Thompson, Ann, '*Hamlet*: Looking Before and After: Why so Many Prequels and Sequels?', in Sarah Annes Brown, Robert I. Lublin, and Lynsey McCulloch, eds., *Reinventing the Renaissance: Shakespeare and his Contemporaries in Adaptation and Performance* (London: Palgrave Macmillan, 2013), 17–31.

Uchino, Tadashi, *Crucible Bodies: Postwar Japanese Performance from Brecht to the New Millennium* (London: Seagull Books, 2009).

Valaskivi, Katja, 'A Brand New Future? Cool Japan and the Social Imaginary of the Branded Nation', *Japan Forum*, 25/4 (2013), 485–504.

Yoshihara, Yukari, 'Tacky "Shakespeares" in Japan', *Multicultural Shakespeare: Translation, Appropriation and Performance*, 10/25 (2013), 83–97.

THE SHAKESPEARE COMPANY JAPAN

Chiba, Katsusuke, *Kieta Yamabito: Shōwa no dentō matagi* (Extinct Mountaineer: The Traditional Matagi Hunter in the Showa Period) (Tokyo: Nōsangyoson Bunka Kyōkai, 2019).

Fackler, Martin, 'Tsunami Warnings, Written in Stone', *The New York Times* (20 April 2011), https://www.nytimes.com/2011/04/21/world/asia/21stones.html?_r=2, accessed 21 June 2020.

Inamasu, Tatsuo, 'The Depths of the Showa Retro Boom', *Japan Spotlight* (November/December 2006), 46–47, https://www.jef.or.jp/journal/pdf/what%27s%20up%20in%20japan.pdf, accessed 20 October 2019.

Kōno, Kōhei, *Showa nosutarujī kaitai – natsukashisa wa dō tsukurareta no ka* (Deconstructing Showa Nostalgia: How the Sense of Familiarity Was Constructed) (Tokyo: Shōbunsha, 2018).

Ministry of Health, Labour and Welfare, 'Summary of Vital Statistics of Japan' (September 2019), https://www.mhlw.go.jp/toukei/saikin/hw/jinkou/kakutei18/dl/04_h2-1.pdf, accessed 20 June 2020.

Motoyama, Tetsuhito, and Konno, Fumiaki, 'The Shakespeare Company Japan and Regional Self-Fashioning', in Kristin Bezio and Anthony Russell, eds., *William Shakespeare and 21st-Century Culture, Politics, and Leadership: Bard Bites* (Cheltenham: Edward Elgar, 2021).

Nebuka, Makoto, *Shirakamisanchi matagi den: Suzuki Tadakatsu no shōgai* (Stories from a Matagi Hunter in Shirakami Sanchi: The Life of Suzuki Tadakatsu) (Tokyo: Yama to Keikokusha, 2018).

Schoch, Richard W., *Not Shakespeare: Bardolatry and Burlesques in the Nineteenth Century* (Cambridge: Cambridge University Press, 2002).

Wells, Stanley, 'Shakespearian Burlesques', *Shakespeare Quarterly*, 16/1 (1965), 49–61.

Wells, Stanley, ed., *Nineteenth-Century Shakespeare Burlesques*, 5 vols. (London: Diploma Press, 1977–78).

Westhead, Rick, 'Japan's Tsunami Recovery Includes Laughing at *King Lear*', *The Star* (8 February 2014), https://www.thestar.com/news/world/2014/02/08/japans_tsunami_recovery_includes_laughing_at_king_lear.html, accessed 16 August 2019.

INDEX

Japanese names are indexed in keeping with the custom of surnames preceding given names. Illustrations are in bold.

adaptations, 2–4
   early, 8–12
Adaptations of Shakespeare: A Critical Anthology of Plays from the Seventeenth Century to the Present, Daniel Fischlin and Mark Fortier, 3–4
Adelman, Janet, 45
Ainu Othello (SCJ), 32, 32 n.8, 277
Akihabara massacre, as inspiration for Kimura, 153, 154–5, 161, 164
Anan Nobuko, 151
angura (Underground Theatre) (also known as shōgekijō), 5, 6, 13, 47, 55
Anzai Tetsuo, 4–5, 11, 47, 283
appropriation, 2, 3
Aum Shinrikyo, sarin gas attack, 20

Bharucha, Rustom, 44
Biberman, Matthew, 156
Brandon, James, 5–6
Brienza, Casey, 151
British Hills, resort, 31, 34–5, 233, 275
Bungakuza (Literature Company), theatre company, 12, 282
Bungei Kyōkai (Literary Arts Association), 10, 11
burlesques, 230, 230 n.5

Cool Japan, 151–2
crimes, mass attacks in Japan, 20, 154–5
Curran, Beverley, 13, 15, 19, 21

Deguchi Norio, 13–14, 23, 24, 50, 53, 295
dialects, *see* languages and dialects

economy, Japan, 19–20, 41
   Economic Miracle, 225–6
Edo Kaoru, 22–3, 37, 38, **42**, 47, 49–57, 272 n.1, 273, 282
   collaboration with Okuizumi, 54–5
   reception in Japan, 56–7
   translation process, 50–1
   writing and rehearsals, 51–5
Eglinton, Mika, 28, 147, 148, 149
Emi Suiin, 8–9

Fischlin, Daniel, 2, 3–4
Fortier, Mark, 2, 3–4
Fujiwara Tatsuya, 18
Fukuda Tsuneari, 5, 12–13, 14, 15
Fukushima Daiichi Nuclear Power Plant, 21, 34

GALLERY LE DECO, performance space, 28–30, 274, 275, 285, 293
Gallimore, Daniel, 8, 9, 11
   'Seven Stages of Shakespeare Reception,' 4, 5–6, 12, 14, 15, 18
gembun itchi movement, 38, 38 n.2
Giulietta (1992), 53, 271
Great East Japan Earthquake (3.11), 20–1, 28, 33–5, 149
   influence on Japanese performances, 20, 34–6, 164, 223, 225, 226–8
Great Hanshin Earthquake, 20

Hamlet (Old Vic 1954), 12, 13
Hamlet, Edo Kaoru translation, 50
Hamlet, Fukuda Tsuneari translation, 12–13
Hamlet, Tsubouchi Shōyō translation, 10–11
HAMLET X SHIBUYA ~ Light, Was Our Revenge Tarnished? (Kakushinhan), 20–1, 26, 27, 28, 147–165
   contemporary social issues, 152–5
   importance of location, 147–8, 154, 157–8
   Kimura's merging approach, 156–7
   revenge theme, 155–6

Index

staging, 28–30
translation, 158–9
Hamlet, Yamagishi Kayō and Doi Shunsho adaptation, 9
'Hot Spring Trilogy' (SCJ), 33–6, 223–4
Hutcheon, Linda, *A Theory of Adaptation,* 2, 3, 156

Ichikawa Sadanji II, 11–12
Imoseyama onna teikin, Chikamatsu Hanji, 5
Inamasu Tatsuo, 225
Inoue Hidenori, 17, 18
Inoue Hisashi, *Tempo Juninen no Shakespeare,* 16, 17

Jean-Jean, theatre, 24, 47, 271, 272
Jiyū Gekijō (Free Theatre), 12, 52
Jōkyō Gekijō, theatre company, 47
jōruri style, 9–10
"J" performance (Japan as Junk), 150–1
Juliet of Tohoku (SCJ), 36, 278
Julius Caesar (Shiizaru kidan: Jiyū no tachi nagori no kireaji) Tsubouchi Shōyō translation, 9

kabuki, 5, 6, 8–9, 11, 16
   Inoue Hidenori's 'Inoue kabuki' style, 18
kachō fūgetsu, 8
Kafka, Franz, 152, 169
Kafka on the Shore, Murakami Haruki, 161
Kahn, Coppélia, 45, 46
kaigyaku (wit/humour), 39
Kakushinhan Theatre Company, 26–8, 161–4, 274–5, *see also HAMLET X SHIBUYA;* Kimura Ryūnosuke
   history and performance style, 147–52
   Pocket series, 27, 162–3, 274, 275
   Studio, 26, 163, 274, 275
kanji script, 148, 223 n.1
katakana, alphabet, 154, 158, 223 n.1
Kawai Shōichirō, 16, 18, 49 n.1, 158, 280, 285, 294, 298
Kawakami Otojirō, 6, 8–9
Kawakami Sadayakko, 6
Kawashima Keizō, 10

Kawatake Toshio, 5
Kawato Michiaki, 7, 8, 10
Kidnie, M.J., 46
Kigeki: Romio to Julietto (A Comedy: Romeo and Juliet), 53, 273, 282
Kimura Ryūnosuke, 26–9, 147, 148–9, 150, 152, 156, 157, 158
   Akihabara massacre, as inspiration, 153, 154–5, 161, 164
   interview, 161–5
   productions in Tokyo area (2019), 282, 285, 289, 293, 297
King Lear (Shakespeare), 43, 45–6, 55
King Lear, Matsuoka Kazuko translation, 14
King Lear, Nahum Tate's 1681 adaptation, 43 n.3
Kinoshita Junji, 33, 234
   Yūzuru (Twilight Crane), 33
Kōchi Yamato, 30
Konno Kaoru, 38
Kudō Kankurō, *Metal Macbeth,* 18

Laera, Margherita, 2, 3, 157
Lamb, Charles and Lamb, Mary, *Tales from Shakespeare,* 7, 8
languages and dialects, 30, 32–3, 32 n.8, 158–9, 230–1, 231 n.7, 234
   kanji script, 148, 223 n.1
   katakana, alphabet, 154, 158, 223 n.1
   Tohoku dialect, 31, 32–3, 34, 230–1
Lear Sushi (SCJ), 36, 278
Lord of the Lies, 18

MacArthur, Michelle, 2
Macbeth (Kakushinhan), 148, 149–50, 151, 152, 274
Macbeth in Osore-zan (Macbeth of Mt. Osore), 31, 276, 277
Maekawa Shirō, 25, 51, 52, 54–5, 273
Maimi, 29–30, **153**
makura (prelude), 38
matagi hunters, 224, 227–8, 229, 231
Matsuoka Kazuko, 7, 14–15, 22, 27, 28, 152–3, 165, 231 n.7
   productions in Tokyo area (2019), 281–2, 285–7, 289–94, 297

Index

Meiji period, 7, 32
   adaptations and translations, 4, 7–11
Meiji University, Shakespeare Project, 23, 56, 295
Mephistopheles no teiri (Mephistopheles's Theorem), 26
Metal Macbeth, 18
Midsummer Night's Dream, A, Noda Hideki adaptation, 17
Midsummer Night's Dream in Matsushima Bay, A (SCJ), 31, 35, 275
Midsummer Night's Dream: Shunjō ukiyo no yume (Spring Fever, the Dreams of the Floating World), Kawashima Keizō, 10
Minami Ryuta, 1, 4, 12, 13, 14, 17
   'Seven Stages of Shakespeare Reception,' 4, 5–6, 12, 14, 15, 18
Much Ado About Nothing, Kawai Shōichirō production, 16, 49 n.1
Much Ado About Nothing, Noda Hideki adaptation, 16, 17
Murakami Takeshi, 5, 13

Nakashima Kazuki, *Lord of the Lies*, 18
National Theatre, Japan, 56, 56 n.3
New King Lear, The (SCJ), 35, 36, 228–9, 277
New Merchant of Venice, The (SCJ), 35, 277
New National Theatre, (NNT) Tokyo, 14, 56, 56 n.3, 283, 286
New Romeo and Juliet, The (SCJ), 20–1, 35, **223**, 223–31, **229**
   dialects, 228, 230–1
   and Great East Japan Earthquake, 223, 225, 226–8
   Shōwa era setting, 224–6
Ninagawa Macbeth, 14, 150
Ninagawa Yukio, 16, 17–18, 27–8, 147, 150, 156, 164
Noda Hideki, 16–17, 293

ochi (witty twist), 39, 40
Odashima Yūshi, 5, 7, 13–14, 15
Ohtani Tomoko, 'Juliet's Girlfriends: The Takarazuka Revue Company and the *Shōjo* Culture', 19

Okuizumi Hikaru, 22, 23–4, 37–8, 51, 52, 53, 272, 282
   collaboration with Edo, 54–5
Osanai Kaoru, 11–12
Othello, Emi Suiin adaptation, 8–9

Poulton, Cody, 21
Powell, Brian, 8, 9, 11, 12

rakugo storytelling, similarities with *The Three Daughters*, 38–42, 46–7
reception, in Japan, 4–7, 56–7, 161–2, 233–4
Reinventing the Renaissance: Shakespeare and his Contemporaries in Adaptation and Performance, Sarah Annes Brown, Robert I. Lublin and Lynsey McCulloch, 4
Richard III (Sandaime, Richado), 16–17
Romeo and Juliet (SCJ 1995), 30–1, 35
Romeo and Juliet (TSC 2012, 2013), 23
Romeo and Juliet, Matsuoka Kazuko translation, 14–15
Romeo and Juliet on the Seashore, (Kakushinhan), 26–7, 28, 274, 275
Romeo and Juliet, Takarazuka Revue adaptation, 19
Rosencrantz and Guildenstern Are Dead, 22, 231 n.7

Saikoku risshihen (Stories of Successful Lives in the West), 7
Saitama Arts Theater, 14, 50, 281
Sakuradoki zeni no yo no naka (Life is as Fragile as Cherry Blossom in a World of Money), Katsu Genzō, 8, 286
Sandaime, Richado, (Richard III), 16–17
Sanders, Julie, 2
Sano Akiko, 13, 14, 15
Satō Keiichi, 24
seigeki (straight play) productions, 8–9
Self-help: With Illustrations of Character and Conduct, Samuel Smiles, 7
Senda Akihiko, 26
Senda Koreya, 47
sewamono (genre of jōruri and kabuki), 9

Index

Shakespeare Company Japan (SCJ), 20–1, 30–6, 31 n.6, 223–231, 233–4, 275–8
    dialects, 32–3, 230–1
    Great East Japan Earthquake and tsunami, 33–5, 223, 225, 226–8
    'Hot Spring Trilogy,' 35–6, 223–4
Shakespeare's Creative Legacies: Artists, Writers, Performers, Readers, Paul Edmondson and Peter Holbrook, 3
Shakespeare Theatre Company (STC), 13–14, 27, 47
'Shakespeare through the Looking-Glass' series (TSC), 22, 24, 44, 55, 56, 272–3
'Shakespeare Tokyo' (Kakushinhan), 148, 163
Shibuya, neighbourhood, 148, 154, 157–8
Shimada Jumpei, 30
Shimamura Hōgetsu, 11
Shimodate Kazumi, 30–6, 30 n.5, 224–5, 228–31, 233–4, 234 n.1, 275, 277, *see also* Shakespeare Company Japan; *The New Romeo and Juliet*
Shinbashi Enbujo Theatre, 18
shingeki (New Theatre) movement, 4, 5, 6, 11–13, 14, 47, 56 n.3
shinpa (shimpa) movement, 5, 6, 8–9, 47
shōgekijō (Little Theatre Movement) (also known as angura), 5, 6, 13, 47, 55
shōjo (young girls) culture, 19
Shōwa era, 224–6, 224 n.2, 230
Shōwa Retro Boom, 225
Sōseki Natsume, 10–11
Suzuki Akinori, 30
Suzuki Masae, 16

Taira Tatsuhiko, 8
Takadō Kaname, 39
Takahashi Yasunari, 7, 9
Takahashi Yutaka, 22
Takarazuka Revue, 19
Tempo Juninen no Shakespeare, Inoue Hisashi, 17–18
terrorism, 20, 154–5
    Akihabara massacre, as inspiration for Kimura, 153, 154–5, 161, 164
Thompson, Ann, 152, 155

Thornbury, Barbara E., 19
Three Daughters of Lear, The (TSC), 20, 37–47, **42**, 43 n.3, **45**
    humour, 39, 54
    as response to early 1990's Japan, 41–5
    similarities with rakugo storytelling, 38–43
    staging, 24–6
3.11 disaster (Great East Japan Earthquake)
    influence on Japanese performances, 20, 34–6, 164, 223, 225, 226–8
Titus Andronicus (Kakushinhan), 27, 150, 151–2, 274
Tohoku dialect, 31, 31 n.7, 32–3, 34, 230, 231
Tohoku region, 24, 24 n.4, 30–1, 33–6, 224, 231, 233, 234
Tokyo, as part of Kakushinhan's concept, 147–9, 163
Tokyo Globe, 5, 14, 23, 280, 291
Tokyo Metropolitan Theatre, 16, 148, 274, 280, 284, 286, 290, 292, 293
Tokyo Shakespeare Company (TSC), 20, 22–3, 22 n.3, 37–8, 271–3, *see also* Edo Kaoru; *The Three Daughters of Lear*
    'Shakespeare through the Looking-Glass' series, 22, 24, 44, 55, 56, 272–3
transculturation, 157
translations
    early, 7–12
    post-Meiji, 12–21
Trial of Macbeth, The (TSC), 52, 54–5, 272, 273
Tsubouchi Shōyō, 5, 9–11, 15, 53, 272
    Hamlet, 10–11
    productions in Tokyo area (2019), 281, 289, 291, 292, 293, 295, 296
    Shiizaru kidan: Jiyū no tachi nagori no kireaji (Caesar's Strange Tale: Residual Sharpness of the Sword of Freedom), 9–10
Tsukasa Mari, 23, **45**
tsunami, 2011, 21, 33–6
Twelfth Night (TSC), 23, 49, 271, 272
Twelfth Night, Matsuoka Kazuko translation, 14
Two Gentlemen of Verona, The (TSC), 23

Index

Uchino Tadashi, 150
ugachi (convey subtle points), 39–40

Wars of the Roses (Kakushinhan 2019), 27, 149, 275
Watanabe Emiko, 12–13

Yamamoto Susumu, 38, 39
Yoshida Kōtarō, 54, 273, 281, 285
Yoshihara Yukari, 18, 150
Yūki Masahide, 46

zero generation, 26, 28, 154